THOR
THE TRIALS OF LOKI

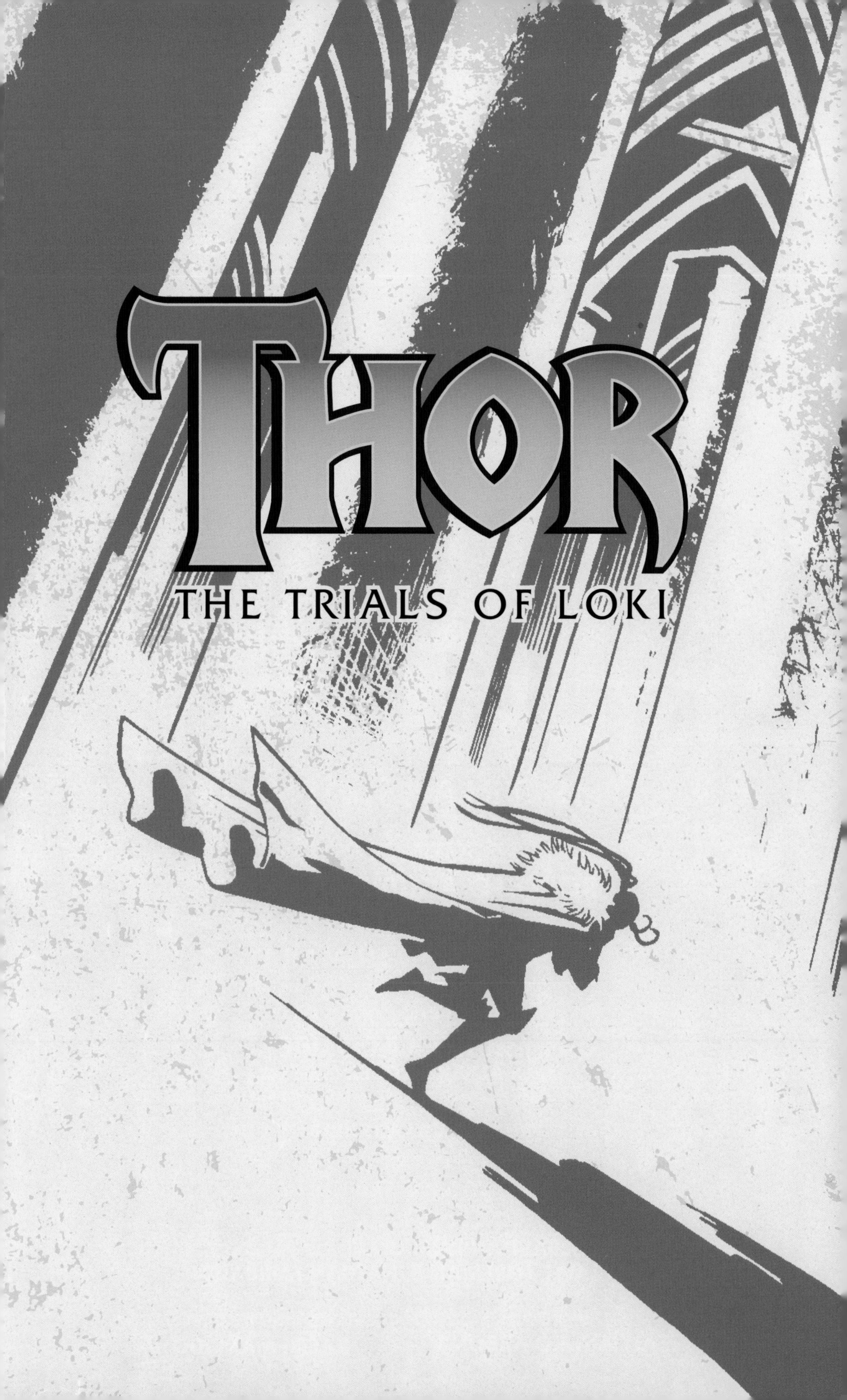

THOR
THE TRIALS OF LOKI

WRITER
ROBERTO AGUIRRE-SACASA

PENCILER
SEBASTIÁN FIUMARA
with **AL BARRIONUEVO** (Issue #4)

INKER
MICHEL LACOMBE
with **ÁLVARO LÓPEZ** (Issue #4)

COLORIST
JOSÉ VILLARRUBIA

LETTERER
VC'S JOE SABINO

COVER ART
SEBASTIÁN FIUMARA (Issue #1) and
TRAVEL FOREMAN & NATHAN FAIRBAIRN

EDITOR
ALEJANDRO ARBONA

SUPERVISING EDITOR
RALPH MACCHIO

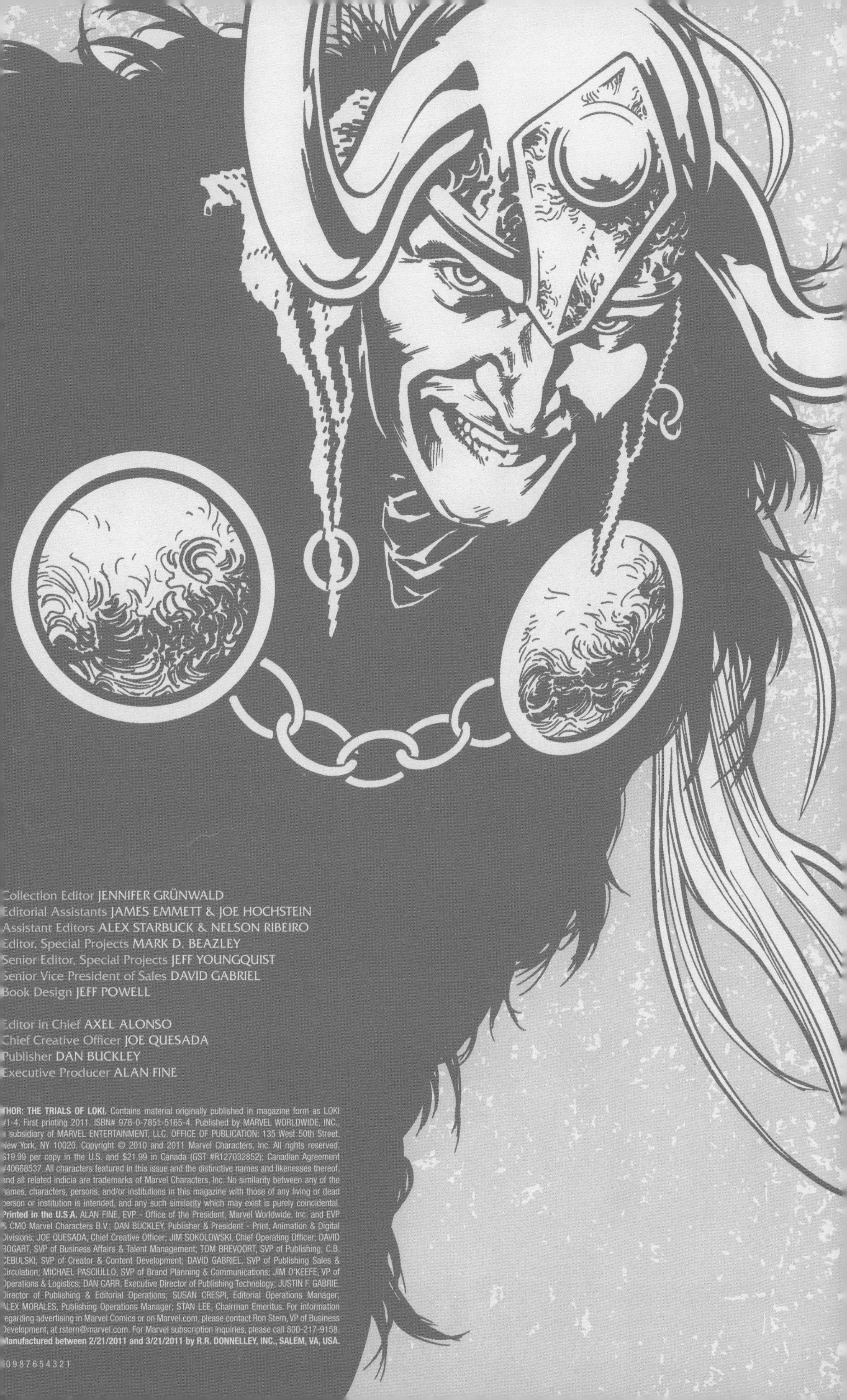

Collection Editor JENNIFER GRÜNWALD
Editorial Assistants JAMES EMMETT & JOE HOCHSTEIN
Assistant Editors ALEX STARBUCK & NELSON RIBEIRO
Editor, Special Projects MARK D. BEAZLEY
Senior Editor, Special Projects JEFF YOUNGQUIST
Senior Vice President of Sales DAVID GABRIEL
Book Design JEFF POWELL

Editor in Chief AXEL ALONSO
Chief Creative Officer JOE QUESADA
Publisher DAN BUCKLEY
Executive Producer ALAN FINE

THOR: THE TRIALS OF LOKI. Contains material originally published in magazine form as LOKI #1-4. First printing 2011. ISBN# 978-0-7851-5165-4. Published by MARVEL WORLDWIDE, INC., a subsidiary of MARVEL ENTERTAINMENT, LLC. OFFICE OF PUBLICATION: 135 West 50th Street, New York, NY 10020.

Printed in the U.S.A. ALAN FINE, EVP - Office of the President, Marvel Worldwide, Inc. and EVP & CMO Marvel Characters B.V.; DAN BUCKLEY, Publisher & President - Print, Animation & Digital Divisions; JOE QUESADA, Chief Creative Officer; JIM SOKOLOWSKI, Chief Operating Officer; DAVID BOGART, SVP of Business Affairs & Talent Management; TOM BREVOORT, SVP of Publishing; C.B. CEBULSKI, SVP of Creator & Content Development; DAVID GABRIEL, SVP of Publishing Sales & Circulation; MICHAEL PASCIULLO, SVP of Brand Planning & Communications; JIM O'KEEFE, VP of Operations & Logistics; DAN CARR, Executive Director of Publishing Technology; JUSTIN F. GABRIE, Director of Publishing & Editorial Operations; SUSAN CRESPI, Editorial Operations Manager; ALEX MORALES, Publishing Operations Manager; STAN LEE, Chairman Emeritus. For information regarding advertising in Marvel Comics or on Marvel.com, please contact Ron Stern, VP of Business Development, at rstern@marvel.com. For Marvel subscription inquiries, please call 800-217-9158. **Manufactured between 2/21/2011 and 3/21/2011 by R.R. DONNELLEY, INC., SALEM, VA, USA.**

10 9 8 7 6 5 4 3 2 1

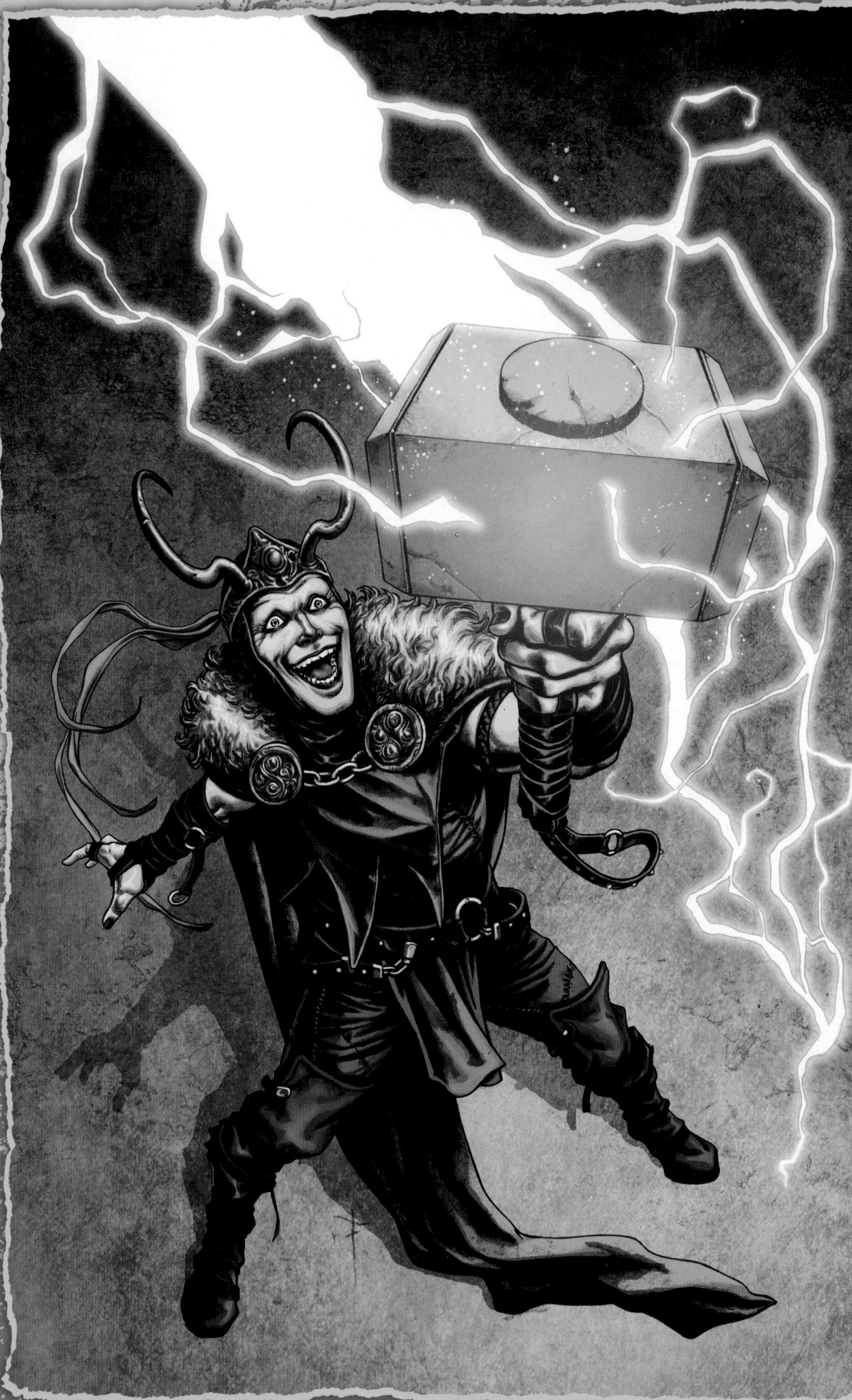

PART ONE
IT SHOULD HAVE BEEN MINE

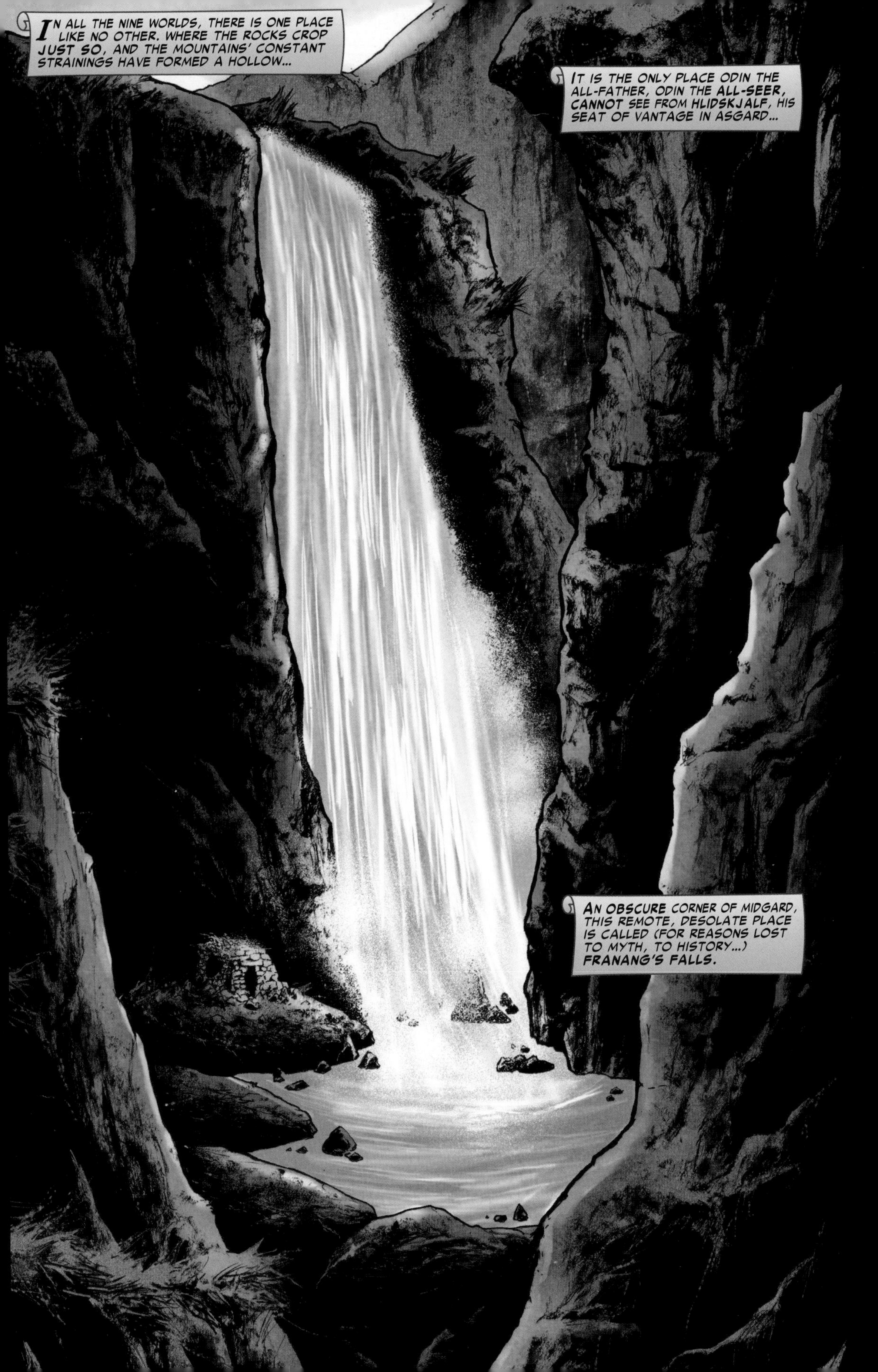
IN ALL THE NINE WORLDS, THERE IS ONE PLACE LIKE NO OTHER. WHERE THE ROCKS CROP JUST SO, AND THE MOUNTAINS' CONSTANT STRAININGS HAVE FORMED A HOLLOW...
IT IS THE ONLY PLACE ODIN THE ALL-FATHER, ODIN THE ALL-SEER, CANNOT SEE FROM HLIDSKJALF, HIS SEAT OF VANTAGE IN ASGARD...
AN OBSCURE CORNER OF MIDGARD, THIS REMOTE, DESOLATE PLACE IS CALLED (FOR REASONS LOST TO MYTH, TO HISTORY...) FRANANG'S FALLS.

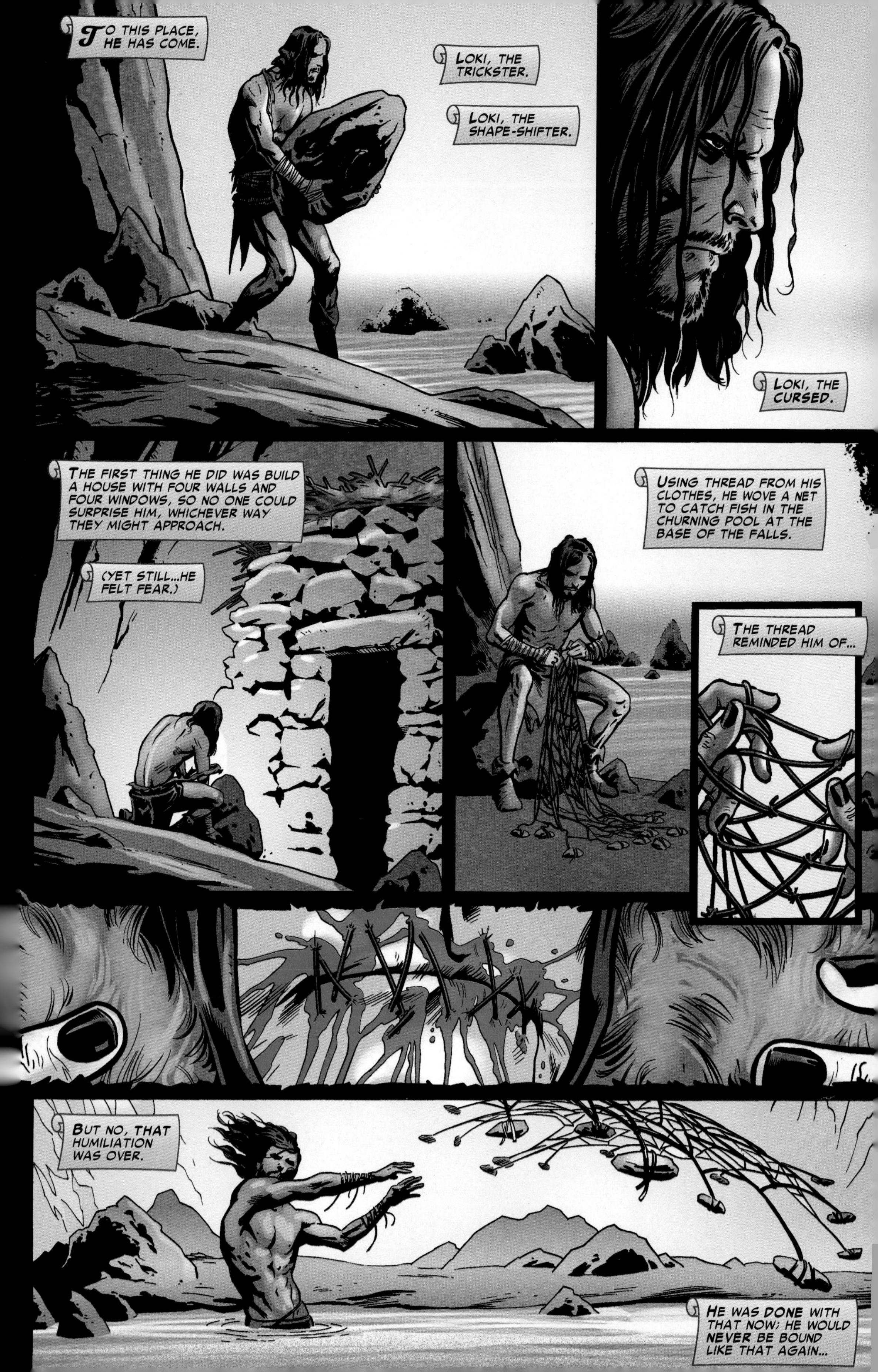

TO THIS PLACE, HE HAS COME.
LOKI, THE TRICKSTER.
LOKI, THE SHAPE-SHIFTER.
LOKI, THE CURSED.
THE FIRST THING HE DID WAS BUILD A HOUSE WITH FOUR WALLS AND FOUR WINDOWS, SO NO ONE COULD SURPRISE HIM, WHICHEVER WAY THEY MIGHT APPROACH.
(YET STILL...HE FELT FEAR.)
USING THREAD FROM HIS CLOTHES, HE WOVE A NET TO CATCH FISH IN THE CHURNING POOL AT THE BASE OF THE FALLS.
THE THREAD REMINDED HIM OF...
BUT NO, THAT HUMILIATION WAS OVER.
HE WAS DONE WITH THAT NOW; HE WOULD NEVER BE BOUND LIKE THAT AGAIN...

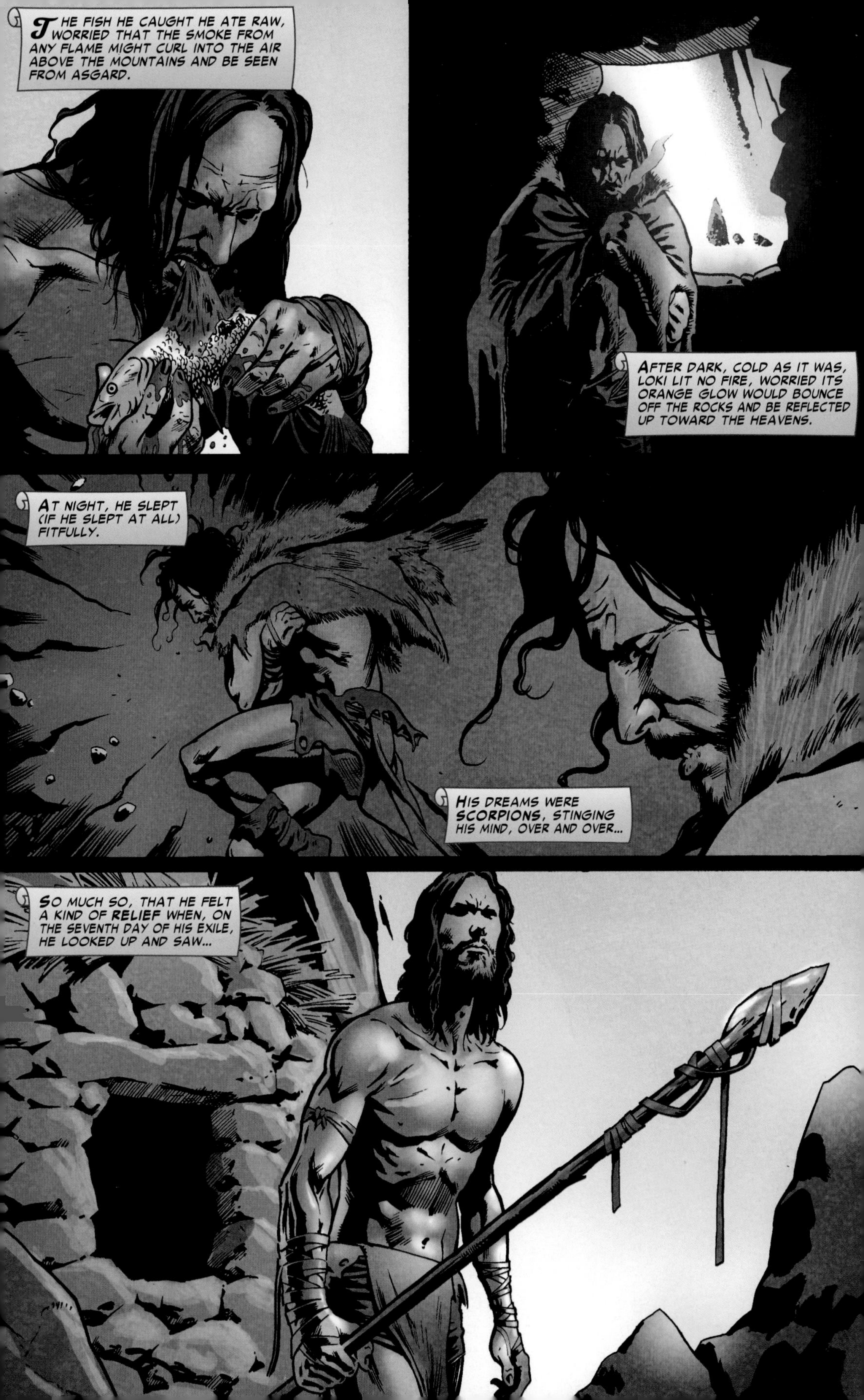
THE FISH HE CAUGHT HE ATE RAW, WORRIED THAT THE SMOKE FROM ANY FLAME MIGHT CURL INTO THE AIR ABOVE THE MOUNTAINS AND BE SEEN FROM ASGARD.
AFTER DARK, COLD AS IT WAS, LOKI LIT NO FIRE, WORRIED ITS ORANGE GLOW WOULD BOUNCE OFF THE ROCKS AND BE REFLECTED UP TOWARD THE HEAVENS.
AT NIGHT, HE SLEPT (IF HE SLEPT AT ALL) FITFULLY.
HIS DREAMS WERE SCORPIONS, STINGING HIS MIND, OVER AND OVER...
SO MUCH SO, THAT HE FELT A KIND OF RELIEF WHEN, ON THE SEVENTH DAY OF HIS EXILE, HE LOOKED UP AND SAW...

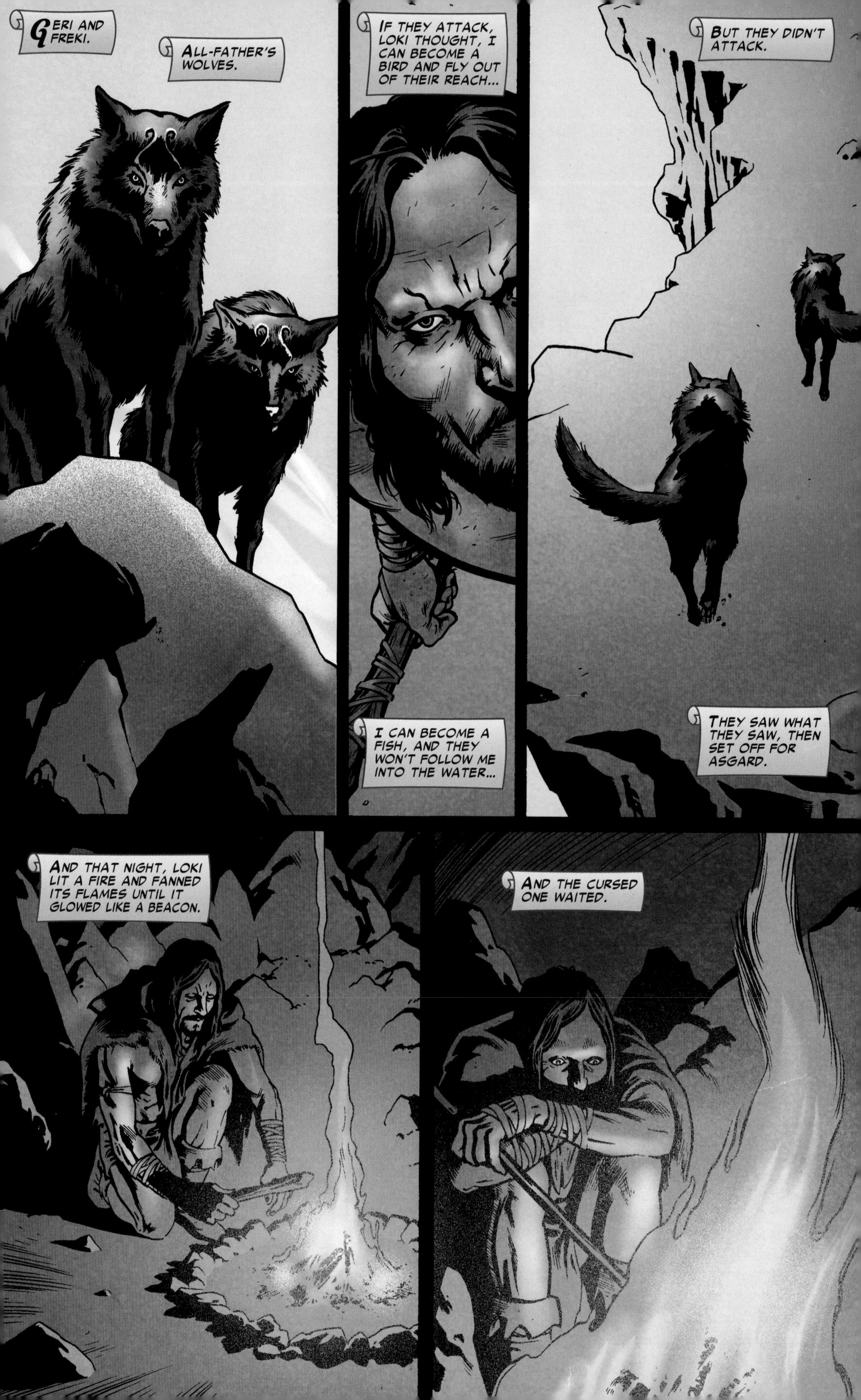
GERI AND FREKI.
ALL-FATHER'S WOLVES.
IF THEY ATTACK, LOKI THOUGHT, I CAN BECOME A BIRD AND FLY OUT OF THEIR REACH...
I CAN BECOME A FISH, AND THEY WON'T FOLLOW ME INTO THE WATER...
BUT THEY DIDN'T ATTACK.
THEY SAW WHAT THEY SAW, THEN SET OFF FOR ASGARD.
AND THAT NIGHT, LOKI LIT A FIRE AND FANNED ITS FLAMES UNTIL IT GLOWED LIKE A BEACON.
AND THE CURSED ONE WAITED.

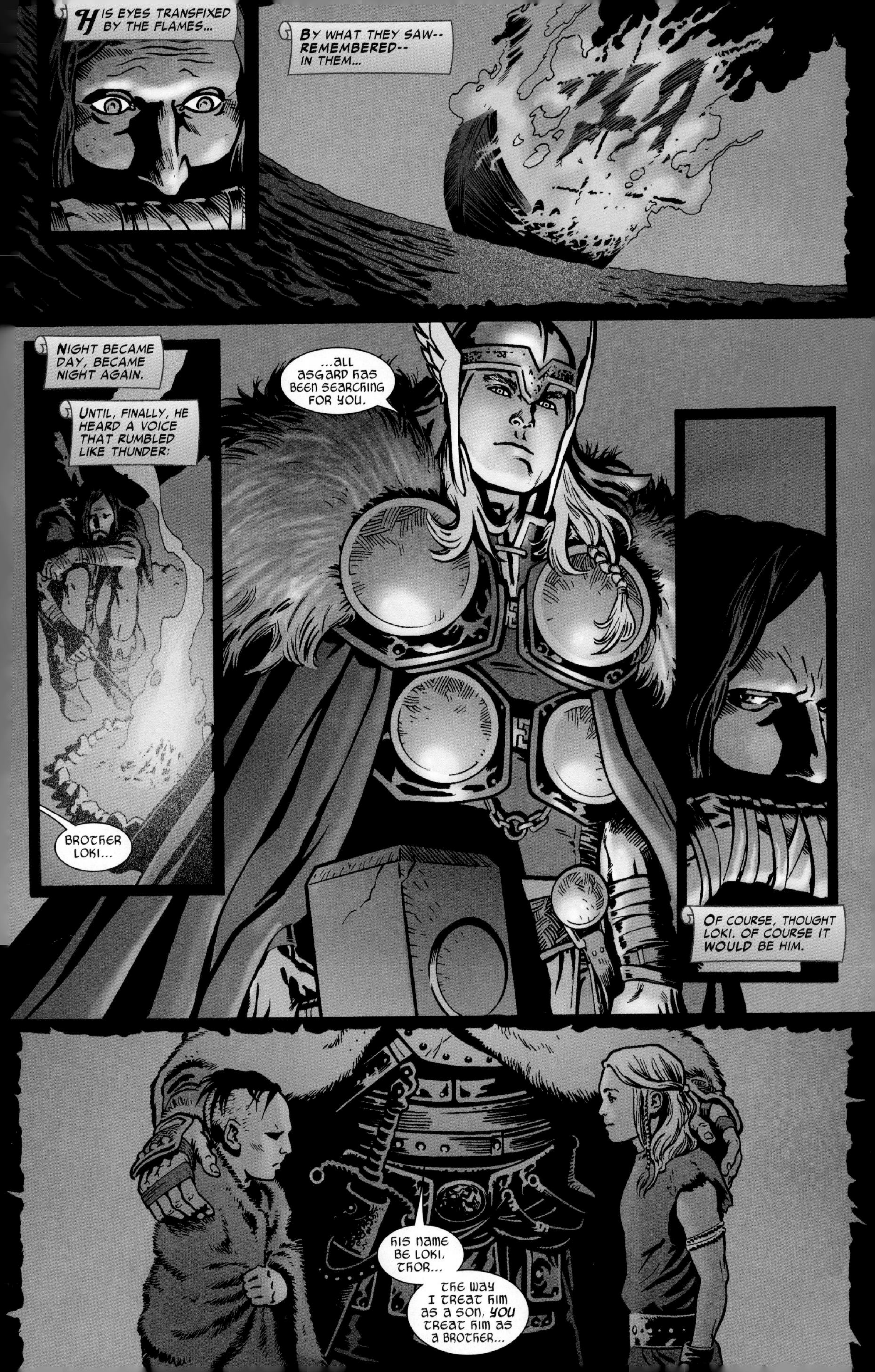
HIS EYES TRANSFIXED BY THE FLAMES...
BY WHAT THEY SAW-- REMEMBERED-- IN THEM...
NIGHT BECAME DAY, BECAME NIGHT AGAIN.
UNTIL, FINALLY, HE HEARD A VOICE THAT RUMBLED LIKE THUNDER:
BROTHER LOKI...
...ALL ASGARD HAS BEEN SEARCHING FOR YOU.
OF COURSE, THOUGHT LOKI. OF COURSE IT WOULD BE HIM.
HIS NAME BE LOKI, THOR...
THE WAY I TREAT HIM AS A SON, YOU TREAT HIM AS A BROTHER...

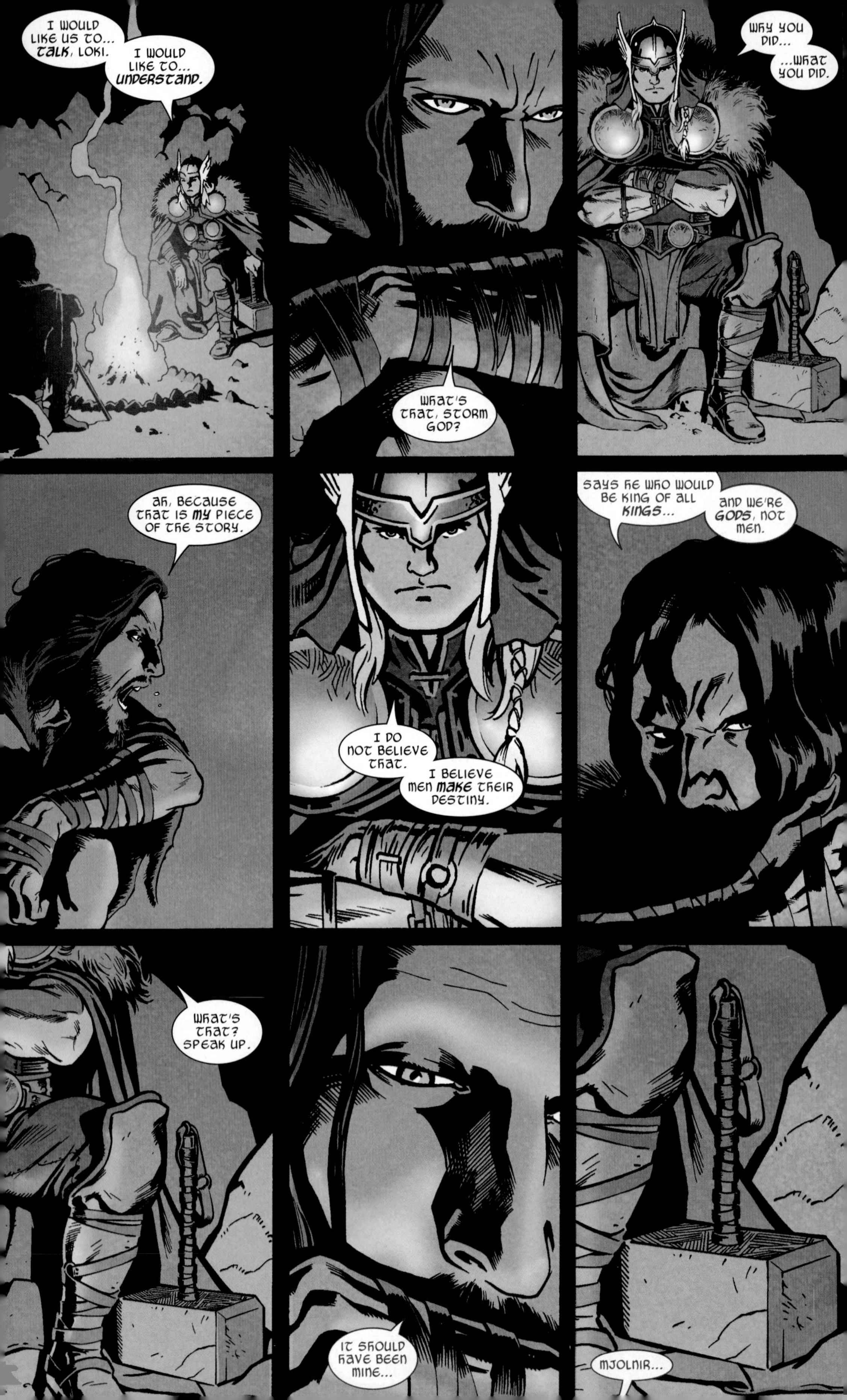
I WOULD LIKE US TO... TALK, LOKI.
I WOULD LIKE TO... UNDERSTAND.
WHAT'S THAT, STORM GOD?
WHY YOU DID...
...WHAT YOU DID.
AH, BECAUSE THAT IS MY PIECE OF THE STORY.
I DO NOT BELIEVE THAT.
I BELIEVE MEN MAKE THEIR DESTINY.
SAYS HE WHO WOULD BE KING OF ALL KINGS...
AND WE'RE GODS, NOT MEN.
WHAT'S THAT? SPEAK UP.
IT SHOULD HAVE BEEN MINE...
MJOLNIR...

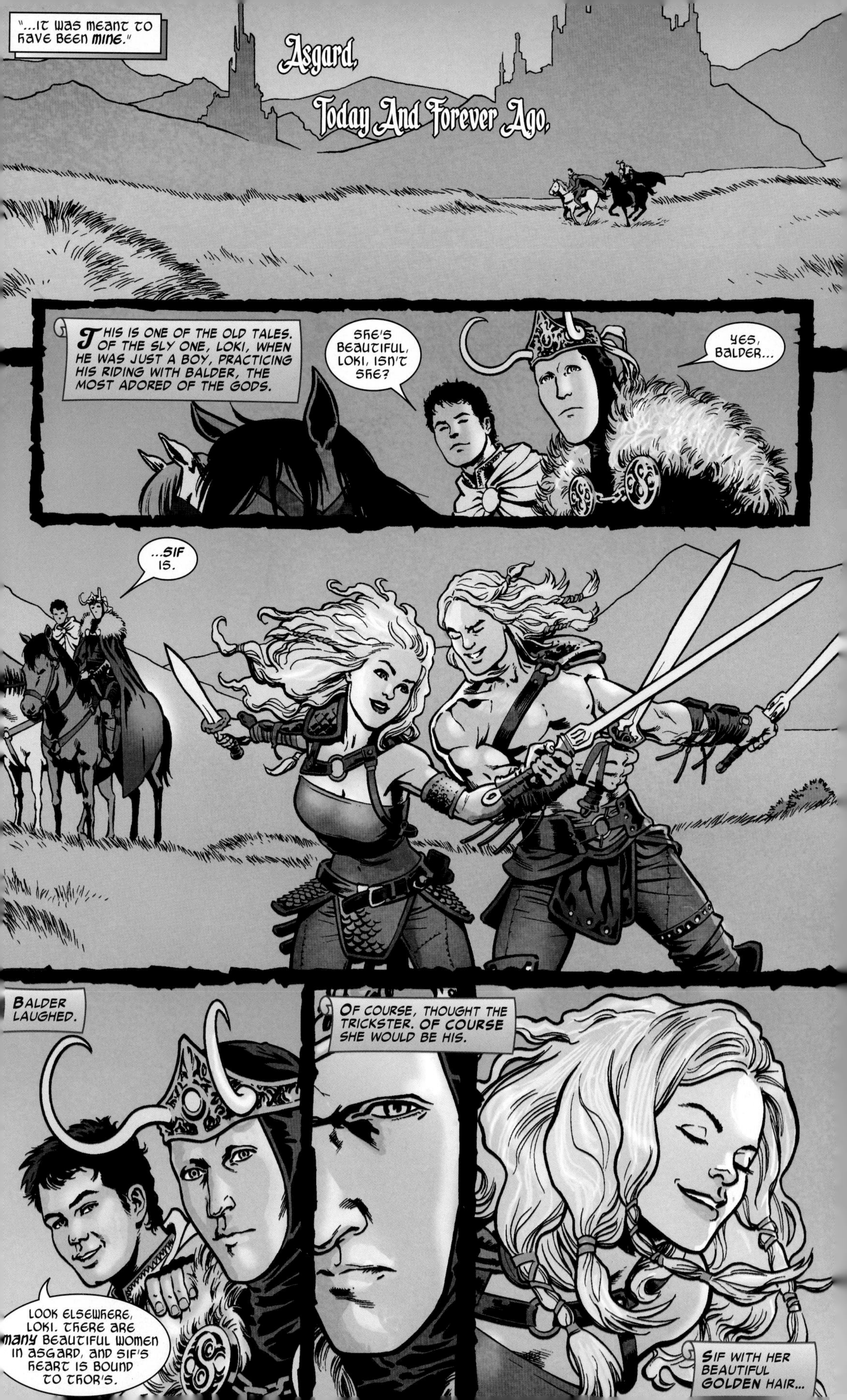
"...It was meant to have been MINE."
Asgard, Today And Forever Ago.
THIS IS ONE OF THE OLD TALES. OF THE SLY ONE, LOKI, WHEN HE WAS JUST A BOY, PRACTICING HIS RIDING WITH BALDER, THE MOST ADORED OF THE GODS.
SHE'S BEAUTIFUL, LOKI, ISN'T SHE?
YES, BALDER...
...SIF IS.
BALDER LAUGHED.
LOOK ELSEWHERE, LOKI. THERE ARE MANY BEAUTIFUL WOMEN IN ASGARD, AND SIF'S HEART IS BOUND TO THOR'S.
OF COURSE, THOUGHT THE TRICKSTER. OF COURSE SHE WOULD BE HIS.
SIF WITH HER BEAUTIFUL GOLDEN HAIR...

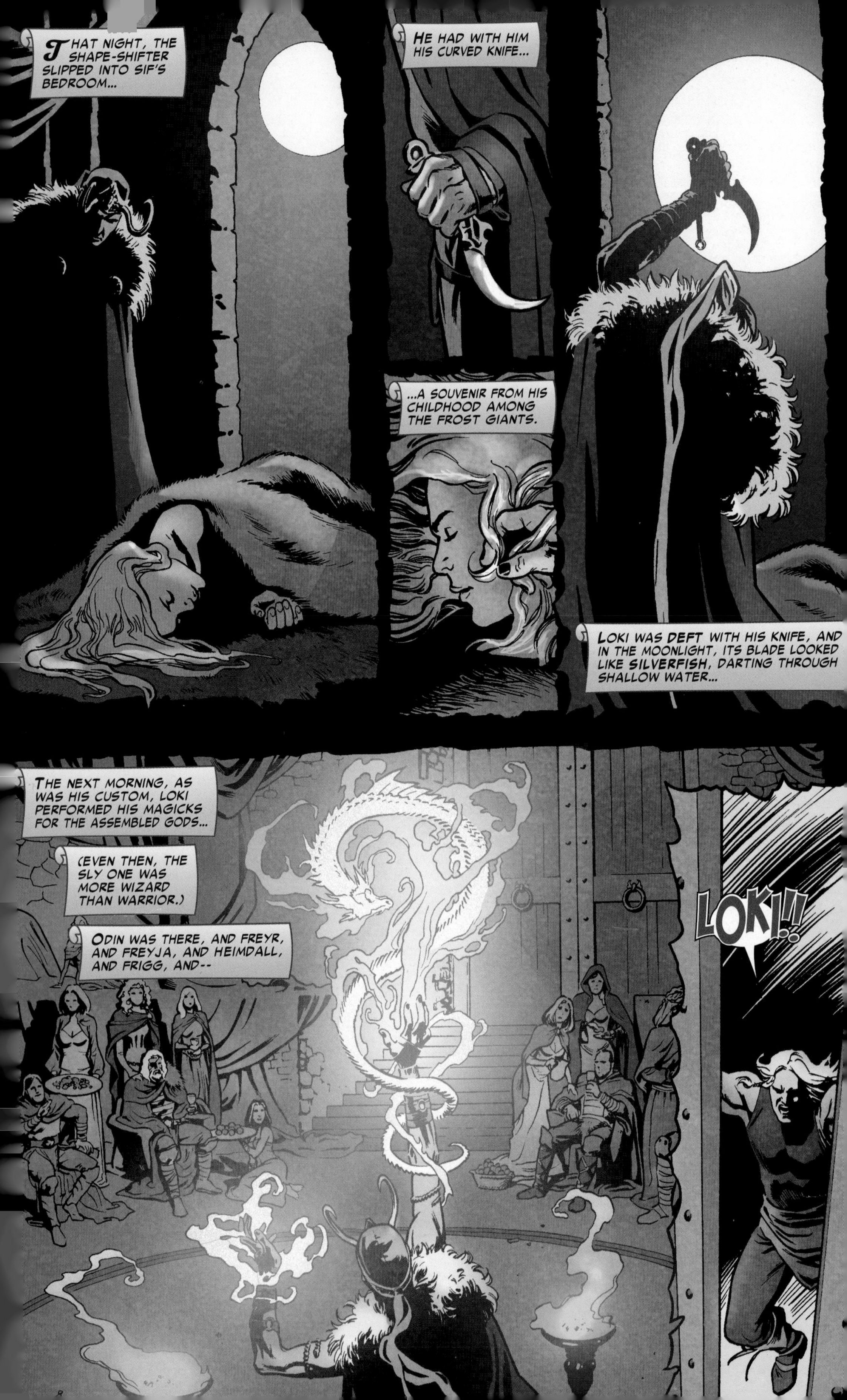
THAT NIGHT, THE SHAPE-SHIFTER SLIPPED INTO SIF'S BEDROOM...
HE HAD WITH HIM HIS CURVED KNIFE...
...A SOUVENIR FROM HIS CHILDHOOD AMONG THE FROST GIANTS.
LOKI WAS DEFT WITH HIS KNIFE, AND IN THE MOONLIGHT, ITS BLADE LOOKED LIKE SILVERFISH, DARTING THROUGH SHALLOW WATER...
THE NEXT MORNING, AS WAS HIS CUSTOM, LOKI PERFORMED HIS MAGICKS FOR THE ASSEMBLED GODS...
(EVEN THEN, THE SLY ONE WAS MORE WIZARD THAN WARRIOR.)
ODIN WAS THERE, AND FREYR, AND FREYJA, AND HEIMDALL, AND FRIGG, AND--
LOKI!!

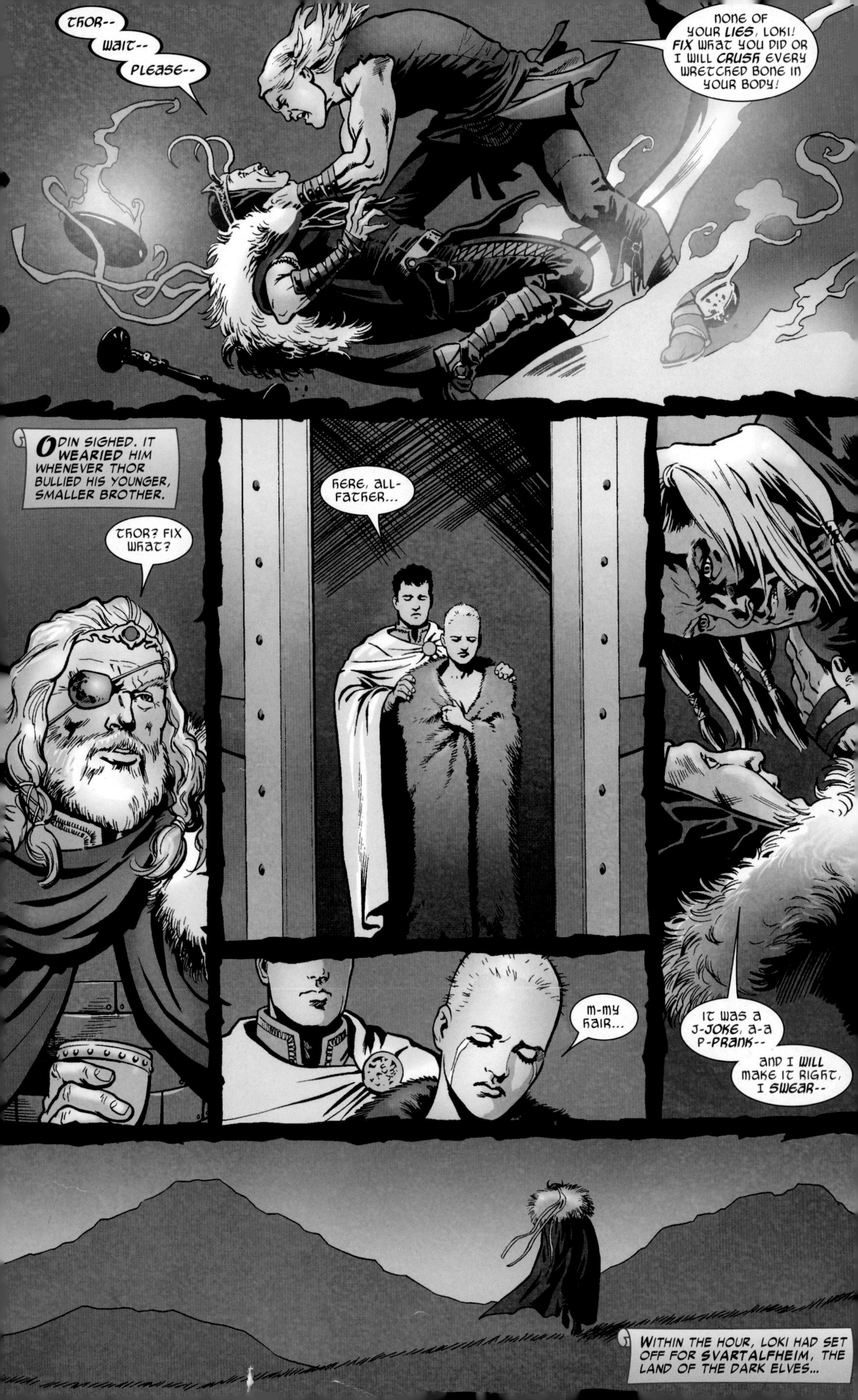
THOR--
WAIT--
PLEASE--
NONE OF YOUR LIES, LOKI! FIX WHAT YOU DID OR I WILL CRUSH EVERY WRETCHED BONE IN YOUR BODY!
ODIN SIGHED. IT WEARIED HIM WHENEVER THOR BULLIED HIS YOUNGER, SMALLER BROTHER.
THOR? FIX WHAT?
HERE, ALL-FATHER...
M-MY HAIR...
IT WAS A J-JOKE, A-A P-PRANK--
AND I WILL MAKE IT RIGHT, I SWEAR--
WITHIN THE HOUR, LOKI HAD SET OFF FOR SVARTALFHEIM, THE LAND OF THE DARK ELVES...

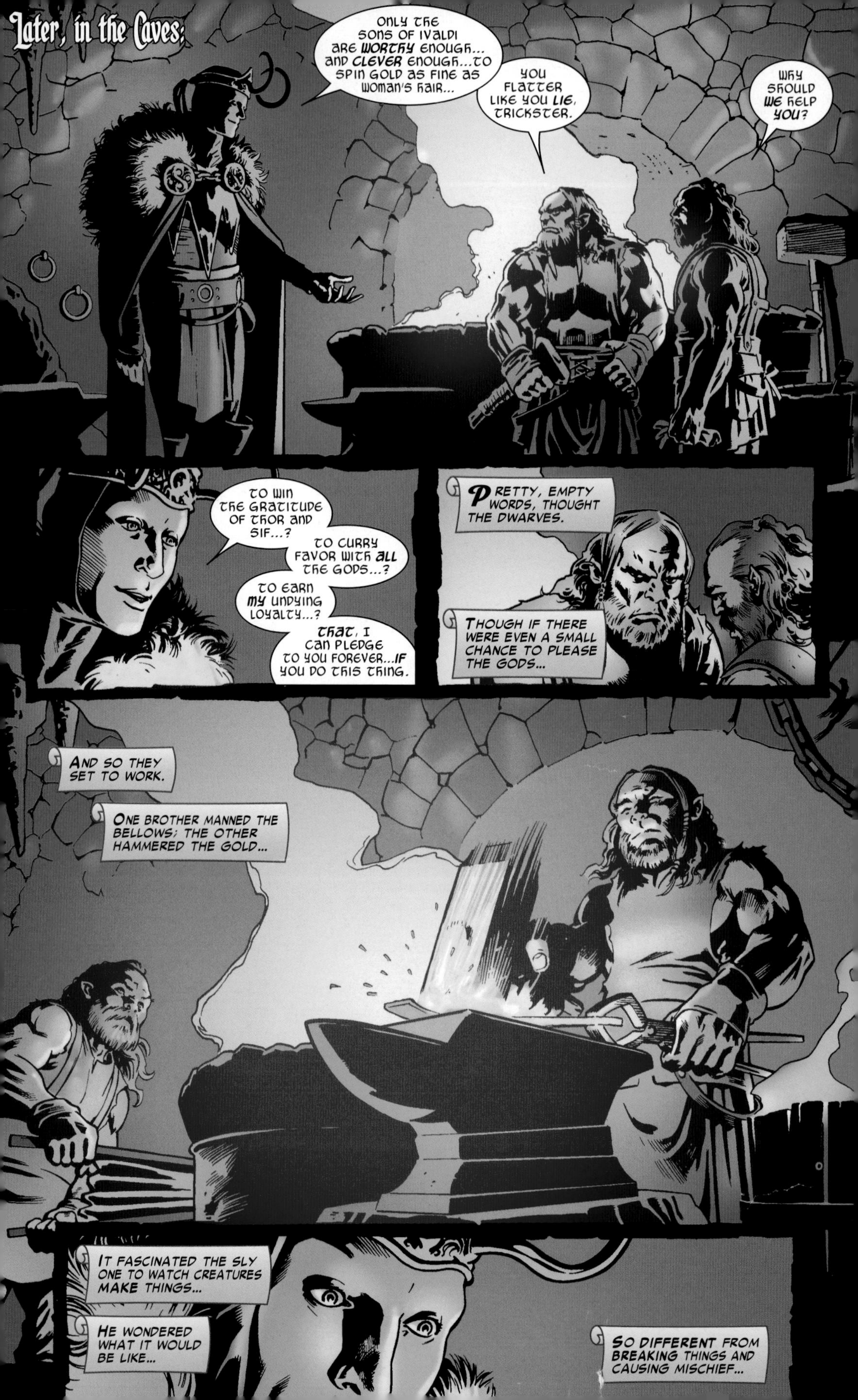
Later, in the Caves:
ONLY THE SONS OF IVALDI ARE WORTHY ENOUGH... AND CLEVER ENOUGH...TO SPIN GOLD AS FINE AS WOMAN'S HAIR...
YOU FLATTER LIKE YOU LIE, TRICKSTER.
WHY SHOULD WE HELP YOU?
TO WIN THE GRATITUDE OF THOR AND SIF...?
TO CURRY FAVOR WITH ALL THE GODS...?
TO EARN MY UNDYING LOYALTY...?
THAT, I CAN PLEDGE TO YOU FOREVER...IF YOU DO THIS THING.
PRETTY, EMPTY WORDS, THOUGHT THE DWARVES.
THOUGH IF THERE WERE EVEN A SMALL CHANCE TO PLEASE THE GODS...
AND SO THEY SET TO WORK.
ONE BROTHER MANNED THE BELLOWS; THE OTHER HAMMERED THE GOLD...
IT FASCINATED THE SLY ONE TO WATCH CREATURES MAKE THINGS...
HE WONDERED WHAT IT WOULD BE LIKE...
SO DIFFERENT FROM BREAKING THINGS AND CAUSING MISCHIEF...

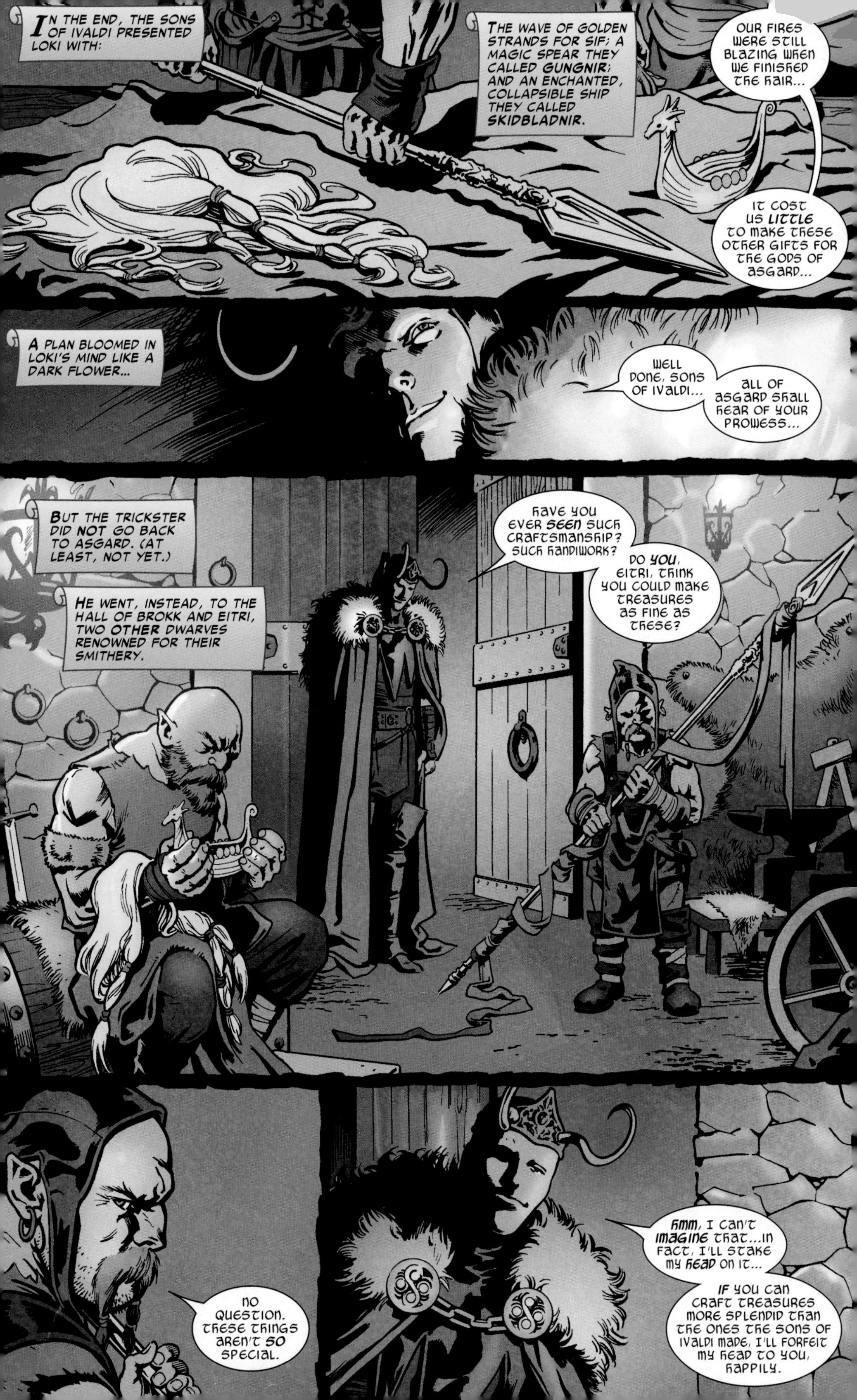
In the end, the sons of Ivaldi presented Loki with:
The wave of golden strands for Sif; a magic spear they called Gungnir; and an enchanted, collapsible ship they called Skidbladnir.
Our fires were still blazing when we finished the hair...
It cost us little to make these other gifts for the gods of Asgard...
A plan bloomed in Loki's mind like a dark flower...
Well done, sons of Ivaldi...
All of Asgard shall hear of your prowess...
But the trickster did not go back to Asgard. (At least, not yet.)
He went, instead, to the hall of Brokk and Eitri, two other dwarves renowned for their smithery.
Have you ever seen such craftsmanship? Such handiwork?
Do you, Eitri, think you could make treasures as fine as these?
No question. These things aren't so special.
Hmm, I can't imagine that...in fact, I'll stake my head on it...
If you can craft treasures more splendid than the ones the sons of Ivaldi made, I'll forfeit my head to you, happily.

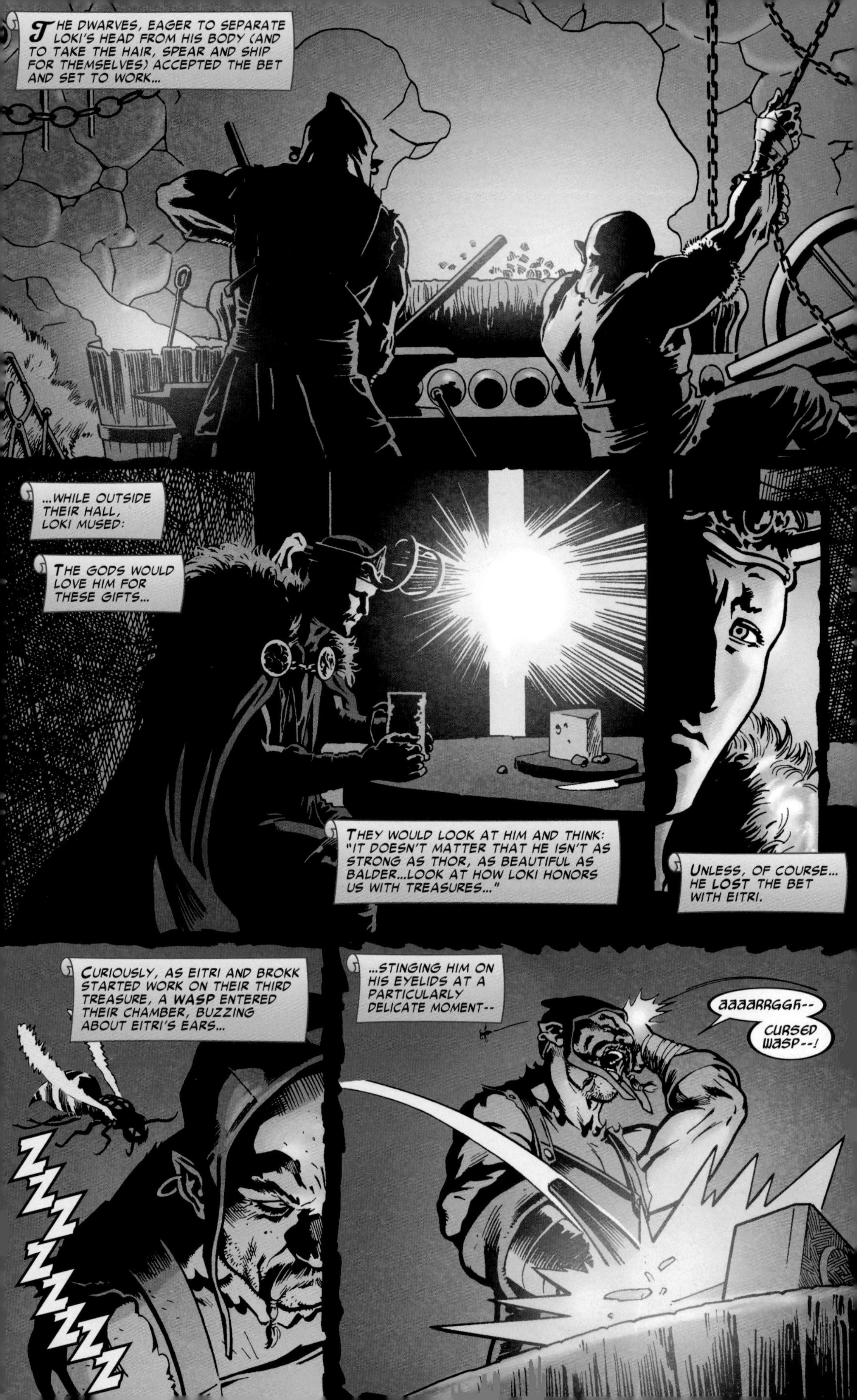
THE DWARVES, EAGER TO SEPARATE LOKI'S HEAD FROM HIS BODY (AND TO TAKE THE HAIR, SPEAR AND SHIP FOR THEMSELVES) ACCEPTED THE BET AND SET TO WORK...
...WHILE OUTSIDE THEIR HALL, LOKI MUSED:
THE GODS WOULD LOVE HIM FOR THESE GIFTS...
THEY WOULD LOOK AT HIM AND THINK: "IT DOESN'T MATTER THAT HE ISN'T AS STRONG AS THOR, AS BEAUTIFUL AS BALDER...LOOK AT HOW LOKI HONORS US WITH TREASURES..."
UNLESS, OF COURSE... HE LOST THE BET WITH EITRI.
CURIOUSLY, AS EITRI AND BROKK STARTED WORK ON THEIR THIRD TREASURE, A WASP ENTERED THEIR CHAMBER, BUZZING ABOUT EITRI'S EARS...
ZZZZZZZZ
...STINGING HIM ON HIS EYELIDS AT A PARTICULARLY DELICATE MOMENT--
AAAARRGGH--
CURSED WASP--!

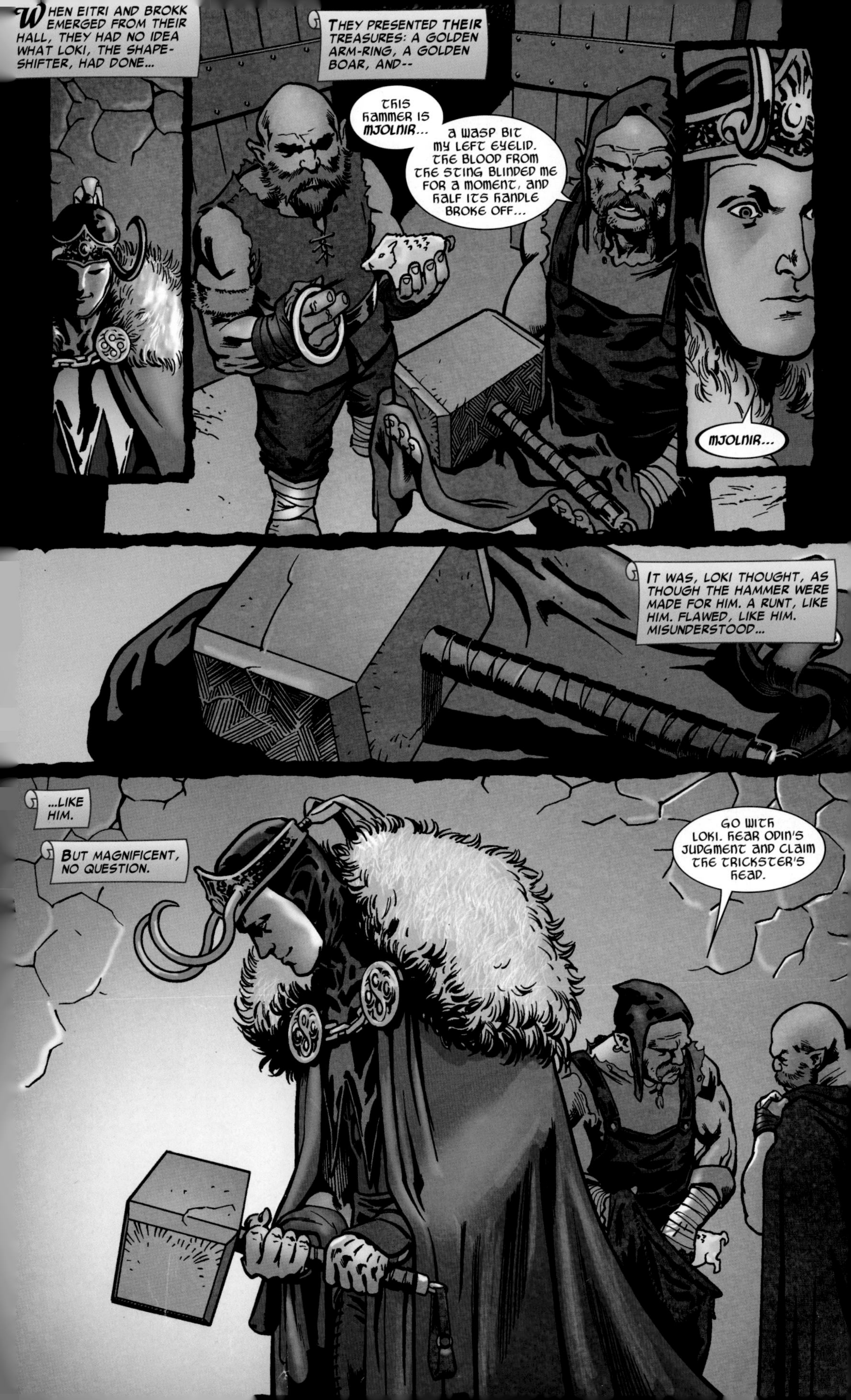
WHEN EITRI AND BROKK EMERGED FROM THEIR HALL, THEY HAD NO IDEA WHAT LOKI, THE SHAPE-SHIFTER, HAD DONE...
THEY PRESENTED THEIR TREASURES: A GOLDEN ARM-RING, A GOLDEN BOAR, AND--
THIS HAMMER IS MJOLNIR...
A WASP BIT MY LEFT EYELID. THE BLOOD FROM THE STING BLINDED ME FOR A MOMENT, AND HALF ITS HANDLE BROKE OFF...
MJOLNIR...
IT WAS, LOKI THOUGHT, AS THOUGH THE HAMMER WERE MADE FOR HIM. A RUNT, LIKE HIM. FLAWED, LIKE HIM. MISUNDERSTOOD...
...LIKE HIM.
BUT MAGNIFICENT, NO QUESTION.
GO WITH LOKI. HEAR ODIN'S JUDGMENT AND CLAIM THE TRICKSTER'S HEAD.

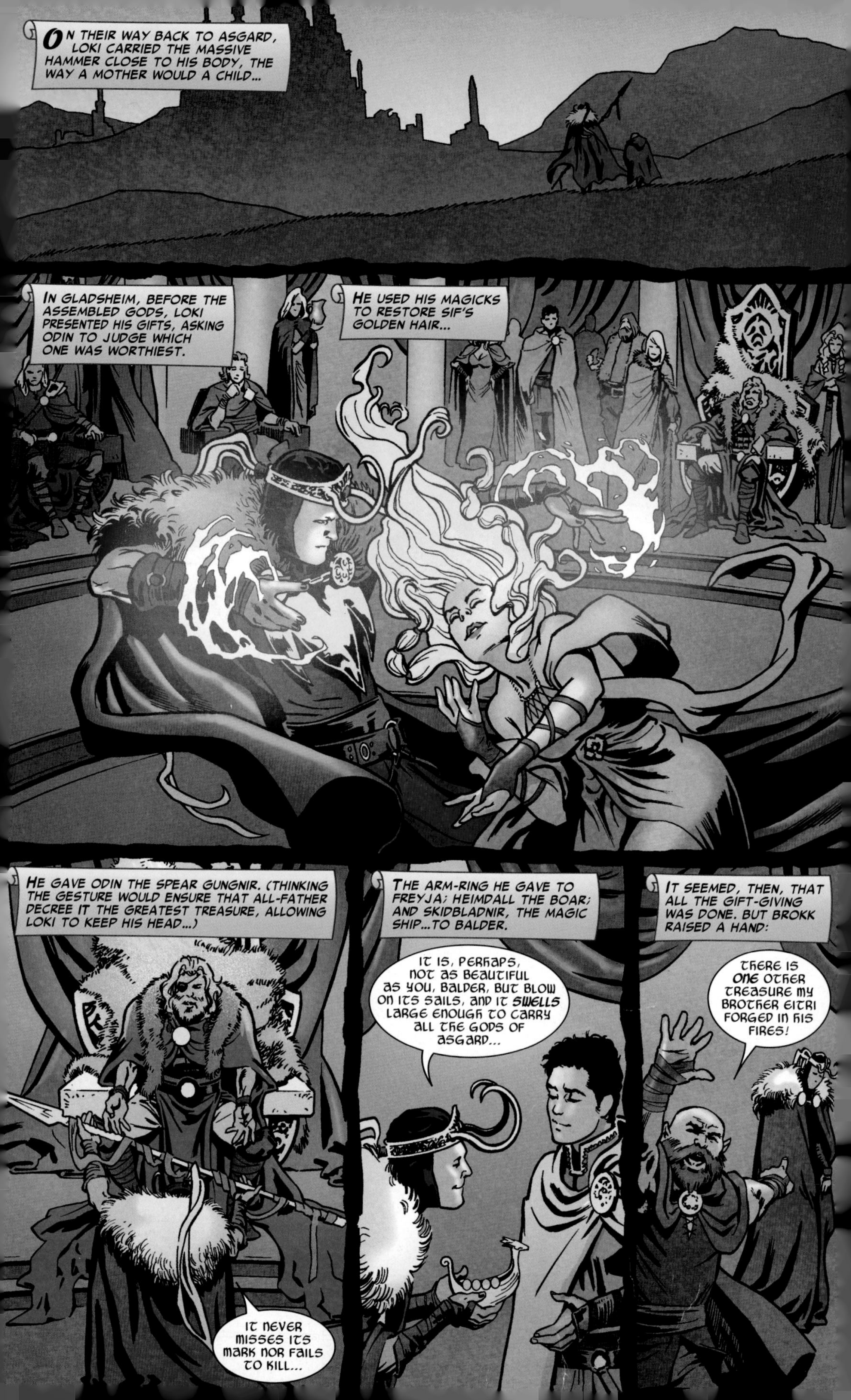
ON THEIR WAY BACK TO ASGARD, LOKI CARRIED THE MASSIVE HAMMER CLOSE TO HIS BODY, THE WAY A MOTHER WOULD A CHILD...
IN GLADSHEIM, BEFORE THE ASSEMBLED GODS, LOKI PRESENTED HIS GIFTS, ASKING ODIN TO JUDGE WHICH ONE WAS WORTHIEST.
HE USED HIS MAGICKS TO RESTORE SIF'S GOLDEN HAIR...
HE GAVE ODIN THE SPEAR GUNGNIR. (THINKING THE GESTURE WOULD ENSURE THAT ALL-FATHER DECREE IT THE GREATEST TREASURE, ALLOWING LOKI TO KEEP HIS HEAD...)
IT NEVER MISSES ITS MARK NOR FAILS TO KILL...
THE ARM-RING HE GAVE TO FREYJA; HEIMDALL THE BOAR; AND SKIDBLADNIR, THE MAGIC SHIP...TO BALDER.
IT IS, PERHAPS, NOT AS BEAUTIFUL AS YOU, BALDER, BUT BLOW ON ITS SAILS, AND IT SWELLS LARGE ENOUGH TO CARRY ALL THE GODS OF ASGARD...
IT SEEMED, THEN, THAT ALL THE GIFT-GIVING WAS DONE. BUT BROKK RAISED A HAND:
THERE IS ONE OTHER TREASURE MY BROTHER EITRI FORGED IN HIS FIRES!

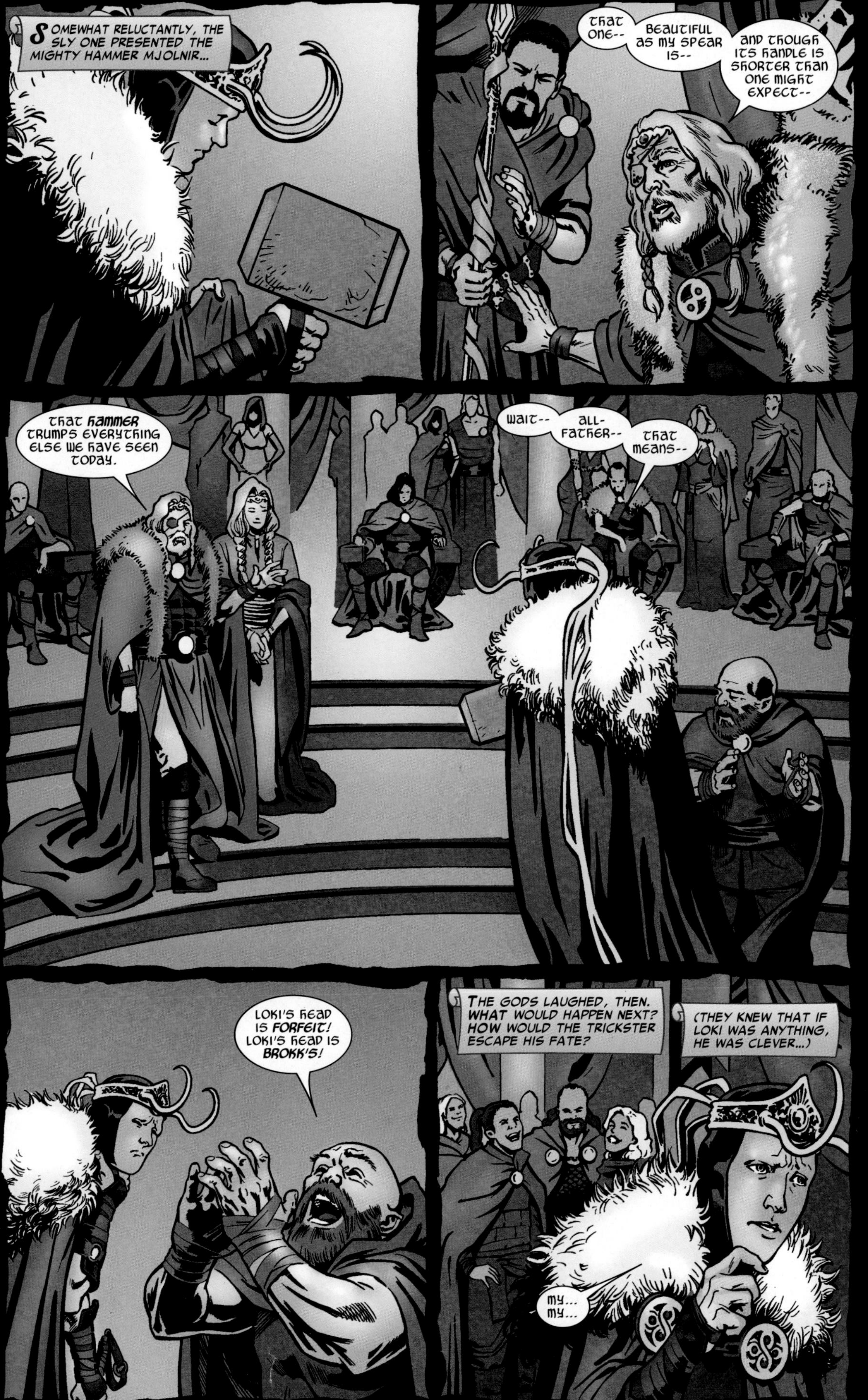
SOMEWHAT RELUCTANTLY, THE SLY ONE PRESENTED THE MIGHTY HAMMER MJOLNIR...
THAT ONE--
BEAUTIFUL AS MY SPEAR IS--
AND THOUGH ITS HANDLE IS SHORTER THAN ONE MIGHT EXPECT--
THAT HAMMER TRUMPS EVERYTHING ELSE WE HAVE SEEN TODAY.
WAIT--
ALL-FATHER--
THAT MEANS--
LOKI'S HEAD IS FORFEIT! LOKI'S HEAD IS BROKK'S!
THE GODS LAUGHED, THEN. WHAT WOULD HAPPEN NEXT? HOW WOULD THE TRICKSTER ESCAPE HIS FATE?
(THEY KNEW THAT IF LOKI WAS ANYTHING, HE WAS CLEVER...)
MY... MY...

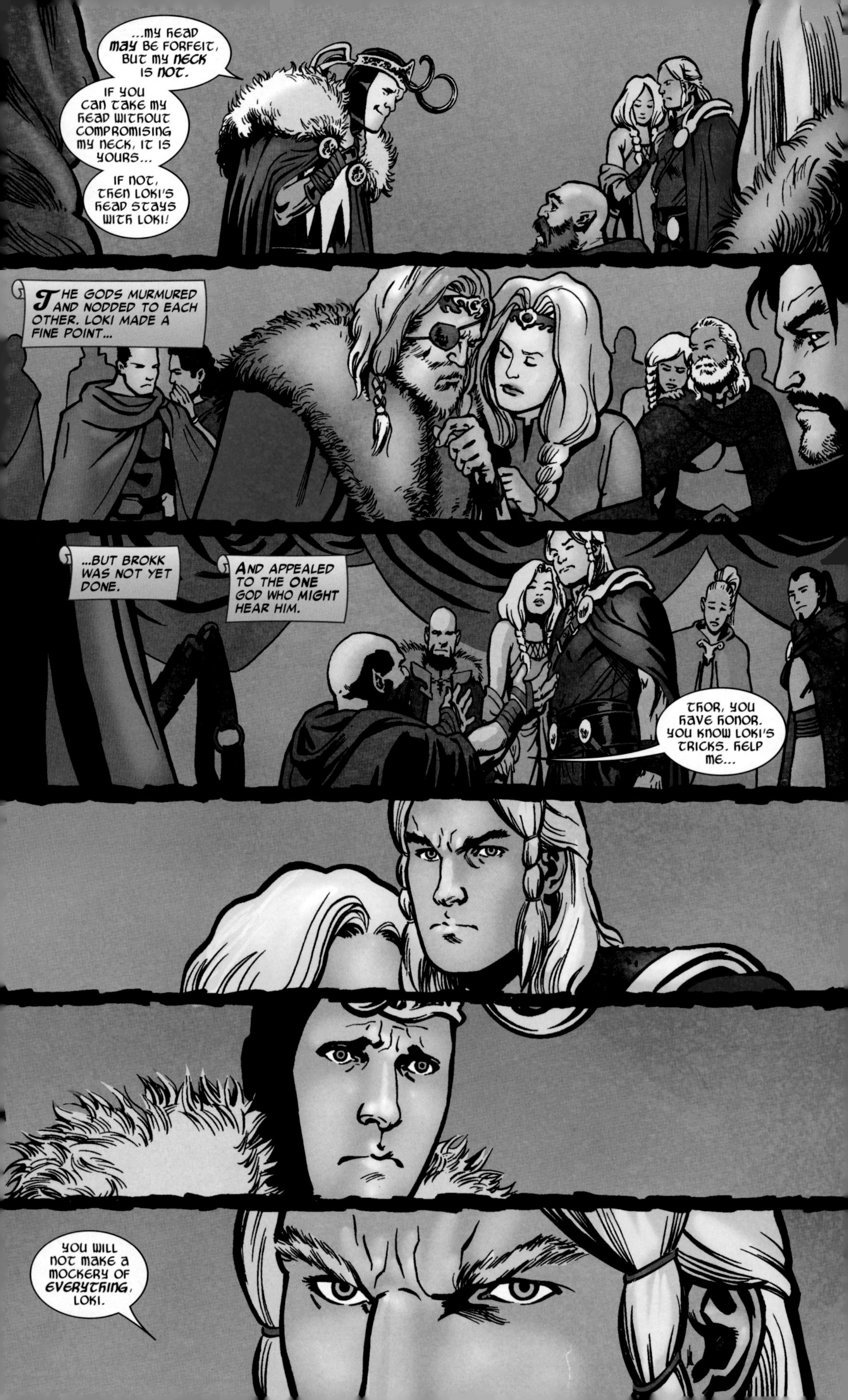
...MY HEAD MAY BE FORFEIT, BUT MY NECK IS NOT.
IF YOU CAN TAKE MY HEAD WITHOUT COMPROMISING MY NECK, IT IS YOURS...
IF NOT, THEN LOKI'S HEAD STAYS WITH LOKI!
THE GODS MURMURED AND NODDED TO EACH OTHER. LOKI MADE A FINE POINT...
...BUT BROKK WAS NOT YET DONE.
AND APPEALED TO THE ONE GOD WHO MIGHT HEAR HIM.
THOR, YOU HAVE HONOR. YOU KNOW LOKI'S TRICKS. HELP ME...
YOU WILL NOT MAKE A MOCKERY OF EVERYTHING, LOKI.

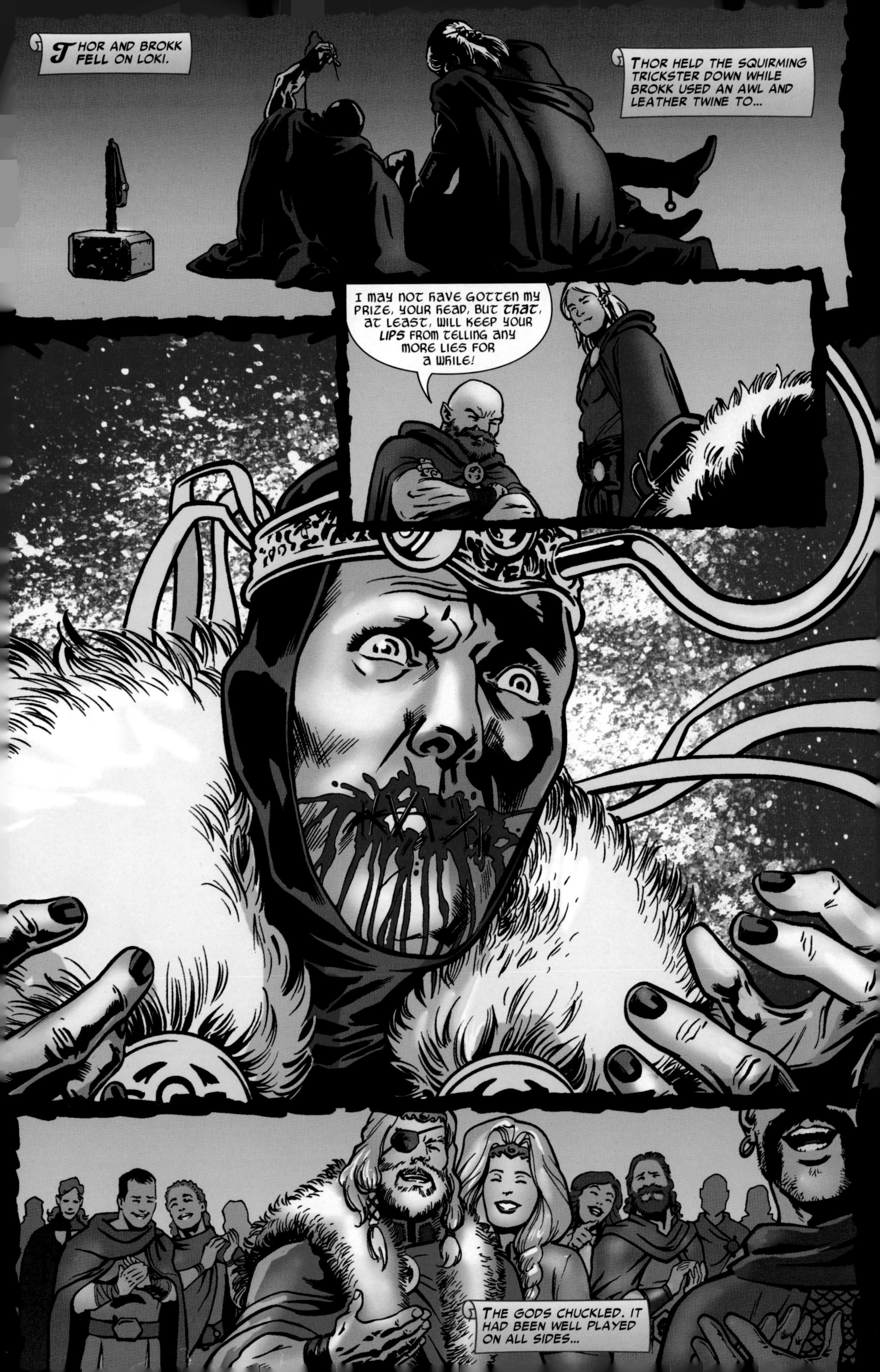
THOR AND BROKK FELL ON LOKI.
THOR HELD THE SQUIRMING TRICKSTER DOWN WHILE BROKK USED AN AWL AND LEATHER TWINE TO...
I MAY NOT HAVE GOTTEN MY PRIZE, YOUR HEAD, BUT THAT, AT LEAST, WILL KEEP YOUR LIPS FROM TELLING ANY MORE LIES FOR A WHILE!
THE GODS CHUCKLED. IT HAD BEEN WELL PLAYED ON ALL SIDES...

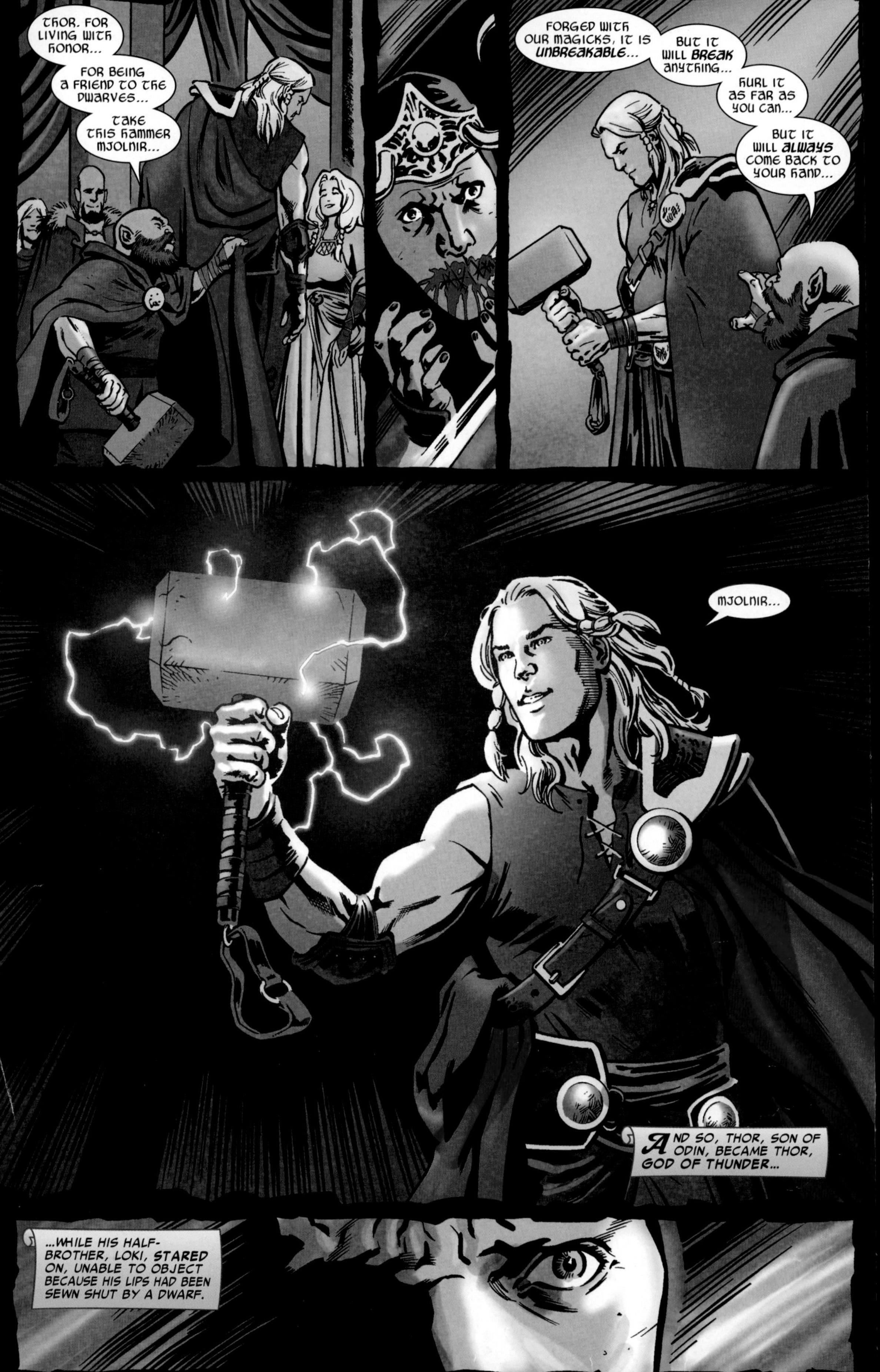
THOR. FOR LIVING WITH HONOR...
FOR BEING A FRIEND TO THE DWARVES...
TAKE THIS HAMMER MJOLNIR...
FORGED WITH OUR MAGICKS, IT IS UNBREAKABLE...
BUT IT WILL BREAK ANYTHING...
HURL IT AS FAR AS YOU CAN...
BUT IT WILL ALWAYS COME BACK TO YOUR HAND...
MJOLNIR...
AND SO, THOR, SON OF ODIN, BECAME THOR, GOD OF THUNDER...
...WHILE HIS HALF-BROTHER, LOKI, STARED ON, UNABLE TO OBJECT BECAUSE HIS LIPS HAD BEEN SEWN SHUT BY A DWARF.

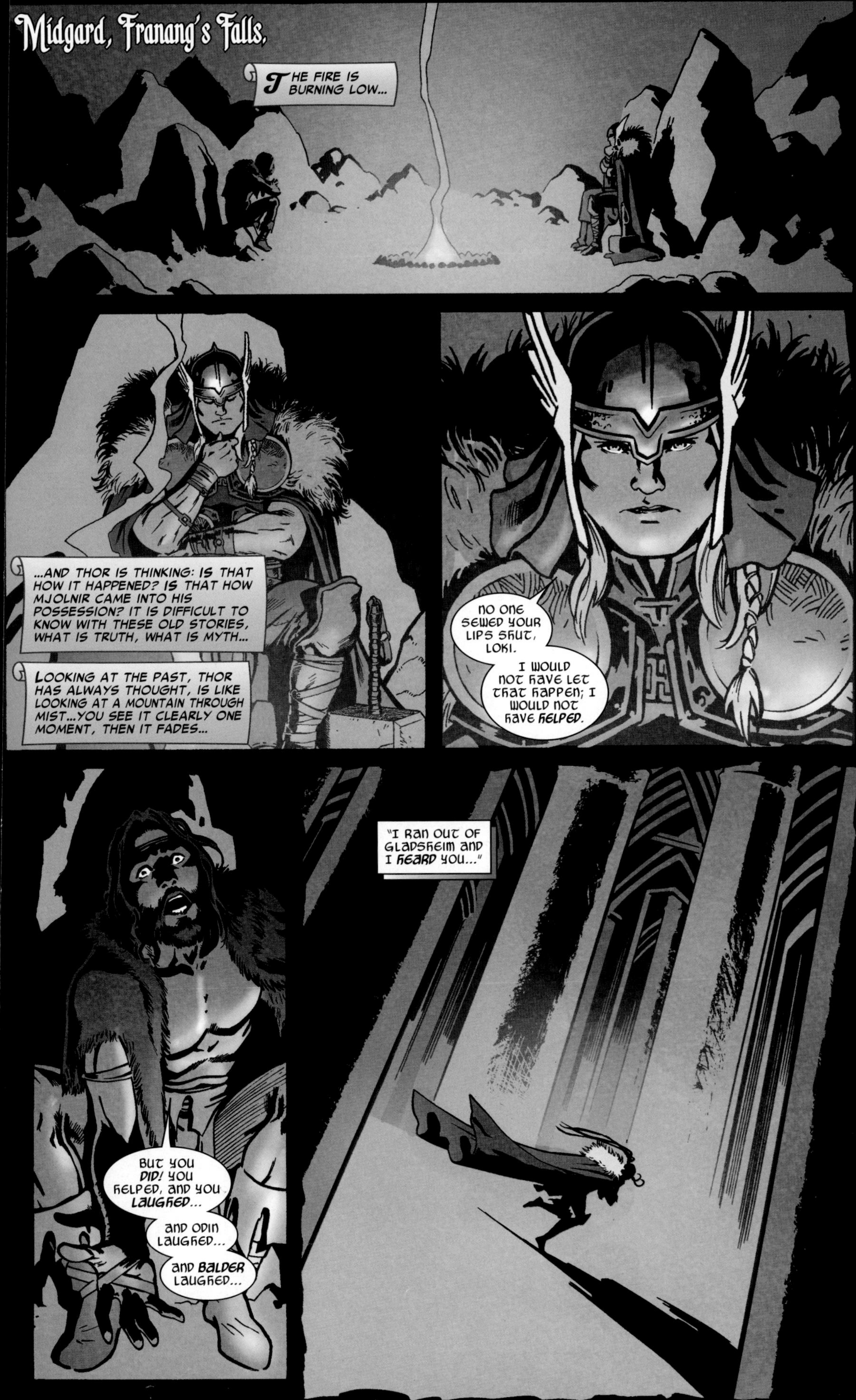
Midgard, Franang's Falls.
THE FIRE IS BURNING LOW...
...AND THOR IS THINKING: IS THAT HOW IT HAPPENED? IS THAT HOW MJOLNIR CAME INTO HIS POSSESSION? IT IS DIFFICULT TO KNOW WITH THESE OLD STORIES, WHAT IS TRUTH, WHAT IS MYTH...
LOOKING AT THE PAST, THOR HAS ALWAYS THOUGHT, IS LIKE LOOKING AT A MOUNTAIN THROUGH MIST...YOU SEE IT CLEARLY ONE MOMENT, THEN IT FADES...
NO ONE SEWED YOUR LIPS SHUT, LOKI.
I WOULD NOT HAVE LET THAT HAPPEN; I WOULD NOT HAVE HELPED.
BUT YOU DID! YOU HELPED, AND YOU LAUGHED...
AND ODIN LAUGHED...
AND BALDER LAUGHED...
"I RAN OUT OF GLADSHEIM AND I HEARD YOU..."

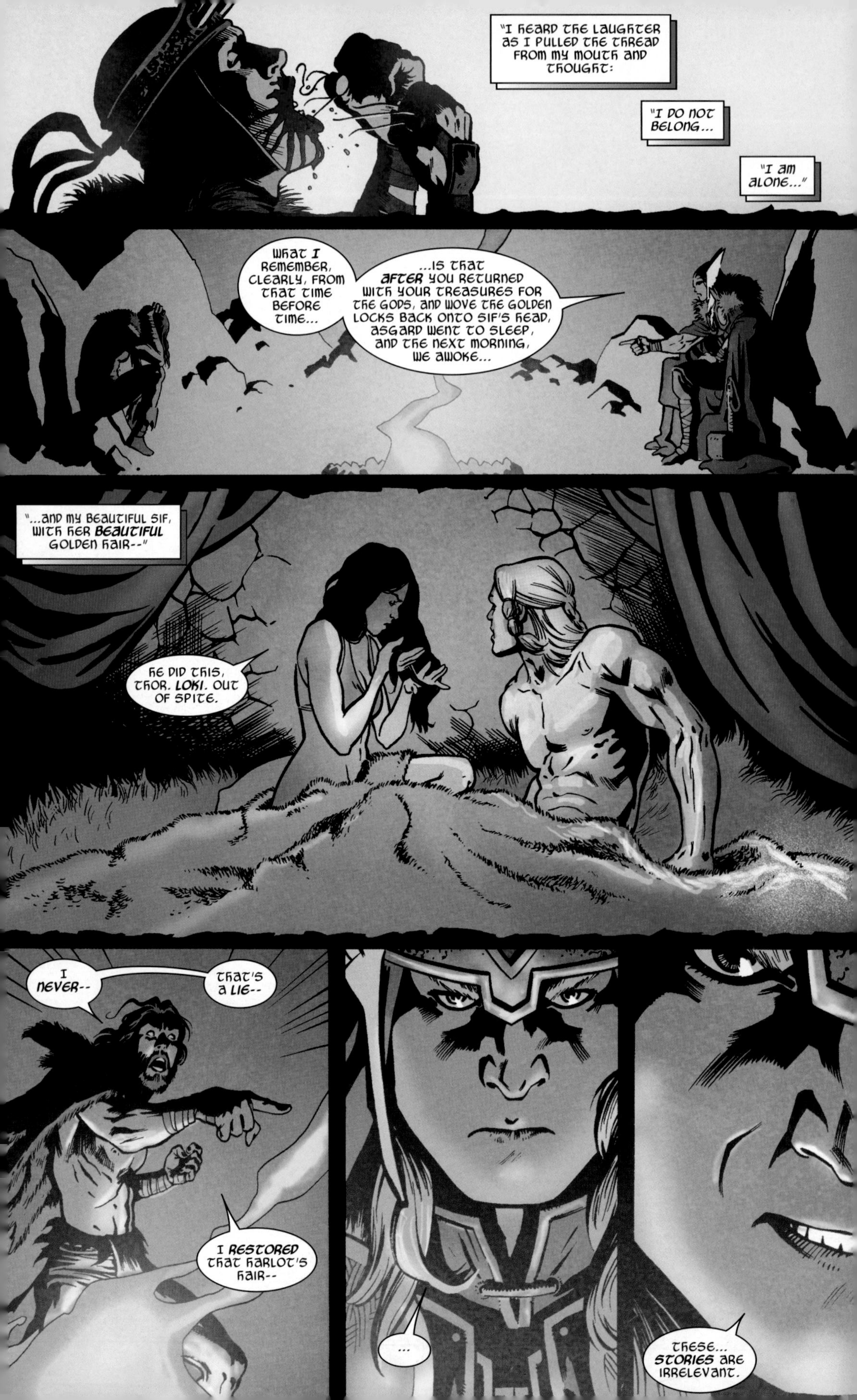
"I HEARD THE LAUGHTER AS I PULLED THE THREAD FROM MY MOUTH AND THOUGHT:
"I DO NOT BELONG...
"I AM ALONE..."
WHAT I REMEMBER, CLEARLY, FROM THAT TIME BEFORE TIME...
...IS THAT AFTER YOU RETURNED WITH YOUR TREASURES FOR THE GODS, AND WOVE THE GOLDEN LOCKS BACK ONTO SIF'S HEAD, ASGARD WENT TO SLEEP, AND THE NEXT MORNING, WE AWOKE...
"...AND MY BEAUTIFUL SIF, WITH HER BEAUTIFUL GOLDEN HAIR--"
HE DID THIS, THOR. LOKI. OUT OF SPITE.
I NEVER--
THAT'S A LIE--
I RESTORED THAT HARLOT'S HAIR--
...
THESE... STORIES ARE IRRELEVANT.

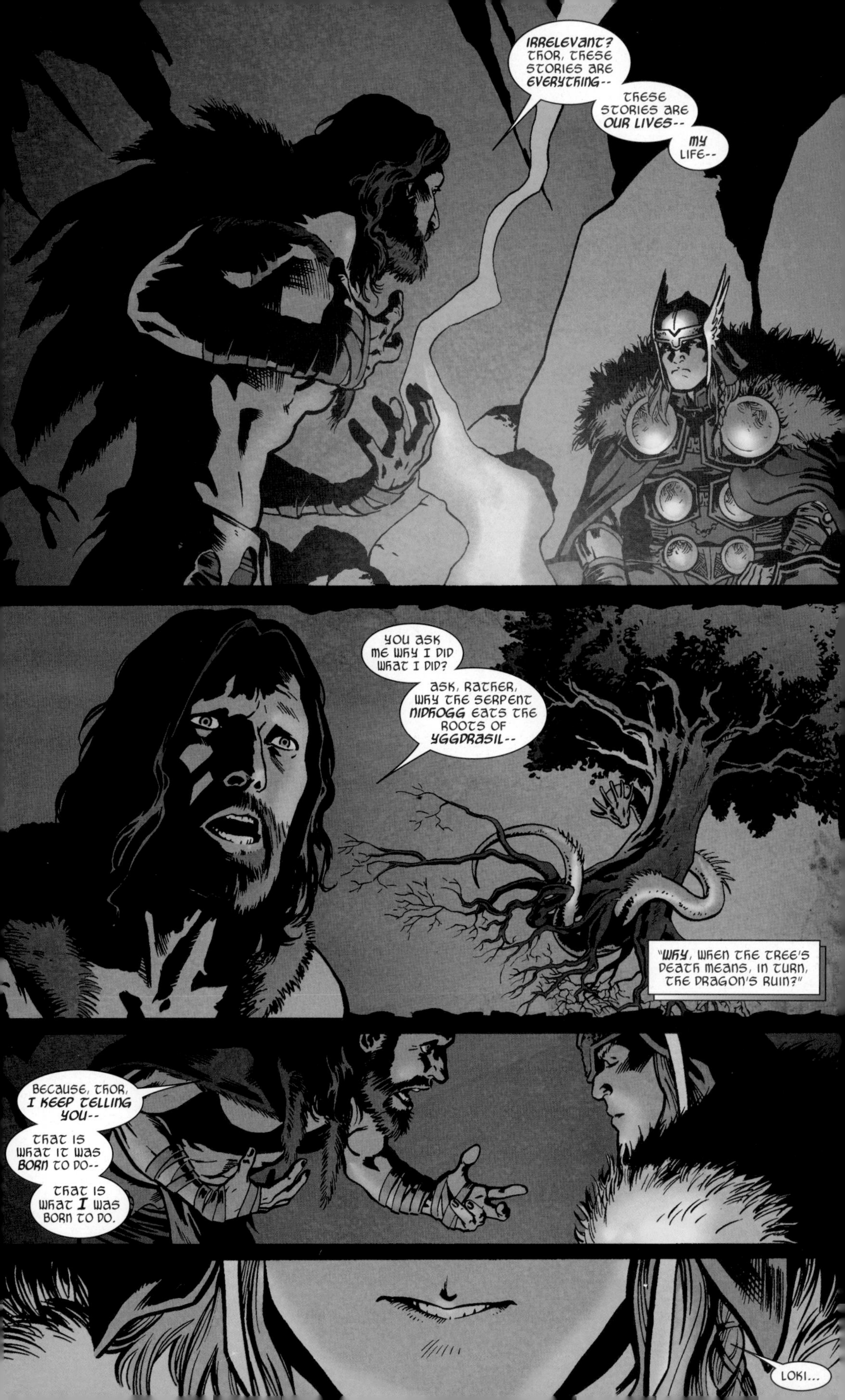
IRRELEVANT? THOR, THESE STORIES ARE EVERYTHING--
THESE STORIES ARE OUR LIVES--
MY LIFE--
YOU ASK ME WHY I DID WHAT I DID?
ASK, RATHER, WHY THE SERPENT NIDHOGG EATS THE ROOTS OF YGGDRASIL--
"WHY, WHEN THE TREE'S DEATH MEANS, IN TURN, THE DRAGON'S RUIN?"
BECAUSE, THOR, I KEEP TELLING YOU--
THAT IS WHAT IT WAS BORN TO DO--
THAT IS WHAT I WAS BORN TO DO.
LOKI...

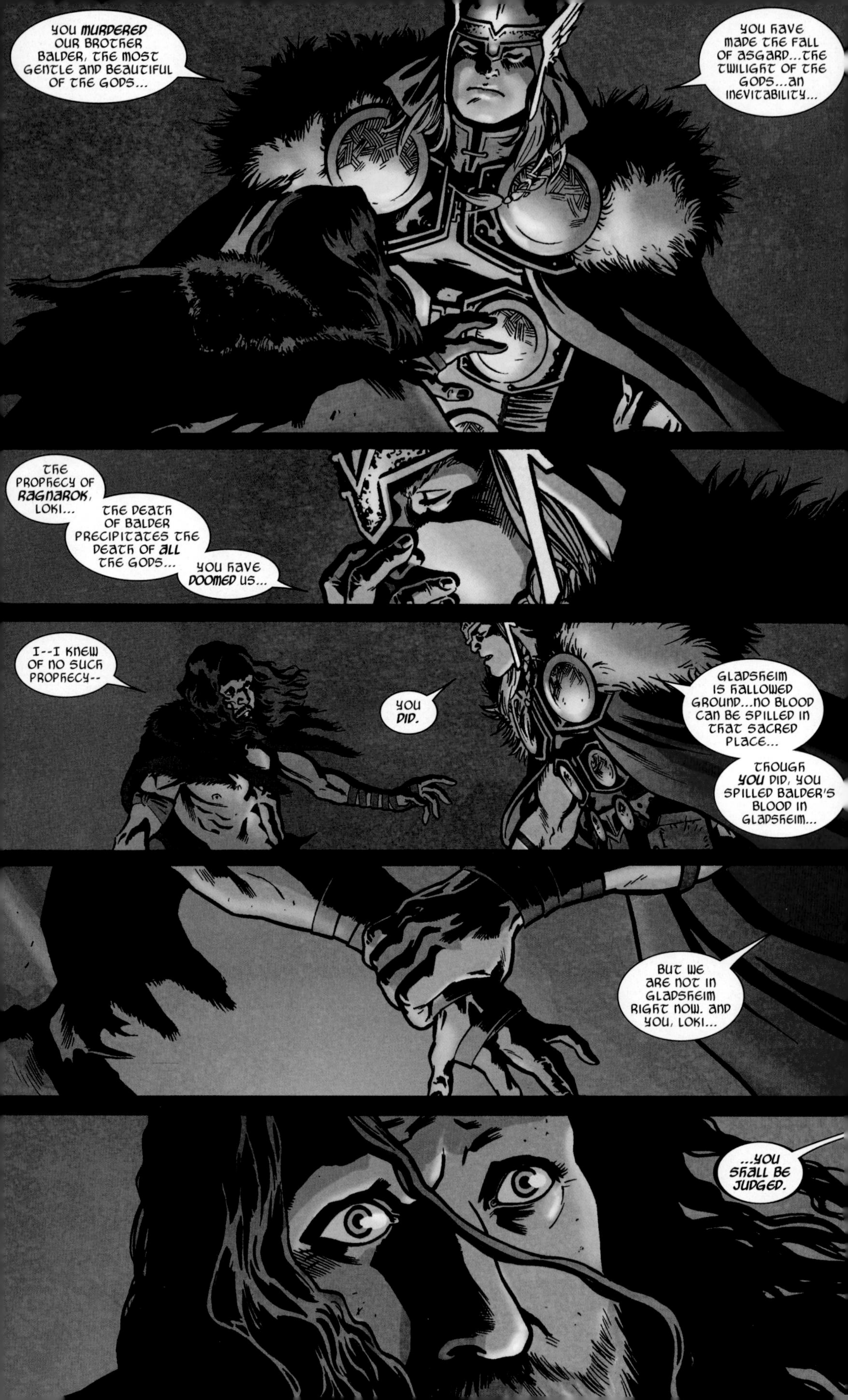
YOU MURDERED OUR BROTHER BALDER, THE MOST GENTLE AND BEAUTIFUL OF THE GODS...
YOU HAVE MADE THE FALL OF ASGARD...THE TWILIGHT OF THE GODS...AN INEVITABILITY...
THE PROPHECY OF RAGNAROK, LOKI...
THE DEATH OF BALDER PRECIPITATES THE DEATH OF ALL THE GODS...
YOU HAVE DOOMED US...
I--I KNEW OF NO SUCH PROPHECY--
YOU DID.
GLADSHEIM IS HALLOWED GROUND...NO BLOOD CAN BE SPILLED IN THAT SACRED PLACE...
THOUGH YOU DID, YOU SPILLED BALDER'S BLOOD IN GLADSHEIM...
BUT WE ARE NOT IN GLADSHEIM RIGHT NOW. AND YOU, LOKI...
...YOU SHALL BE JUDGED.

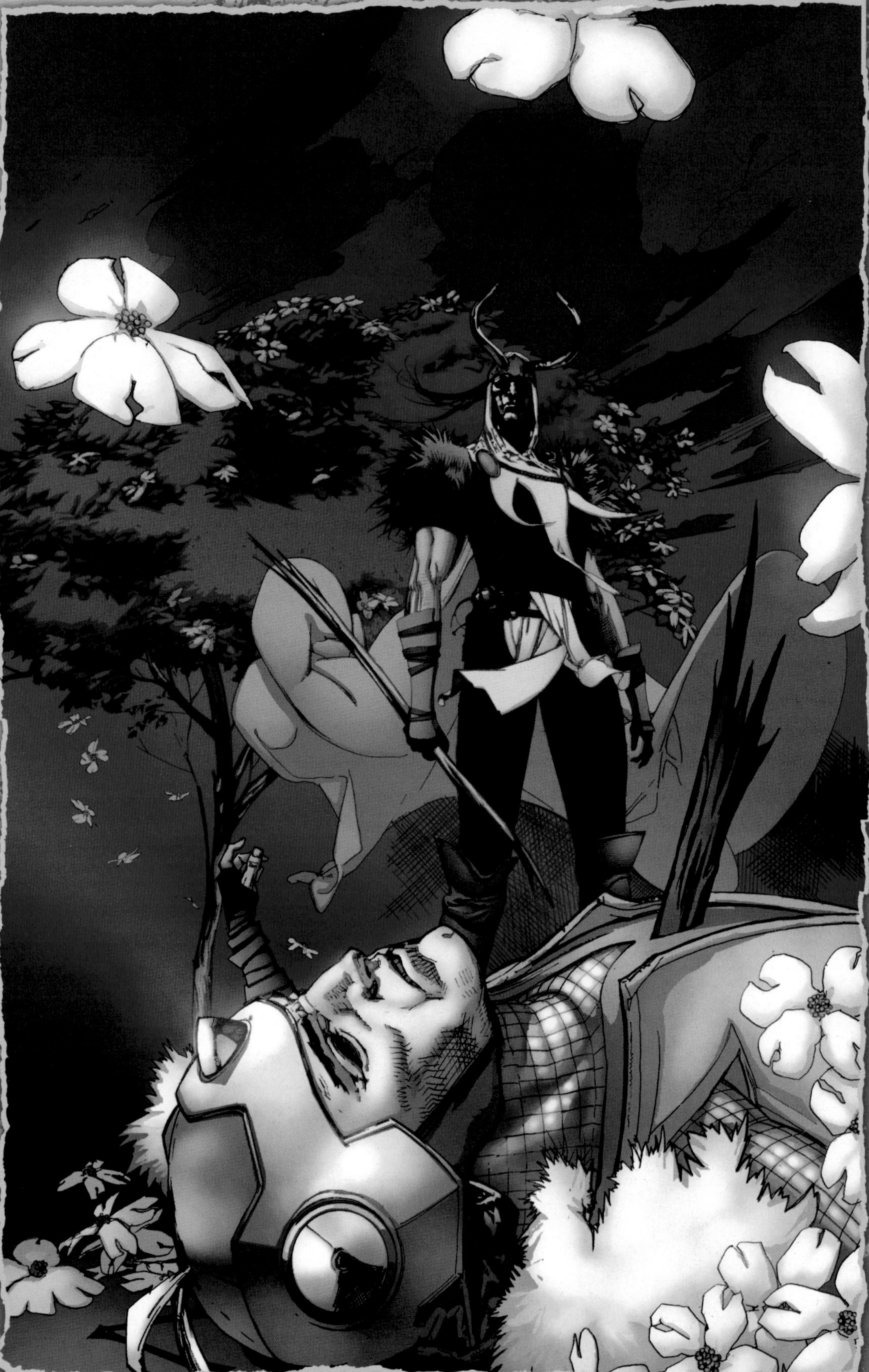

PART TWO
BLOOD DEMANDS BLOOD

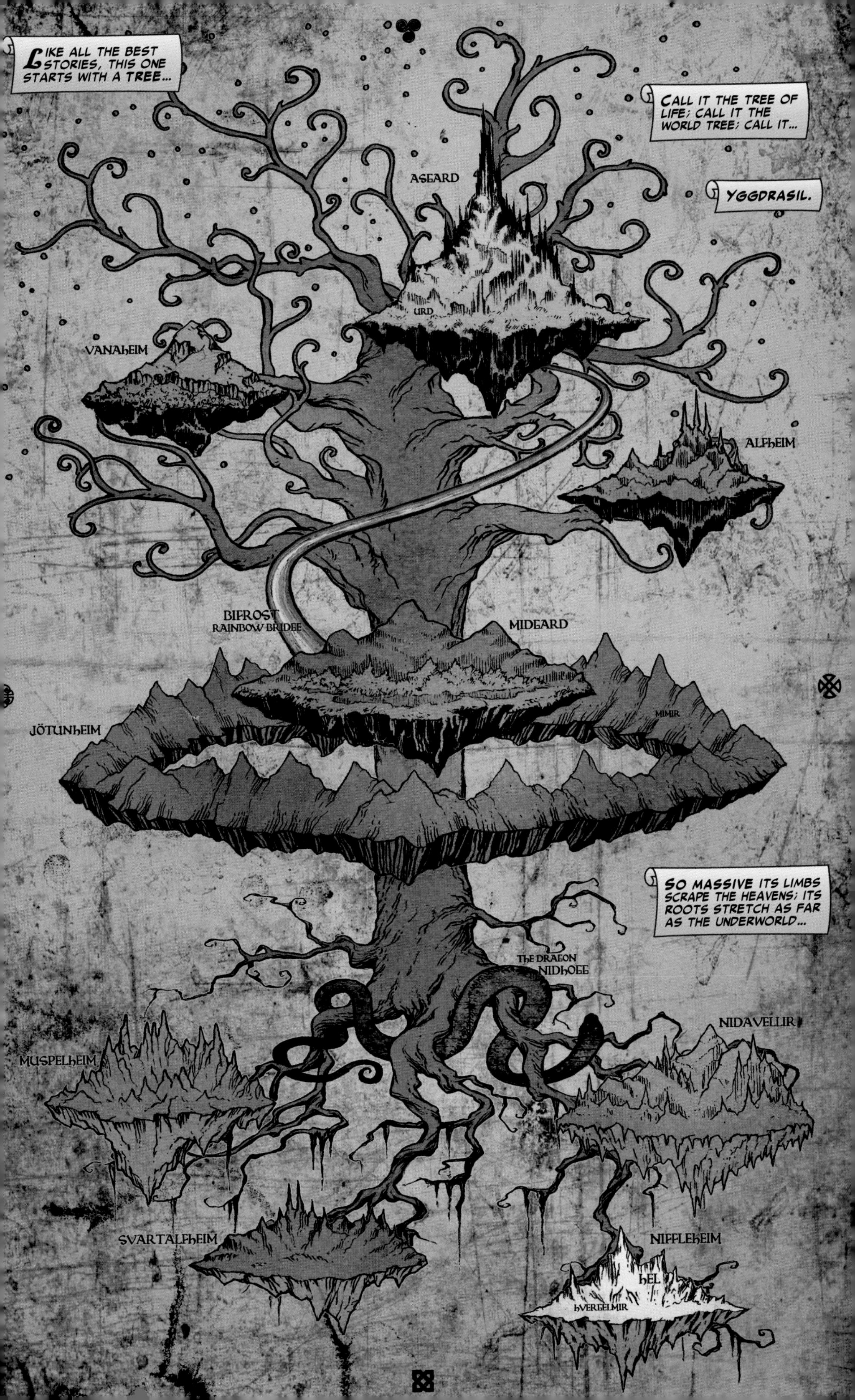

LIKE ALL THE BEST STORIES, THIS ONE STARTS WITH A TREE...
CALL IT THE TREE OF LIFE; CALL IT THE WORLD TREE; CALL IT...
YGGDRASIL.
ASGARD
URD
VANAHEIM
ALFHEIM
BIFROST
RAINBOW BRIDGE
MIDGARD
JÖTUNHEIM
MIMIR
SO MASSIVE ITS LIMBS SCRAPE THE HEAVENS; ITS ROOTS STRETCH AS FAR AS THE UNDERWORLD...
THE DRAGON
NIDHOGG
NIDAVELLIR
MUSPELHEIM
SVARTALFHEIM
NIFFLEHEIM
HEL
HVERGELMIR

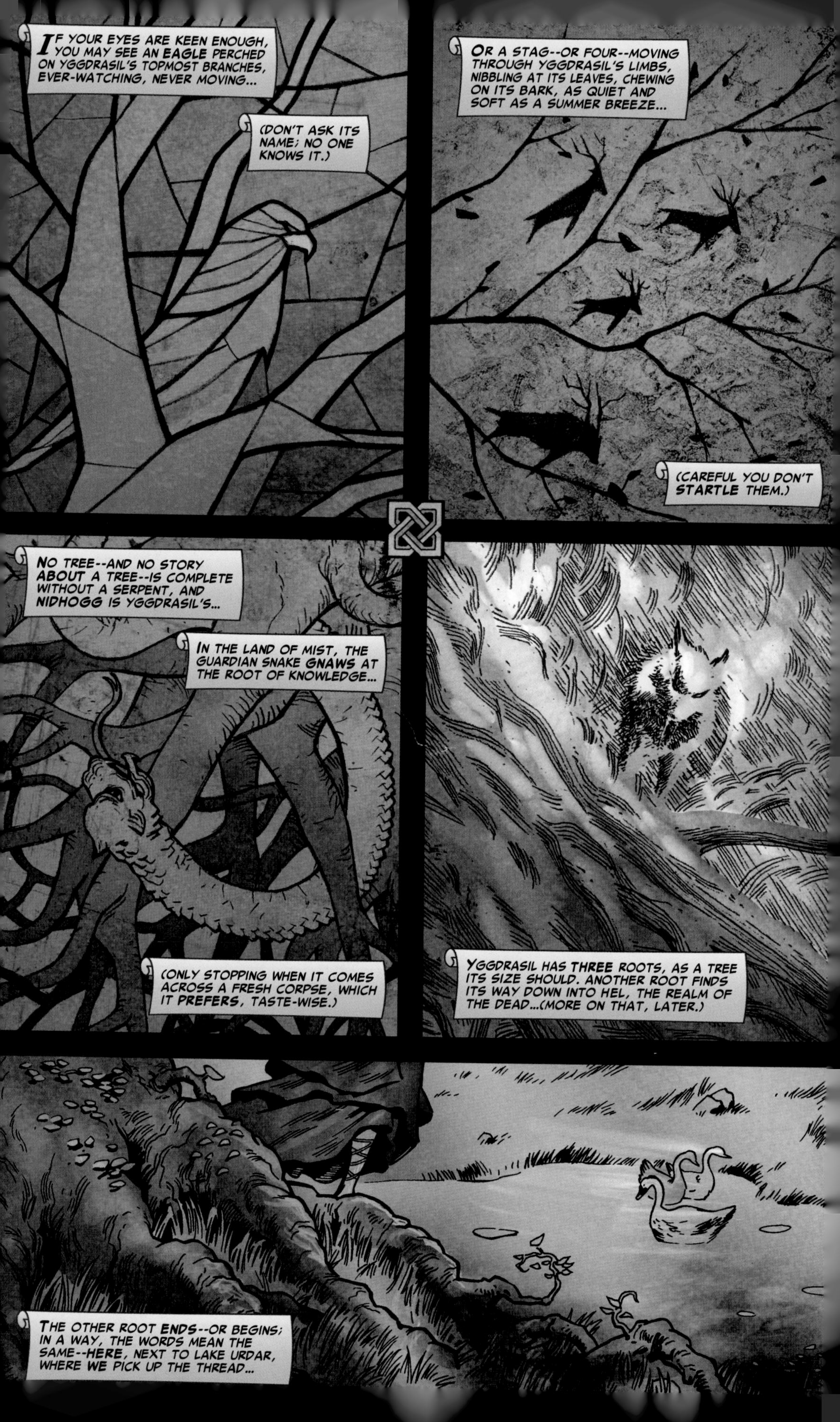
IF YOUR EYES ARE KEEN ENOUGH, YOU MAY SEE AN EAGLE PERCHED ON YGGDRASIL'S TOPMOST BRANCHES, EVER-WATCHING, NEVER MOVING...
(DON'T ASK ITS NAME; NO ONE KNOWS IT.)
OR A STAG--OR FOUR--MOVING THROUGH YGGDRASIL'S LIMBS, NIBBLING AT ITS LEAVES, CHEWING ON ITS BARK, AS QUIET AND SOFT AS A SUMMER BREEZE...
(CAREFUL YOU DON'T STARTLE THEM.)
NO TREE--AND NO STORY ABOUT A TREE--IS COMPLETE WITHOUT A SERPENT, AND NIDHOGG IS YGGDRASIL'S...
IN THE LAND OF MIST, THE GUARDIAN SNAKE GNAWS AT THE ROOT OF KNOWLEDGE...
(ONLY STOPPING WHEN IT COMES ACROSS A FRESH CORPSE, WHICH IT PREFERS, TASTE-WISE.)
YGGDRASIL HAS THREE ROOTS, AS A TREE ITS SIZE SHOULD. ANOTHER ROOT FINDS ITS WAY DOWN INTO HEL, THE REALM OF THE DEAD...(MORE ON THAT, LATER.)
THE OTHER ROOT ENDS--OR BEGINS; IN A WAY, THE WORDS MEAN THE SAME--HERE, NEXT TO LAKE URDAR, WHERE WE PICK UP THE THREAD...

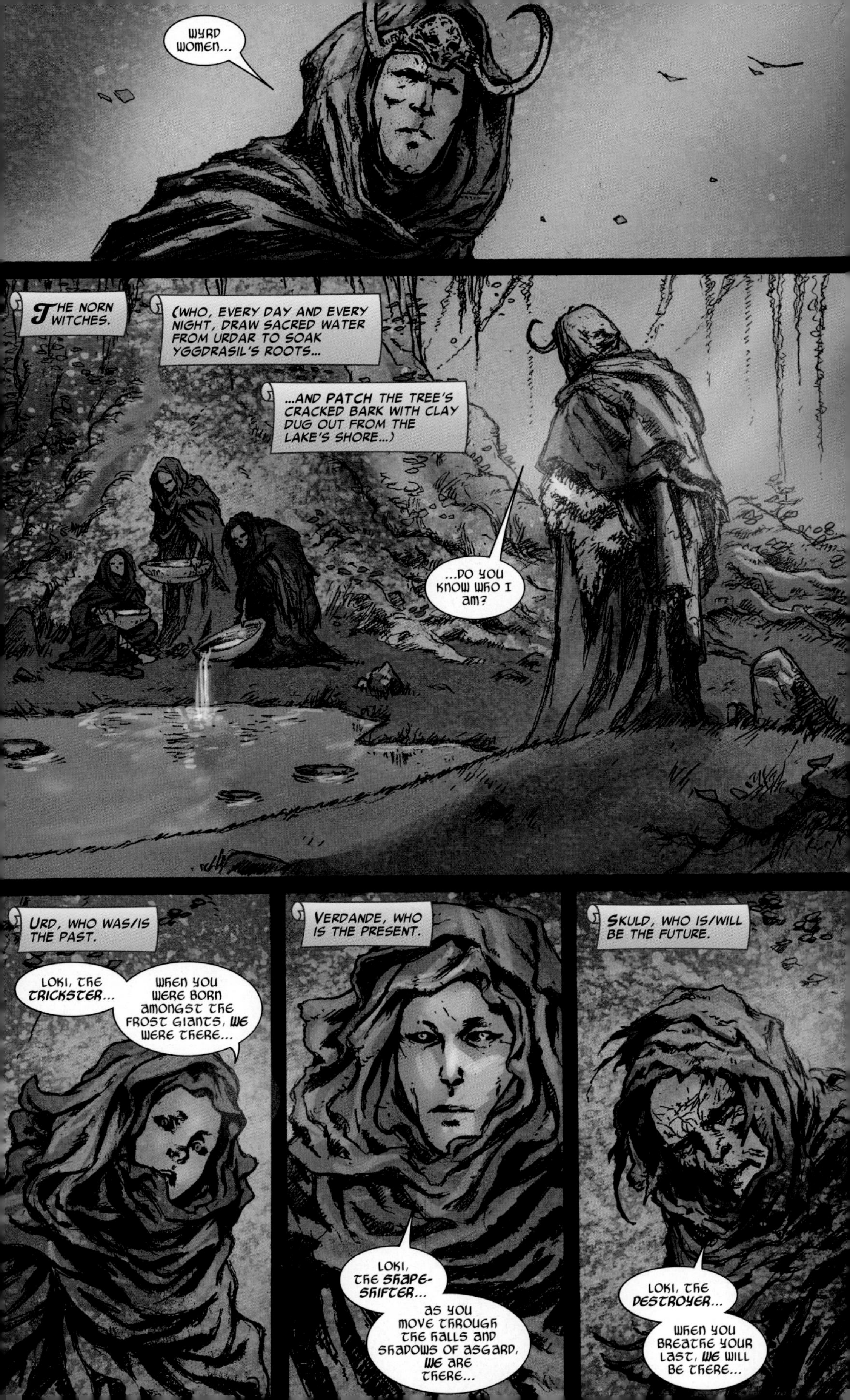
WYRD WOMEN...
THE NORN WITCHES.
(WHO, EVERY DAY AND EVERY NIGHT, DRAW SACRED WATER FROM URDAR TO SOAK YGGDRASIL'S ROOTS...
...AND PATCH THE TREE'S CRACKED BARK WITH CLAY DUG OUT FROM THE LAKE'S SHORE...)
...DO YOU KNOW WHO I AM?
URD, WHO WAS/IS THE PAST.
LOKI, THE TRICKSTER...
WHEN YOU WERE BORN AMONGST THE FROST GIANTS, WE WERE THERE...
VERDANDE, WHO IS THE PRESENT.
LOKI, THE SHAPE-SHIFTER...
AS YOU MOVE THROUGH THE HALLS AND SHADOWS OF ASGARD, WE ARE THERE...
SKULD, WHO IS/WILL BE THE FUTURE.
LOKI, THE DESTROYER...
WHEN YOU BREATHE YOUR LAST, WE WILL BE THERE...

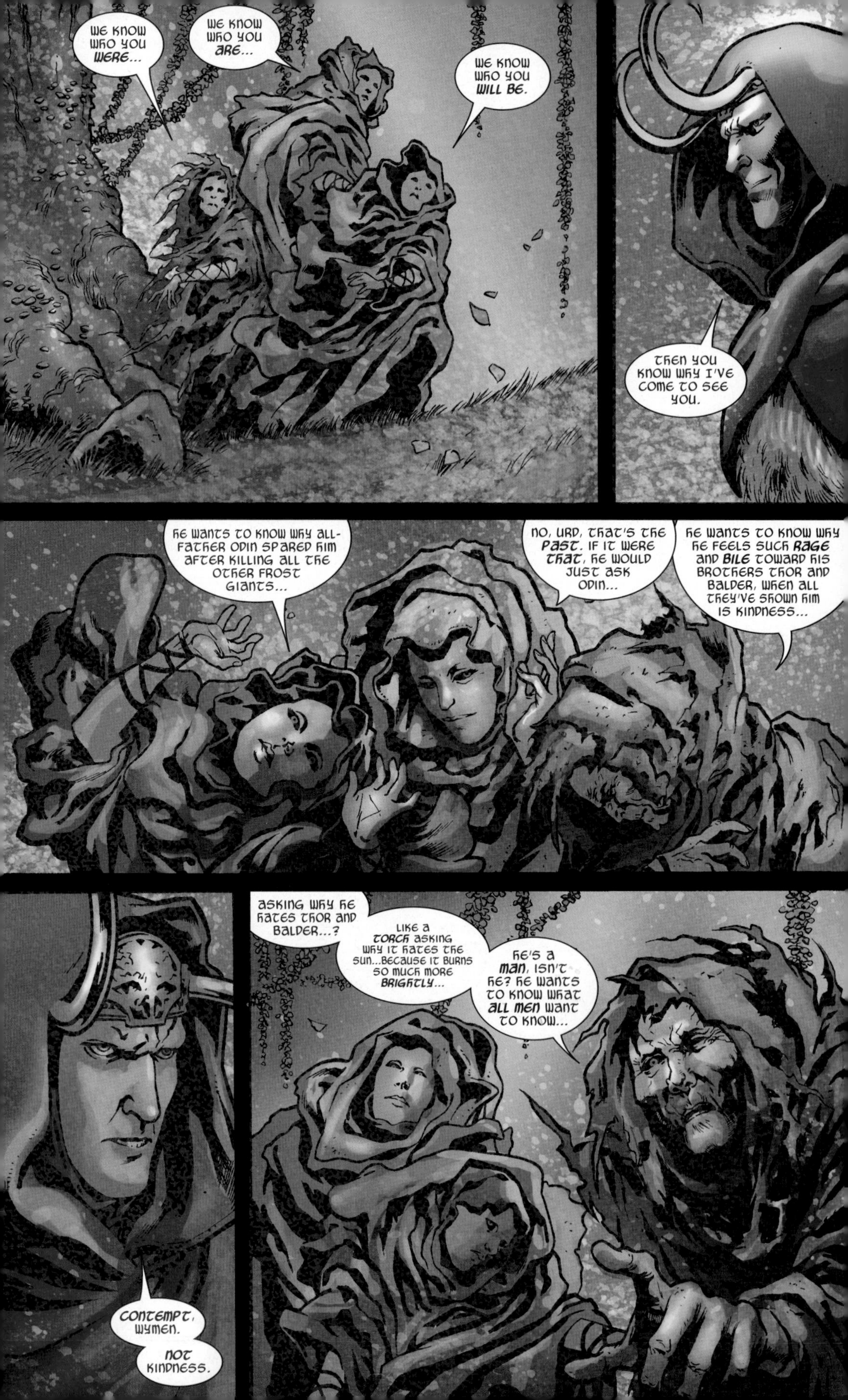
WE KNOW WHO YOU WERE...
WE KNOW WHO YOU ARE...
WE KNOW WHO YOU WILL BE.
THEN YOU KNOW WHY I'VE COME TO SEE YOU.
HE WANTS TO KNOW WHY ALL-FATHER ODIN SPARED HIM AFTER KILLING ALL THE OTHER FROST GIANTS...
NO, URD, THAT'S THE PAST. IF IT WERE THAT, HE WOULD JUST ASK ODIN...
HE WANTS TO KNOW WHY HE FEELS SUCH RAGE AND BILE TOWARD HIS BROTHERS THOR AND BALDER, WHEN ALL THEY'VE SHOWN HIM IS KINDNESS...
CONTEMPT, WYMEN.
NOT KINDNESS.
ASKING WHY HE HATES THOR AND BALDER...?
LIKE A TORCH ASKING WHY IT HATES THE SUN...BECAUSE IT BURNS SO MUCH MORE BRIGHTLY...
HE'S A MAN, ISN'T HE? HE WANTS TO KNOW WHAT ALL MEN WANT TO KNOW...

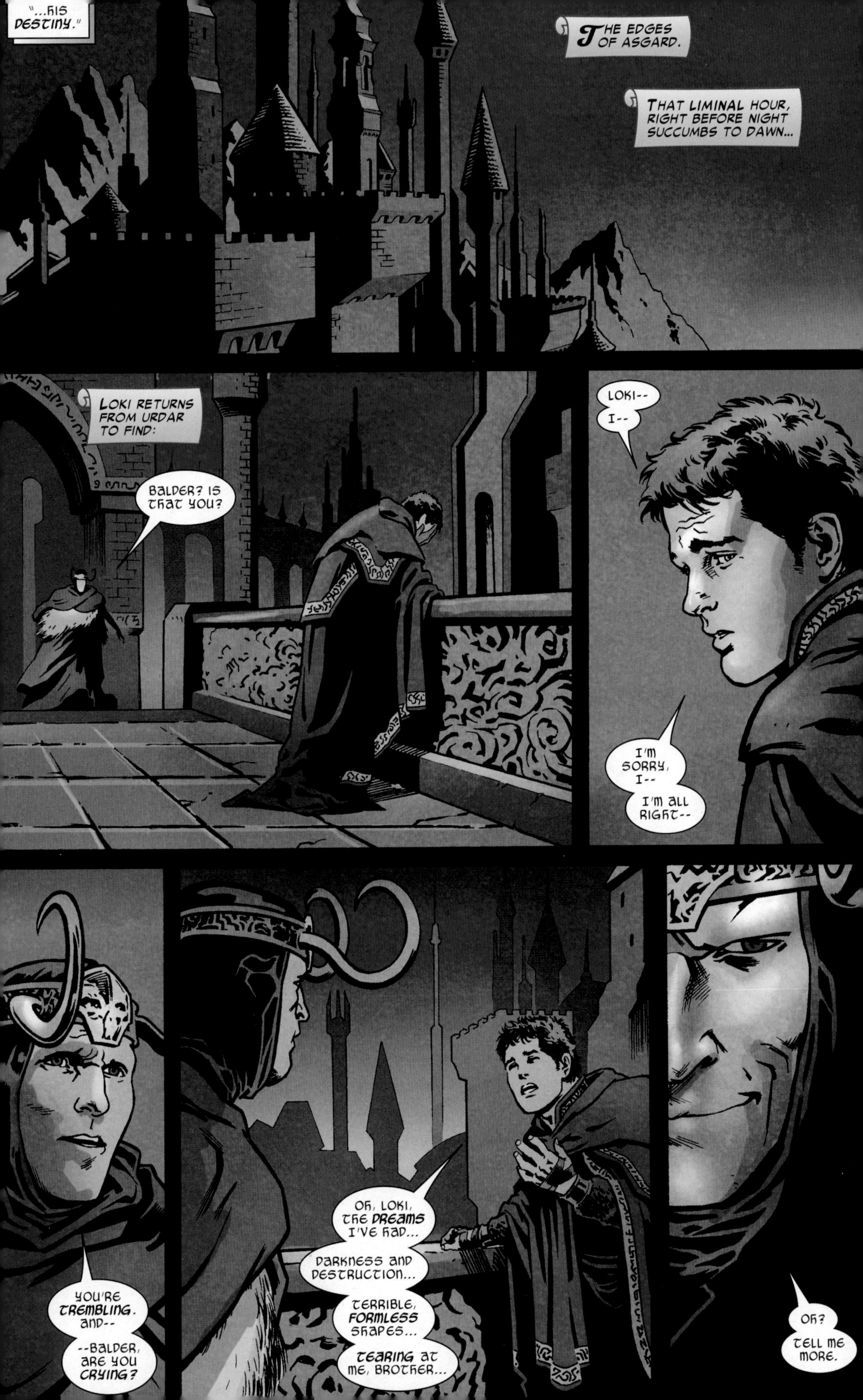
"...HIS DESTINY."
THE EDGES OF ASGARD.
THAT LIMINAL HOUR, RIGHT BEFORE NIGHT SUCCUMBS TO DAWN...
LOKI RETURNS FROM URDAR TO FIND:
BALDER? IS THAT YOU?
LOKI--
I--
I'M SORRY, I--
I'M ALL RIGHT--
YOU'RE TREMBLING. AND--
--BALDER, ARE YOU CRYING?
OH, LOKI, THE DREAMS I'VE HAD...
DARKNESS AND DESTRUCTION...
TERRIBLE, FORMLESS SHAPES...
TEARING AT ME, BROTHER...
OH?
TELL ME MORE.

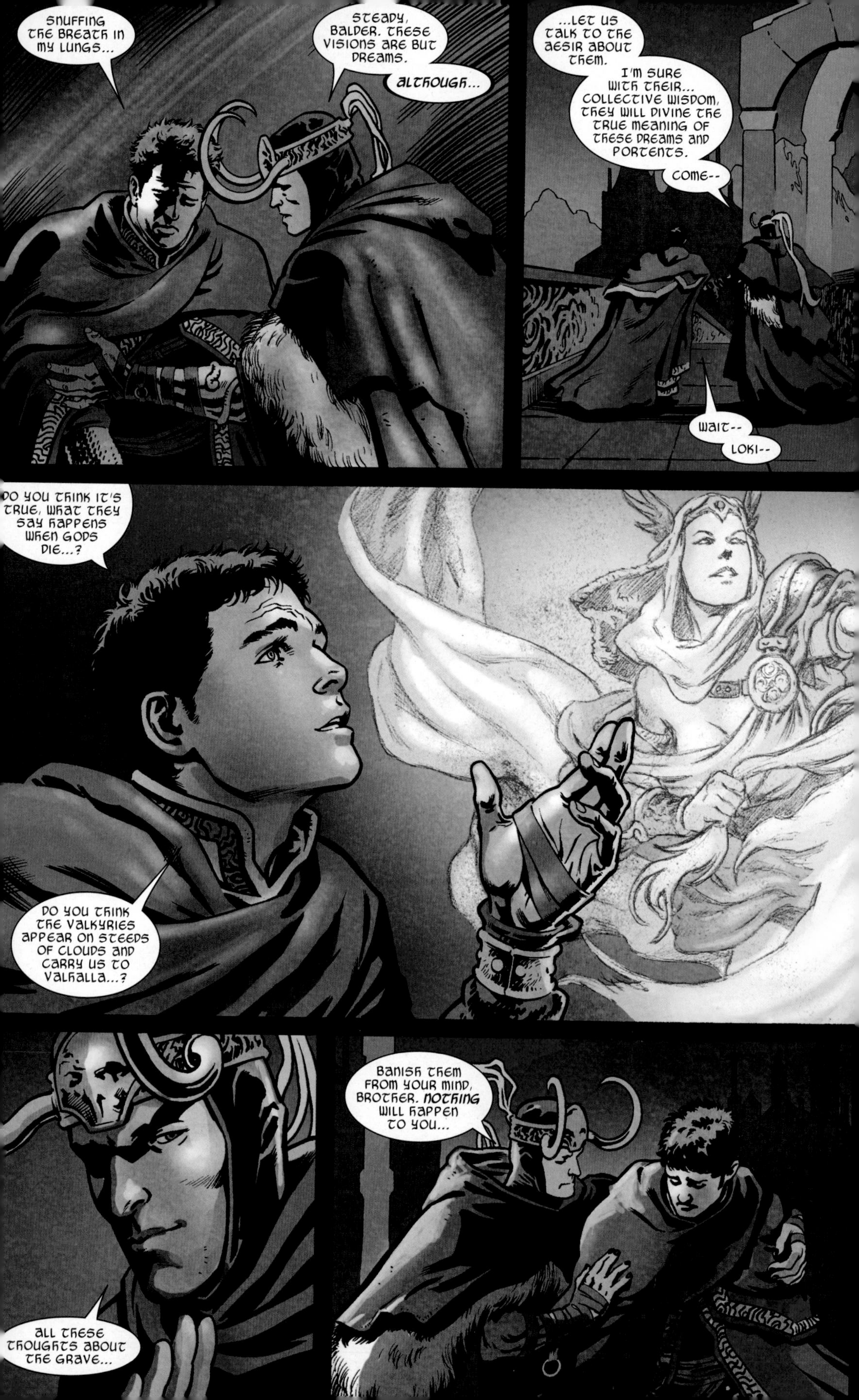
SNUFFING THE BREATH IN MY LUNGS...
STEADY, BALDER. THESE VISIONS ARE BUT DREAMS.
ALTHOUGH...
...LET US TALK TO THE AESIR ABOUT THEM.
I'M SURE WITH THEIR... COLLECTIVE WISDOM, THEY WILL DIVINE THE TRUE MEANING OF THESE DREAMS AND PORTENTS.
COME--
WAIT--
LOKI--
DO YOU THINK IT'S TRUE, WHAT THEY SAY HAPPENS WHEN GODS DIE...?
DO YOU THINK THE VALKYRIES APPEAR ON STEEDS OF CLOUDS AND CARRY US TO VALHALLA...?
ALL THESE THOUGHTS ABOUT THE GRAVE...
BANISH THEM FROM YOUR MIND, BROTHER. NOTHING WILL HAPPEN TO YOU...

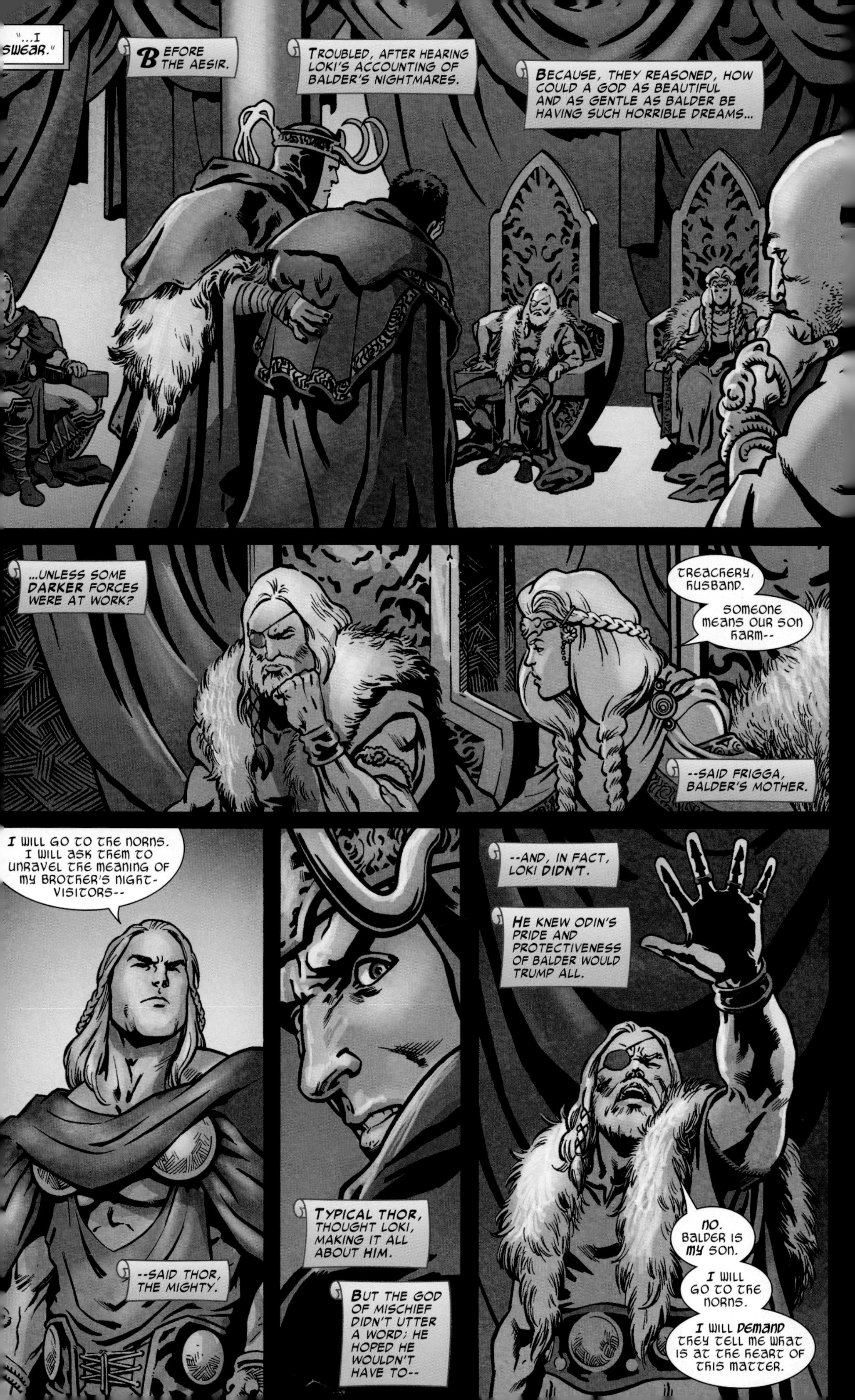
"...I SWEAR."
BEFORE THE AESIR.
TROUBLED, AFTER HEARING LOKI'S ACCOUNTING OF BALDER'S NIGHTMARES.
BECAUSE, THEY REASONED, HOW COULD A GOD AS BEAUTIFUL AND AS GENTLE AS BALDER BE HAVING SUCH HORRIBLE DREAMS...
...UNLESS SOME DARKER FORCES WERE AT WORK?
TREACHERY, HUSBAND.
SOMEONE MEANS OUR SON HARM--
--SAID FRIGGA, BALDER'S MOTHER.
I WILL GO TO THE NORNS. I WILL ASK THEM TO UNRAVEL THE MEANING OF MY BROTHER'S NIGHT-VISITORS--
--SAID THOR, THE MIGHTY.
TYPICAL THOR, THOUGHT LOKI, MAKING IT ALL ABOUT HIM.
BUT THE GOD OF MISCHIEF DIDN'T UTTER A WORD; HE HOPED HE WOULDN'T HAVE TO--
--AND, IN FACT, LOKI DIDN'T.
HE KNEW ODIN'S PRIDE AND PROTECTIVENESS OF BALDER WOULD TRUMP ALL.
NO. BALDER IS MY SON.
I WILL GO TO THE NORNS.
I WILL DEMAND THEY TELL ME WHAT IS AT THE HEART OF THIS MATTER.

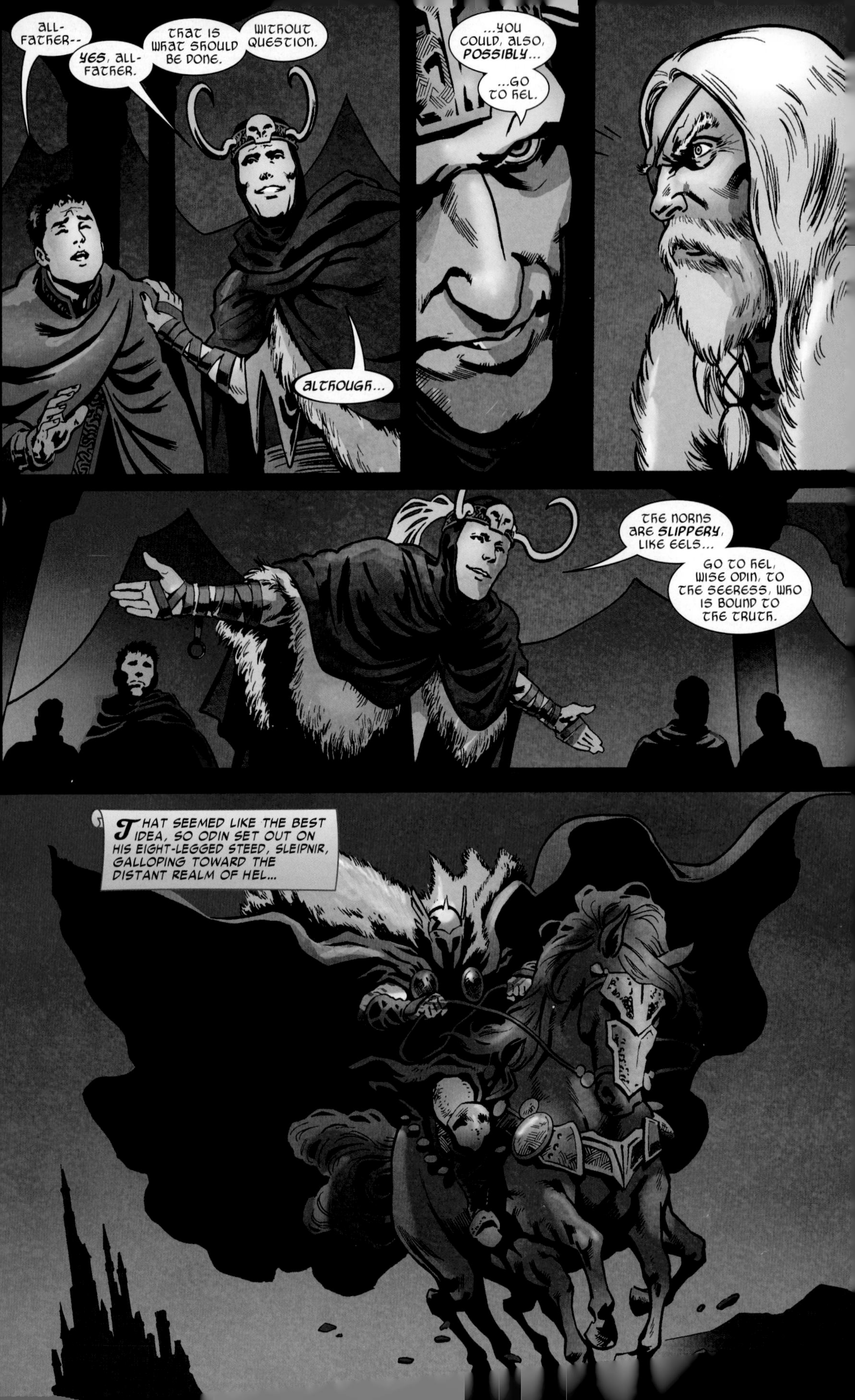
ALL-FATHER--
YES, ALL-FATHER.
THAT IS WHAT SHOULD BE DONE.
WITHOUT QUESTION.
ALTHOUGH...
...YOU COULD, ALSO, POSSIBLY...
...GO TO HEL.
THE NORNS ARE SLIPPERY, LIKE EELS...
GO TO HEL, WISE ODIN, TO THE SEERESS, WHO IS BOUND TO THE TRUTH.
THAT SEEMED LIKE THE BEST IDEA, SO ODIN SET OUT ON HIS EIGHT-LEGGED STEED, SLEIPNIR, GALLOPING TOWARD THE DISTANT REALM OF HEL...

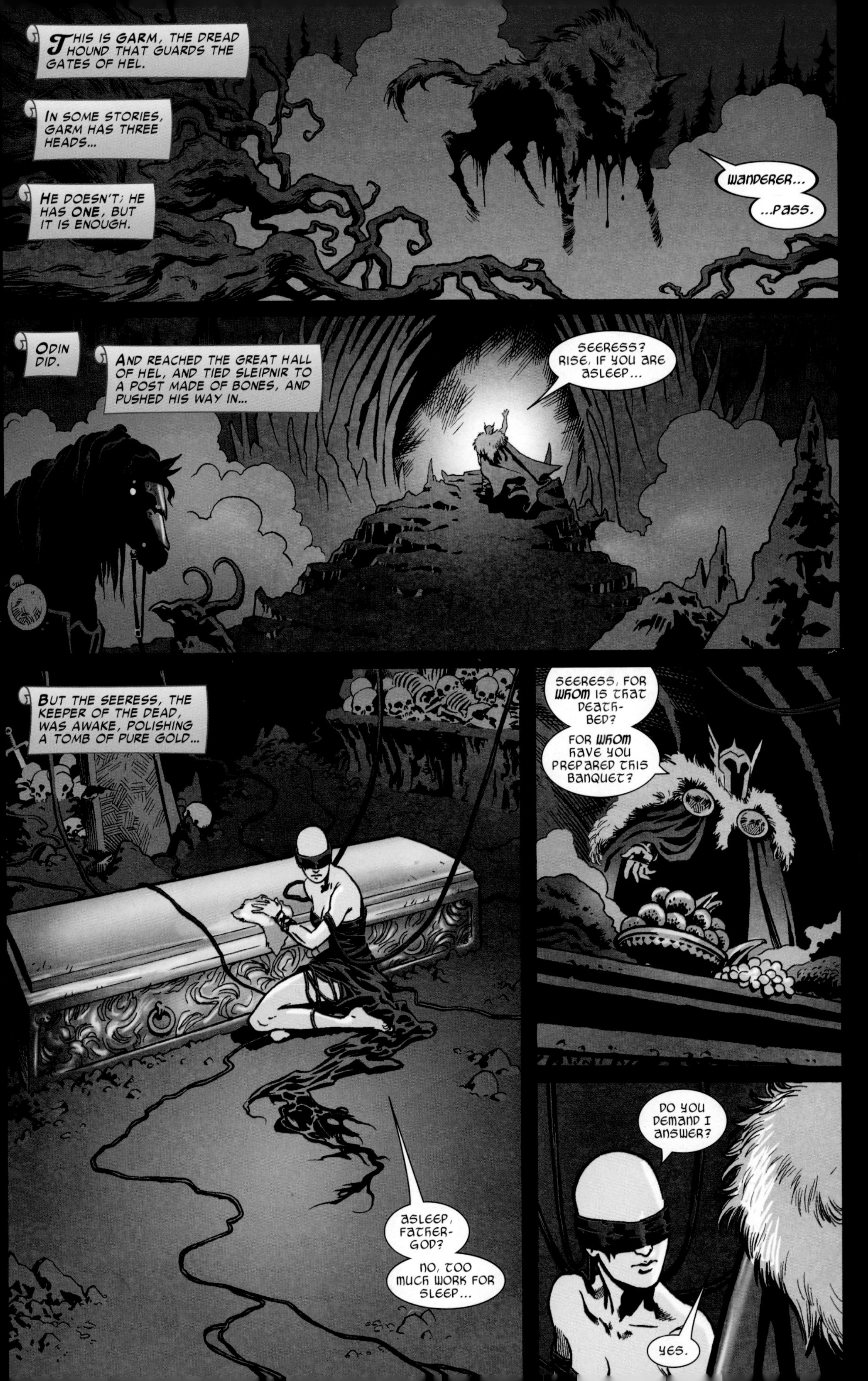

This is GARM, the dread hound that guards the gates of Hel.
In some stories, Garm has three heads...
He doesn't; he has ONE, but it is enough.
Wanderer...
...pass.
Odin did.
And reached the great hall of Hel, and tied Sleipnir to a post made of bones, and pushed his way in...
Seeress? Rise, if you are asleep...
But the seeress, the keeper of the dead, was awake, polishing a tomb of pure gold...
Asleep, Father-God?
No, too much work for sleep...
Seeress, for WHOM is that death-bed?
For WHOM have you prepared this banquet?
Do you demand I answer?
Yes.

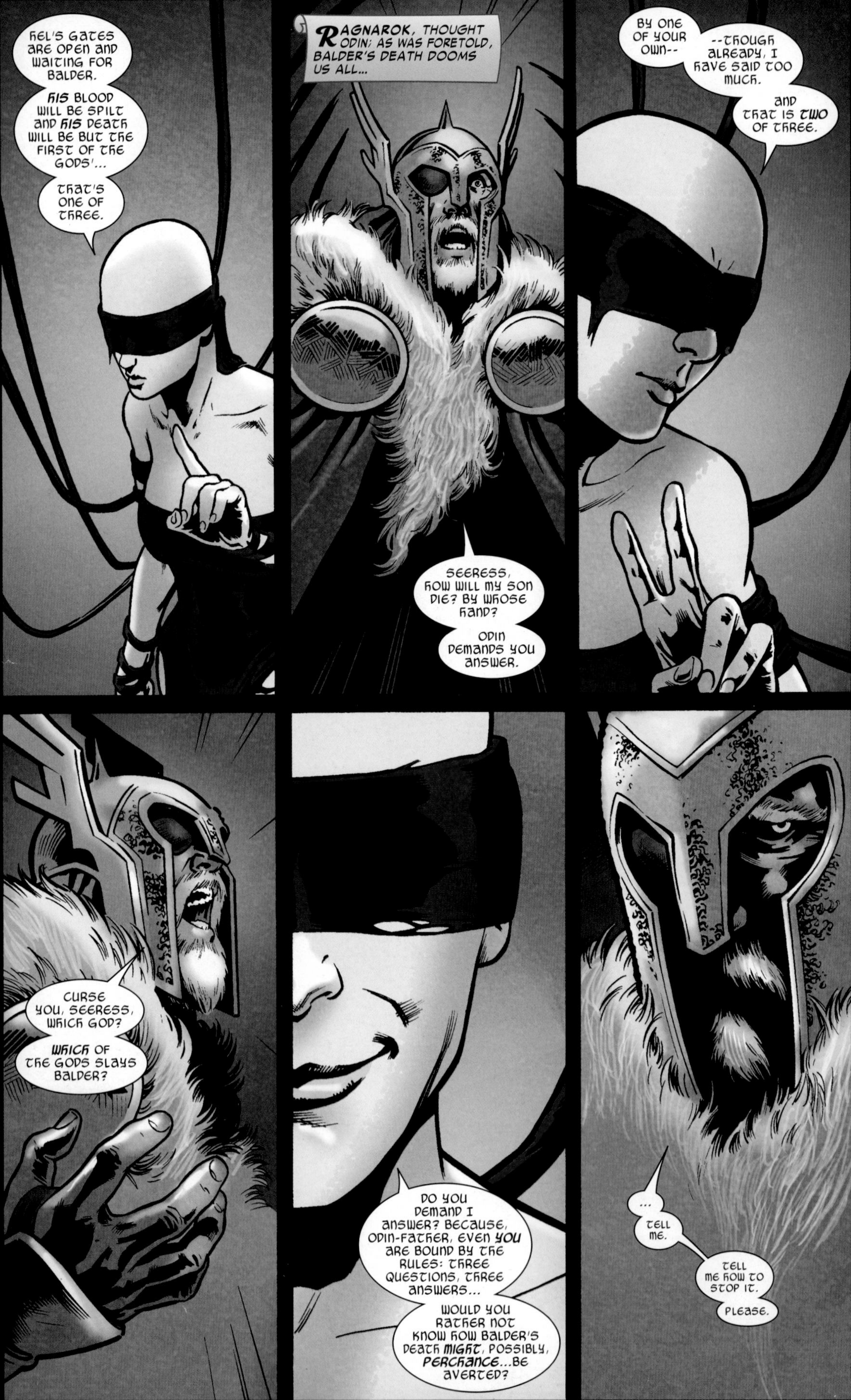
HEL'S GATES ARE OPEN AND WAITING FOR BALDER.
HIS BLOOD WILL BE SPILT AND HIS DEATH WILL BE BUT THE FIRST OF THE GODS'...
THAT'S ONE OF THREE.
RAGNAROK, THOUGHT ODIN; AS WAS FORETOLD, BALDER'S DEATH DOOMS US ALL...
SEERESS, HOW WILL MY SON DIE? BY WHOSE HAND?
ODIN DEMANDS YOU ANSWER.
BY ONE OF YOUR OWN--
--THOUGH ALREADY, I HAVE SAID TOO MUCH.
AND THAT IS TWO OF THREE.
CURSE YOU, SEERESS, WHICH GOD?
WHICH OF THE GODS SLAYS BALDER?
DO YOU DEMAND I ANSWER? BECAUSE, ODIN-FATHER, EVEN YOU ARE BOUND BY THE RULES: THREE QUESTIONS, THREE ANSWERS...
WOULD YOU RATHER NOT KNOW HOW BALDER'S DEATH MIGHT, POSSIBLY, PERCHANCE...BE AVERTED?
...
TELL ME.
TELL ME HOW TO STOP IT.
PLEASE.

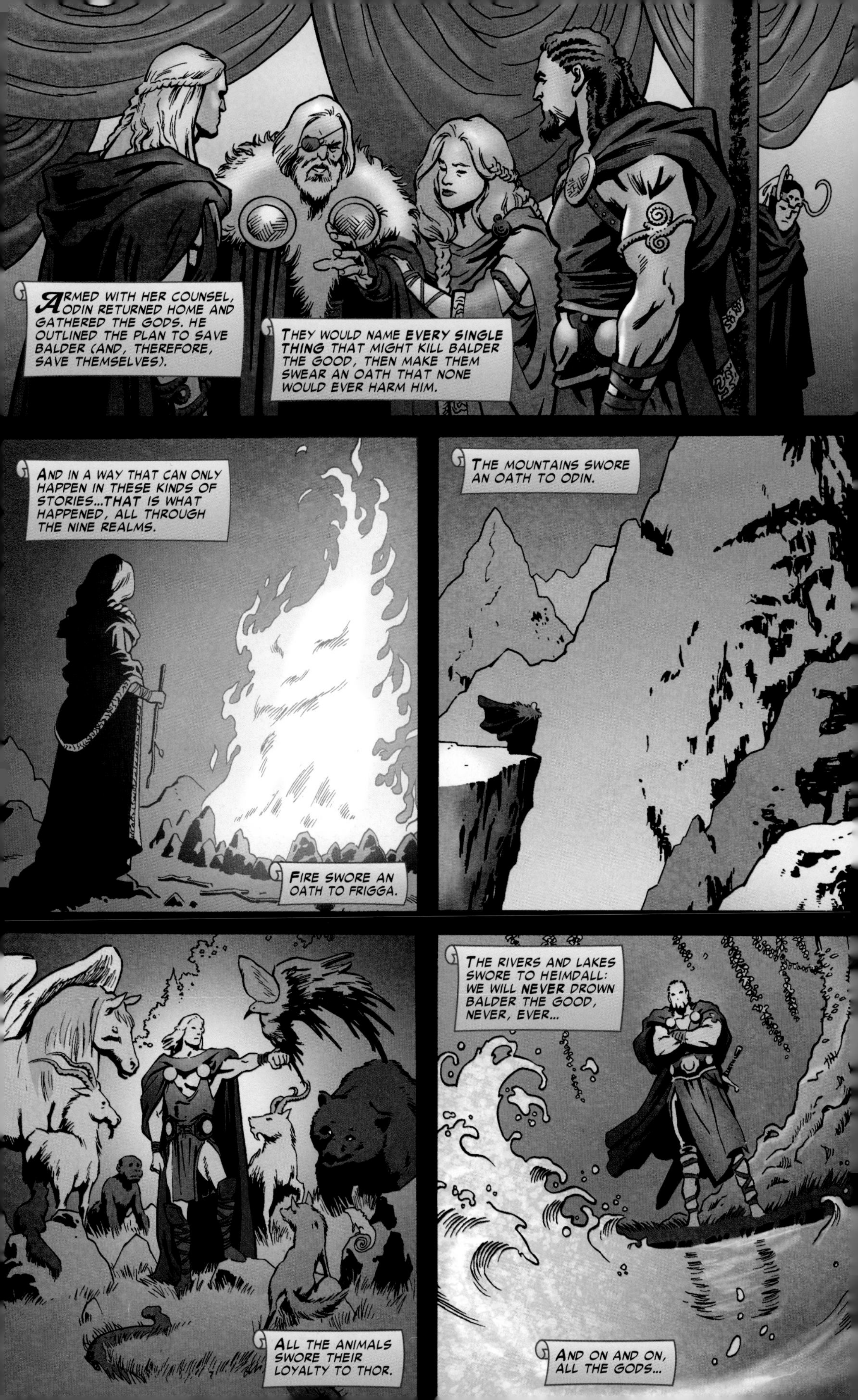
ARMED WITH HER COUNSEL, ODIN RETURNED HOME AND GATHERED THE GODS. HE OUTLINED THE PLAN TO SAVE BALDER (AND, THEREFORE, SAVE THEMSELVES).
THEY WOULD NAME EVERY SINGLE THING THAT MIGHT KILL BALDER THE GOOD, THEN MAKE THEM SWEAR AN OATH THAT NONE WOULD EVER HARM HIM.
AND IN A WAY THAT CAN ONLY HAPPEN IN THESE KINDS OF STORIES...THAT IS WHAT HAPPENED, ALL THROUGH THE NINE REALMS.
FIRE SWORE AN OATH TO FRIGGA.
THE MOUNTAINS SWORE AN OATH TO ODIN.
ALL THE ANIMALS SWORE THEIR LOYALTY TO THOR.
THE RIVERS AND LAKES SWORE TO HEIMDALL: WE WILL NEVER DROWN BALDER THE GOOD, NEVER, EVER...
AND ON AND ON, ALL THE GODS...

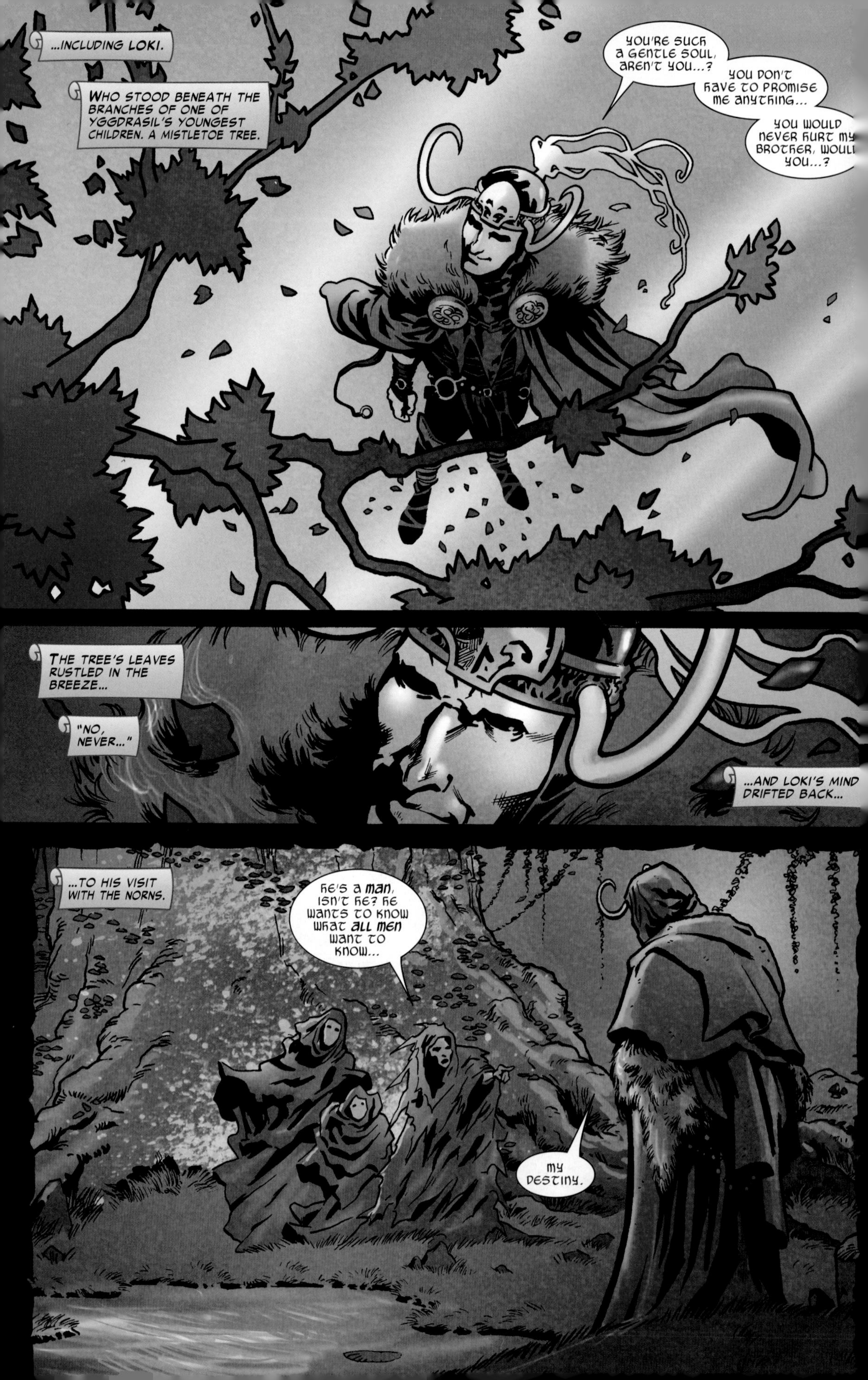
...INCLUDING LOKI.
WHO STOOD BENEATH THE BRANCHES OF ONE OF YGGDRASIL'S YOUNGEST CHILDREN. A MISTLETOE TREE.
YOU'RE SUCH A GENTLE SOUL, AREN'T YOU...?
YOU DON'T HAVE TO PROMISE ME ANYTHING...
YOU WOULD NEVER HURT MY BROTHER, WOULD YOU...?
THE TREE'S LEAVES RUSTLED IN THE BREEZE...
"NO, NEVER..."
...AND LOKI'S MIND DRIFTED BACK...
...TO HIS VISIT WITH THE NORNS.
HE'S A MAN, ISN'T HE? HE WANTS TO KNOW WHAT ALL MEN WANT TO KNOW...
MY DESTINY.

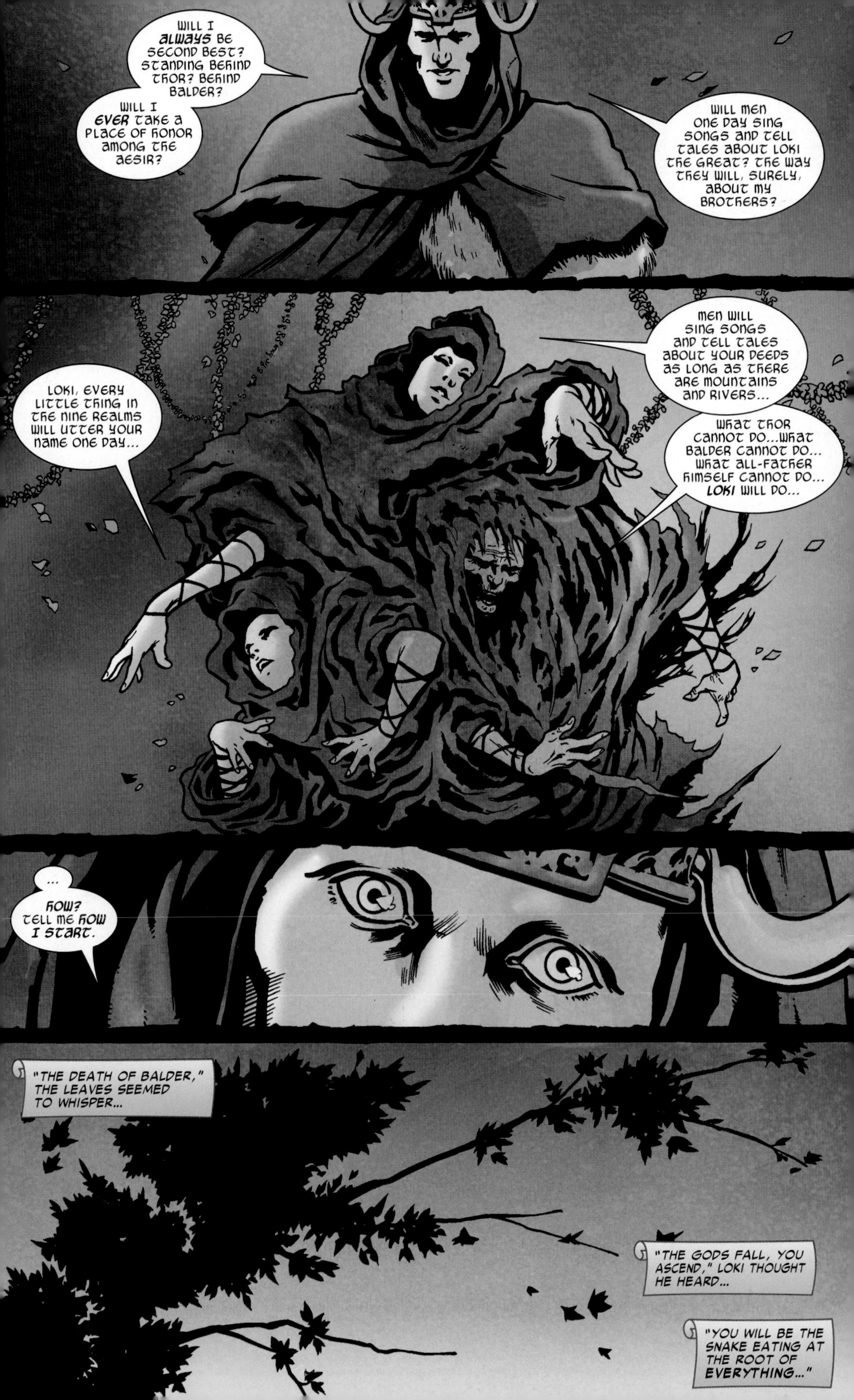
WILL I ALWAYS BE SECOND BEST? STANDING BEHIND THOR? BEHIND BALDER?
WILL I EVER TAKE A PLACE OF HONOR AMONG THE AESIR?
WILL MEN ONE DAY SING SONGS AND TELL TALES ABOUT LOKI THE GREAT? THE WAY THEY WILL, SURELY, ABOUT MY BROTHERS?
MEN WILL SING SONGS AND TELL TALES ABOUT YOUR DEEDS AS LONG AS THERE ARE MOUNTAINS AND RIVERS...
LOKI, EVERY LITTLE THING IN THE NINE REALMS WILL UTTER YOUR NAME ONE DAY...
WHAT THOR CANNOT DO...WHAT BALDER CANNOT DO... WHAT ALL-FATHER HIMSELF CANNOT DO... LOKI WILL DO...
...
HOW? TELL ME HOW I START.
"THE DEATH OF BALDER," THE LEAVES SEEMED TO WHISPER...
"THE GODS FALL, YOU ASCEND," LOKI THOUGHT HE HEARD...
"YOU WILL BE THE SNAKE EATING AT THE ROOT OF EVERYTHING..."

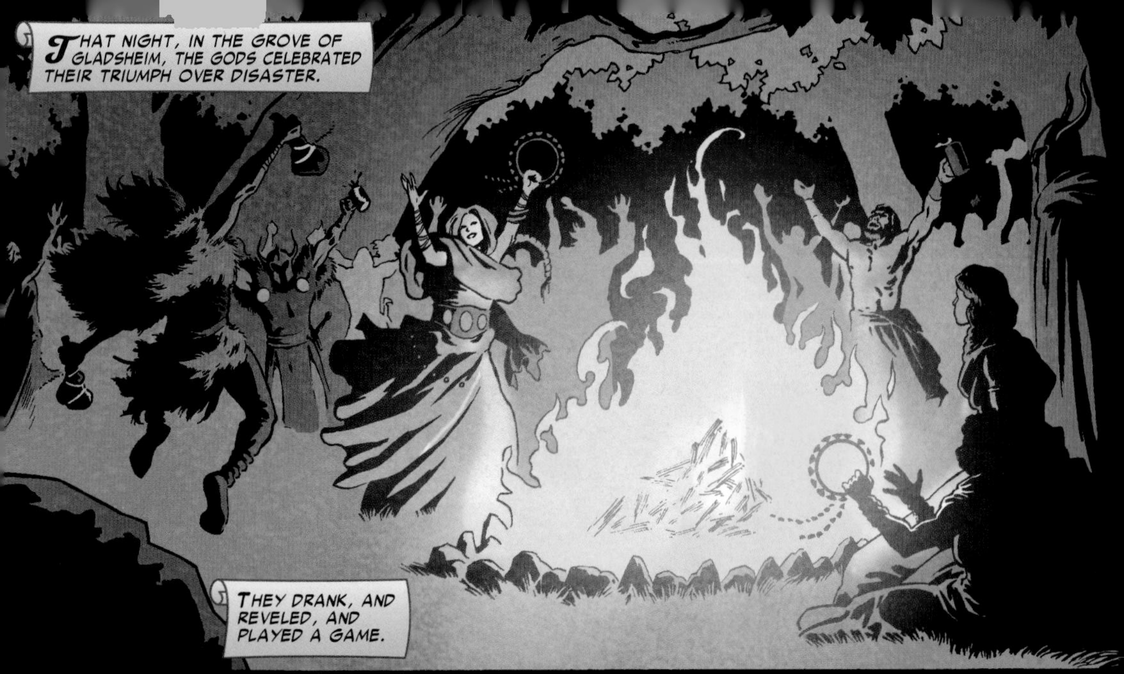
THAT NIGHT, IN THE GROVE OF GLADSHEIM, THE GODS CELEBRATED THEIR TRIUMPH OVER DISASTER.
THEY DRANK, AND REVELED, AND PLAYED A GAME.

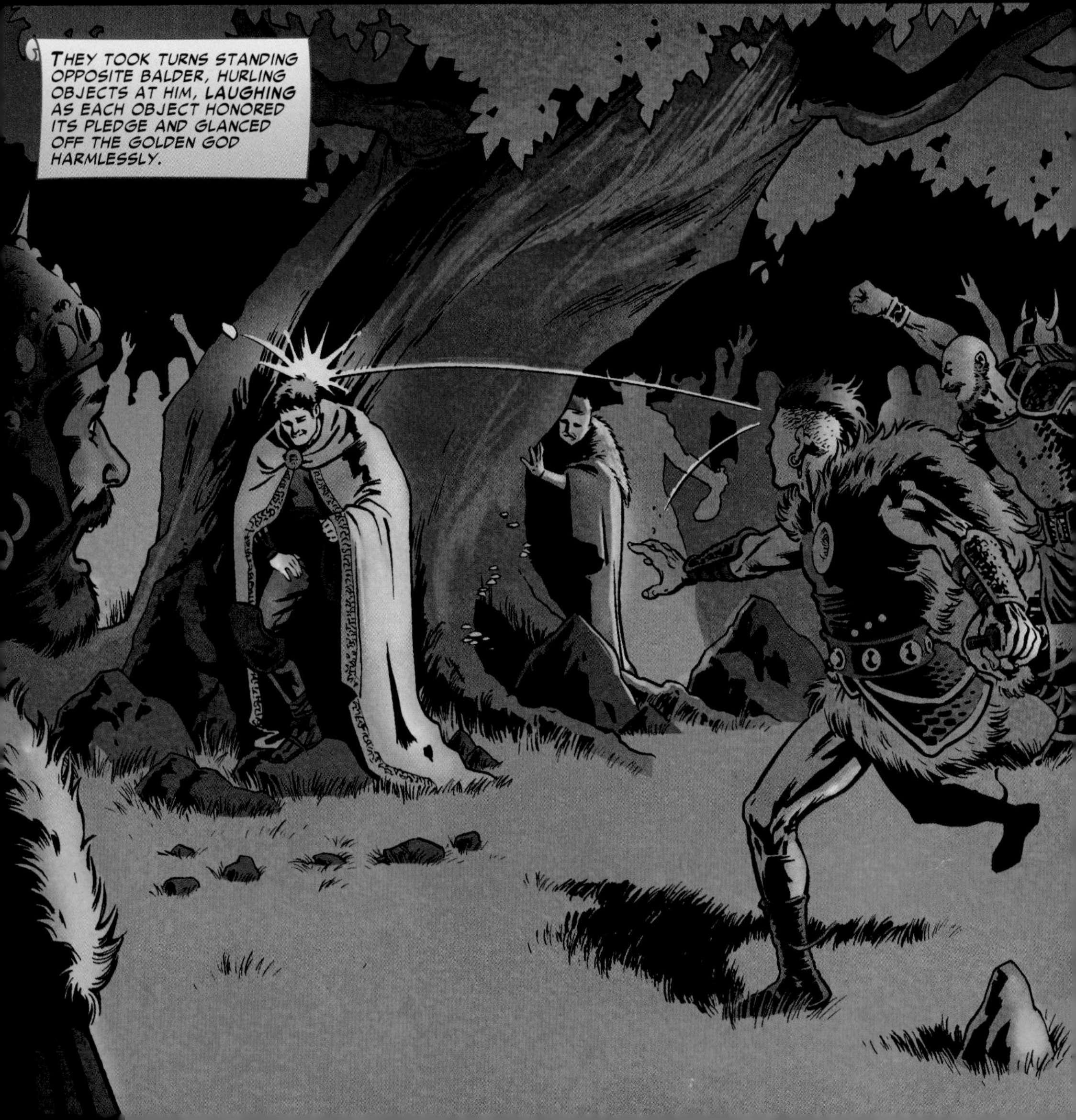
THEY TOOK TURNS STANDING OPPOSITE BALDER, HURLING OBJECTS AT HIM, LAUGHING AS EACH OBJECT HONORED ITS PLEDGE AND GLANCED OFF THE GOLDEN GOD HARMLESSLY.

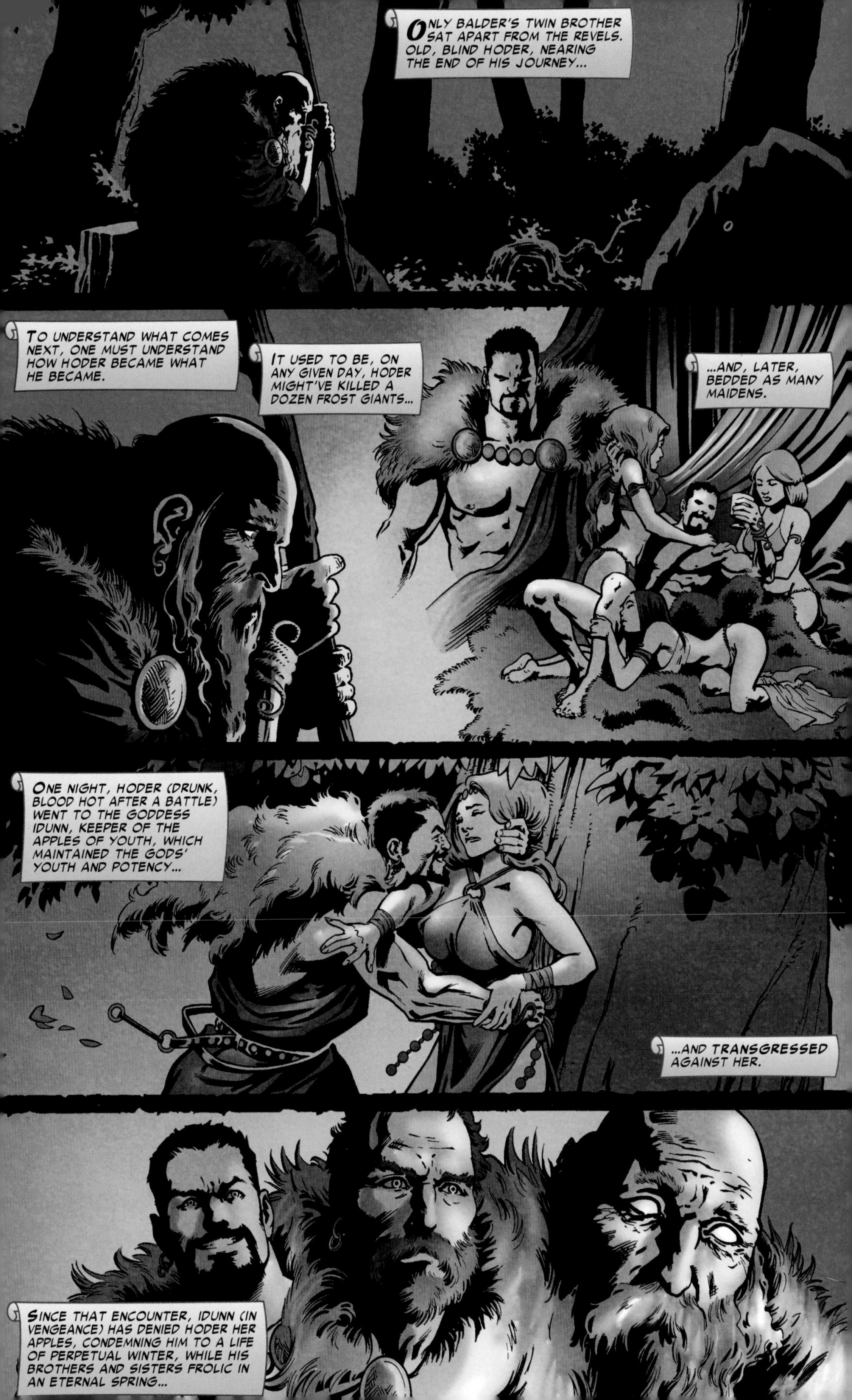
ONLY BALDER'S TWIN BROTHER SAT APART FROM THE REVELS. OLD, BLIND HODER, NEARING THE END OF HIS JOURNEY...
TO UNDERSTAND WHAT COMES NEXT, ONE MUST UNDERSTAND HOW HODER BECAME WHAT HE BECAME.
IT USED TO BE, ON ANY GIVEN DAY, HODER MIGHT'VE KILLED A DOZEN FROST GIANTS...
...AND, LATER, BEDDED AS MANY MAIDENS.
ONE NIGHT, HODER (DRUNK, BLOOD HOT AFTER A BATTLE) WENT TO THE GODDESS IDUNN, KEEPER OF THE APPLES OF YOUTH, WHICH MAINTAINED THE GODS' YOUTH AND POTENCY...
...AND TRANSGRESSED AGAINST HER.
SINCE THAT ENCOUNTER, IDUNN (IN VENGEANCE) HAS DENIED HODER HER APPLES, CONDEMNING HIM TO A LIFE OF PERPETUAL WINTER, WHILE HIS BROTHERS AND SISTERS FROLIC IN AN ETERNAL SPRING...

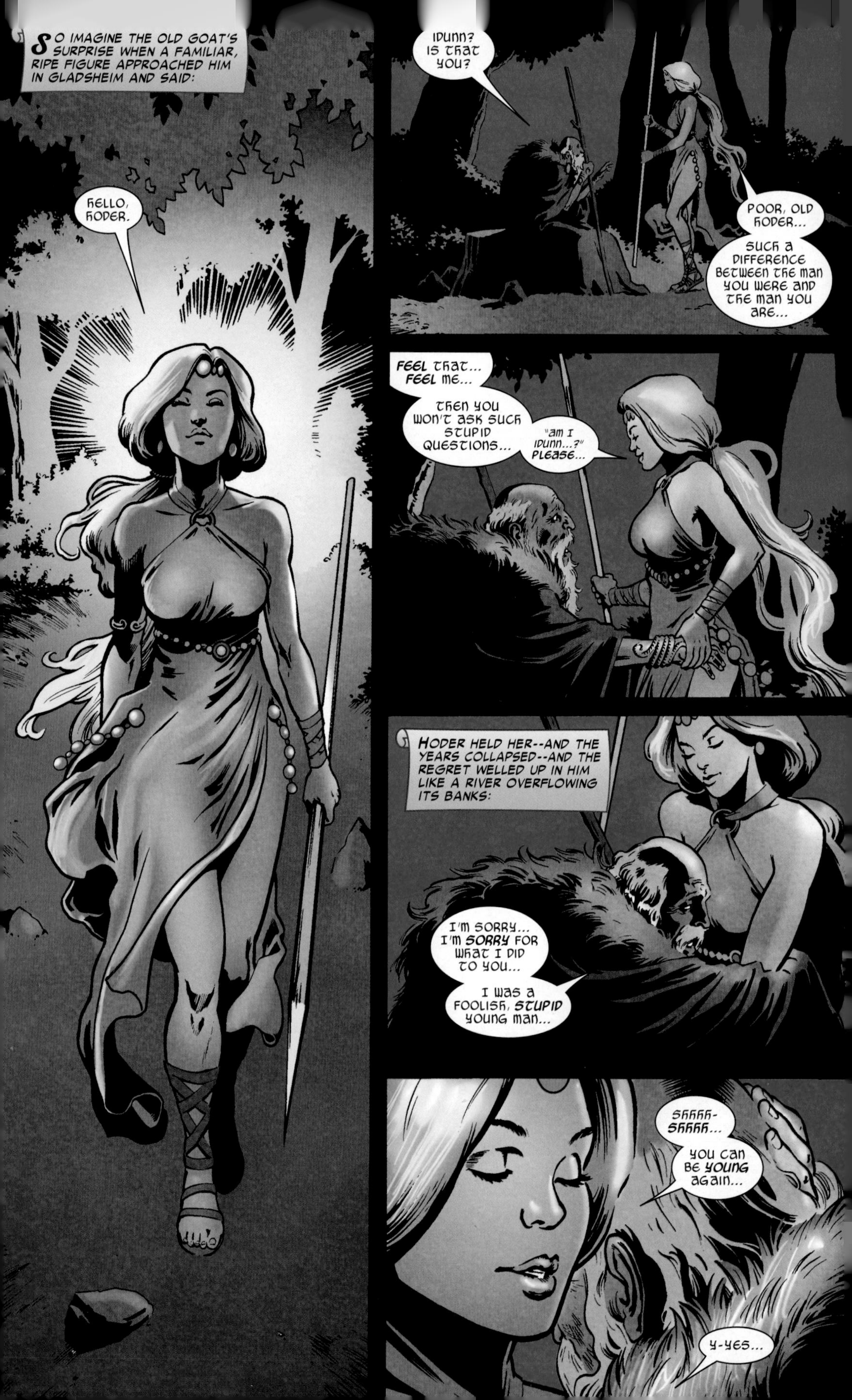
SO IMAGINE THE OLD GOAT'S SURPRISE WHEN A FAMILIAR, RIPE FIGURE APPROACHED HIM IN GLADSHEIM AND SAID:
HELLO, HODER.
IDUNN? IS THAT YOU?
POOR, OLD HODER...
SUCH A DIFFERENCE BETWEEN THE MAN YOU WERE AND THE MAN YOU ARE...
FEEL THAT... FEEL ME...
THEN YOU WON'T ASK SUCH STUPID QUESTIONS...
"AM I IDUNN...?" PLEASE...
HODER HELD HER--AND THE YEARS COLLAPSED--AND THE REGRET WELLED UP IN HIM LIKE A RIVER OVERFLOWING ITS BANKS:
I'M SORRY... I'M SORRY FOR WHAT I DID TO YOU...
I WAS A FOOLISH, STUPID YOUNG MAN...
SHHHH-SHHHH...
YOU CAN BE YOUNG AGAIN...
Y-YES...

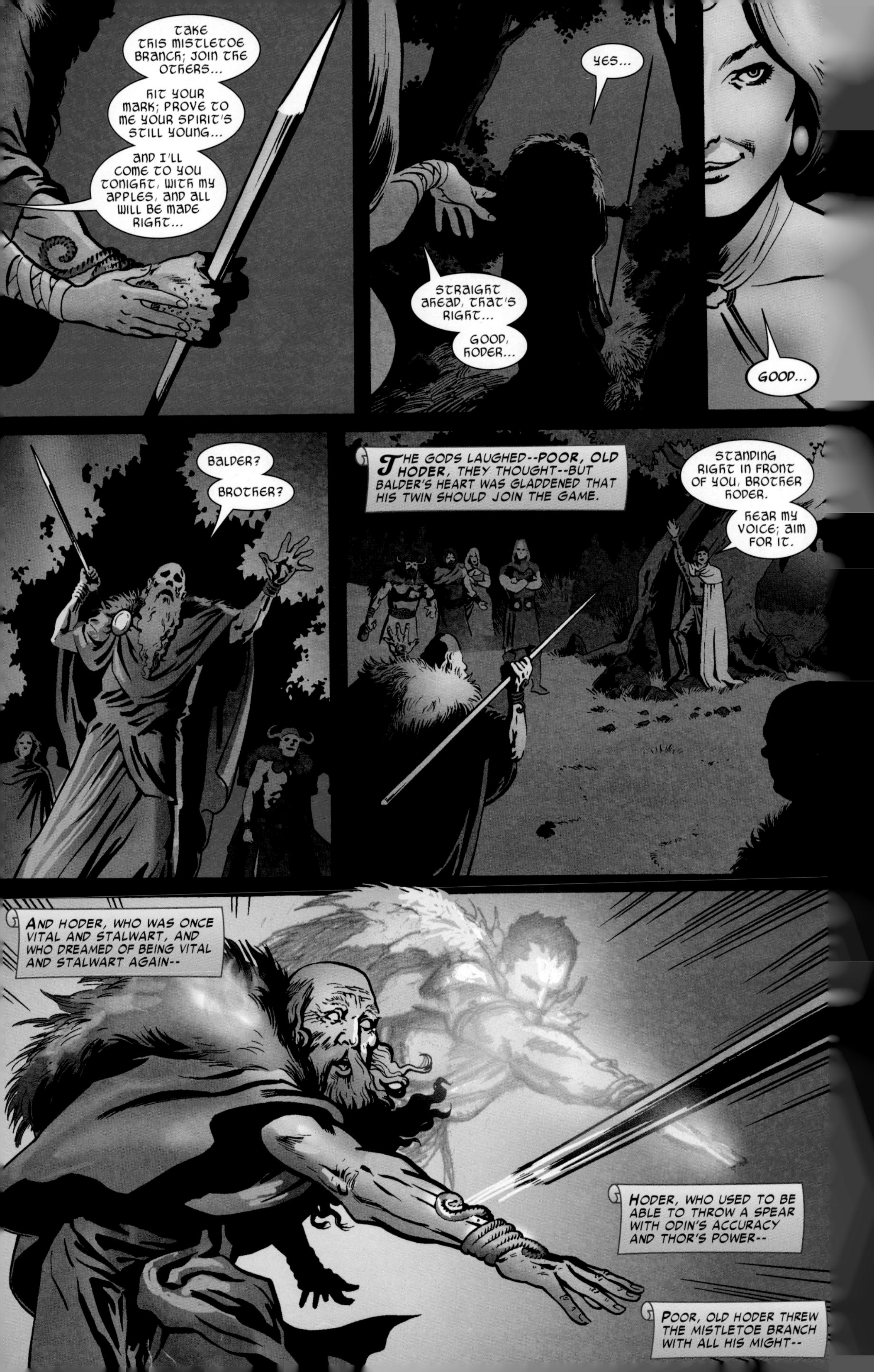
TAKE THIS MISTLETOE BRANCH; JOIN THE OTHERS...
HIT YOUR MARK; PROVE TO ME YOUR SPIRIT'S STILL YOUNG...
AND I'LL COME TO YOU TONIGHT, WITH MY APPLES, AND ALL WILL BE MADE RIGHT...
YES...
STRAIGHT AHEAD, THAT'S RIGHT...
GOOD, HODER...
GOOD...
BALDER?
BROTHER?
THE GODS LAUGHED--POOR, OLD HODER, THEY THOUGHT--BUT BALDER'S HEART WAS GLADDENED THAT HIS TWIN SHOULD JOIN THE GAME.
STANDING RIGHT IN FRONT OF YOU, BROTHER HODER.
HEAR MY VOICE; AIM FOR IT.
AND HODER, WHO WAS ONCE VITAL AND STALWART, AND WHO DREAMED OF BEING VITAL AND STALWART AGAIN--
HODER, WHO USED TO BE ABLE TO THROW A SPEAR WITH ODIN'S ACCURACY AND THOR'S POWER--
POOR, OLD HODER THREW THE MISTLETOE BRANCH WITH ALL HIS MIGHT--

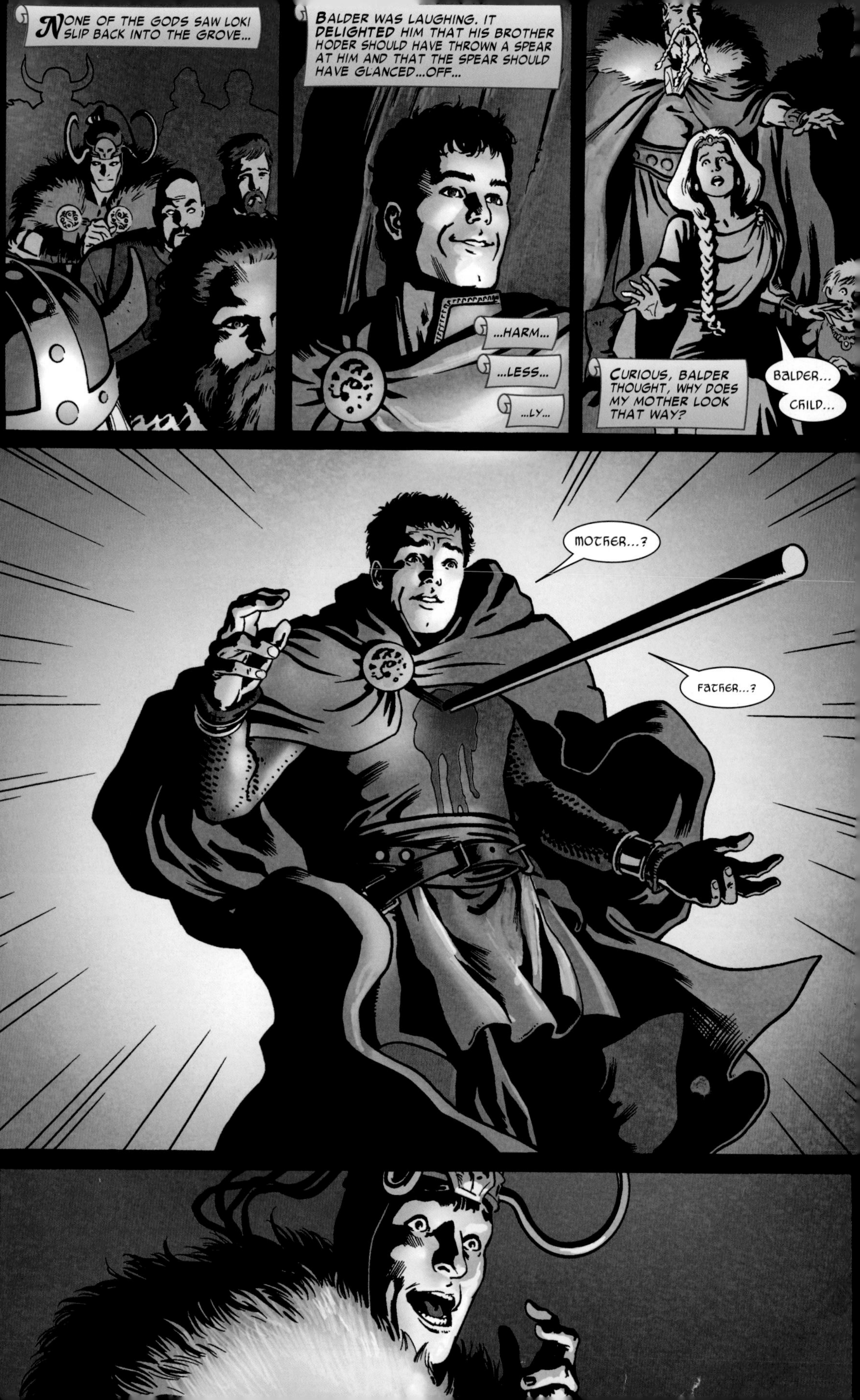
NONE OF THE GODS SAW LOKI SLIP BACK INTO THE GROVE...
BALDER WAS LAUGHING. IT DELIGHTED HIM THAT HIS BROTHER HODER SHOULD HAVE THROWN A SPEAR AT HIM AND THAT THE SPEAR SHOULD HAVE GLANCED...OFF...
...HARM...
...LESS...
...LY...
CURIOUS, BALDER THOUGHT, WHY DOES MY MOTHER LOOK THAT WAY?
BALDER...
CHILD...
MOTHER...?
FATHER...?

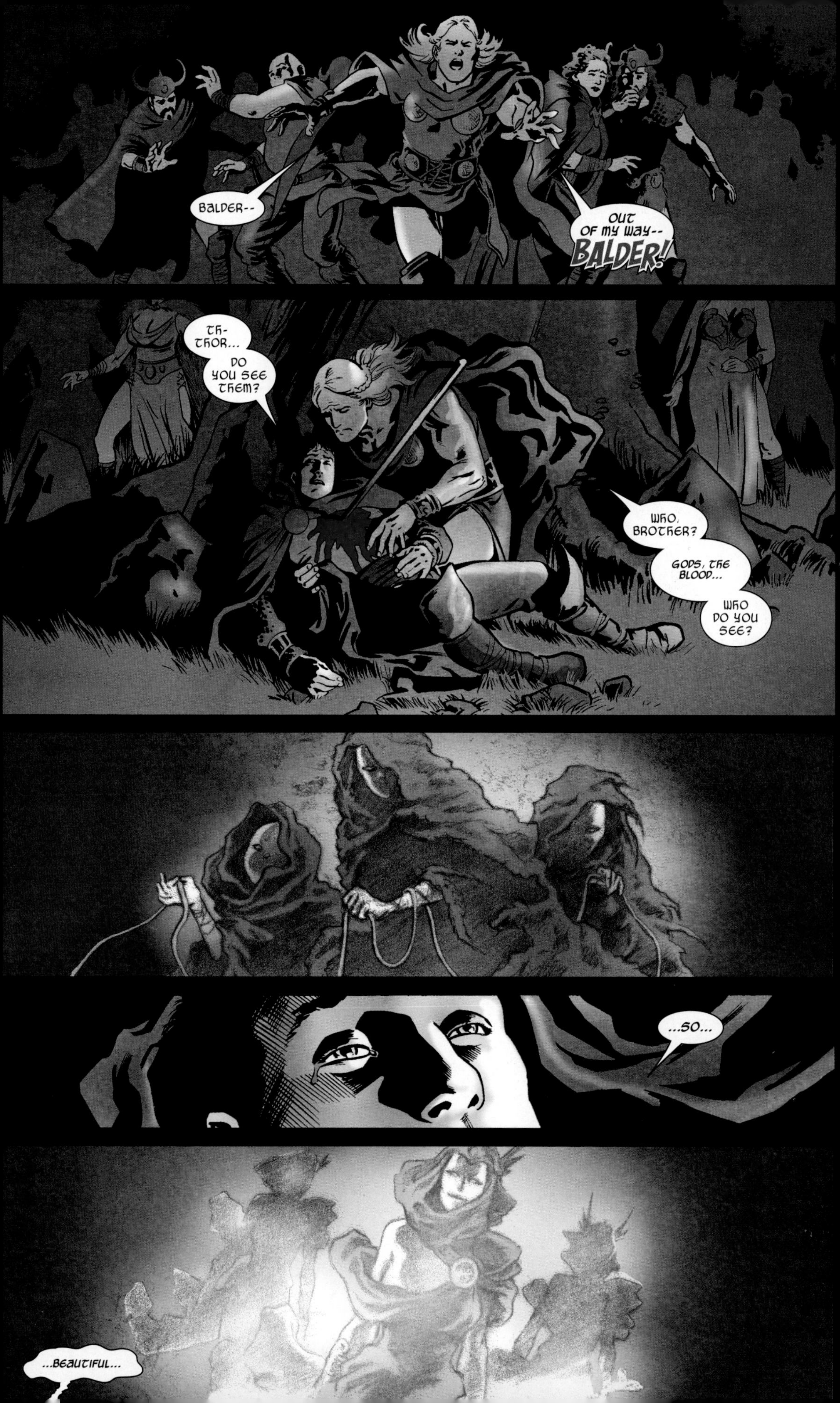
BALDER--
OUT OF MY WAY-- BALDER!
TH-THOR... DO YOU SEE THEM?
WHO, BROTHER?
GODS, THE BLOOD...
WHO DO YOU SEE?
...SO...
...BEAUTIFUL...

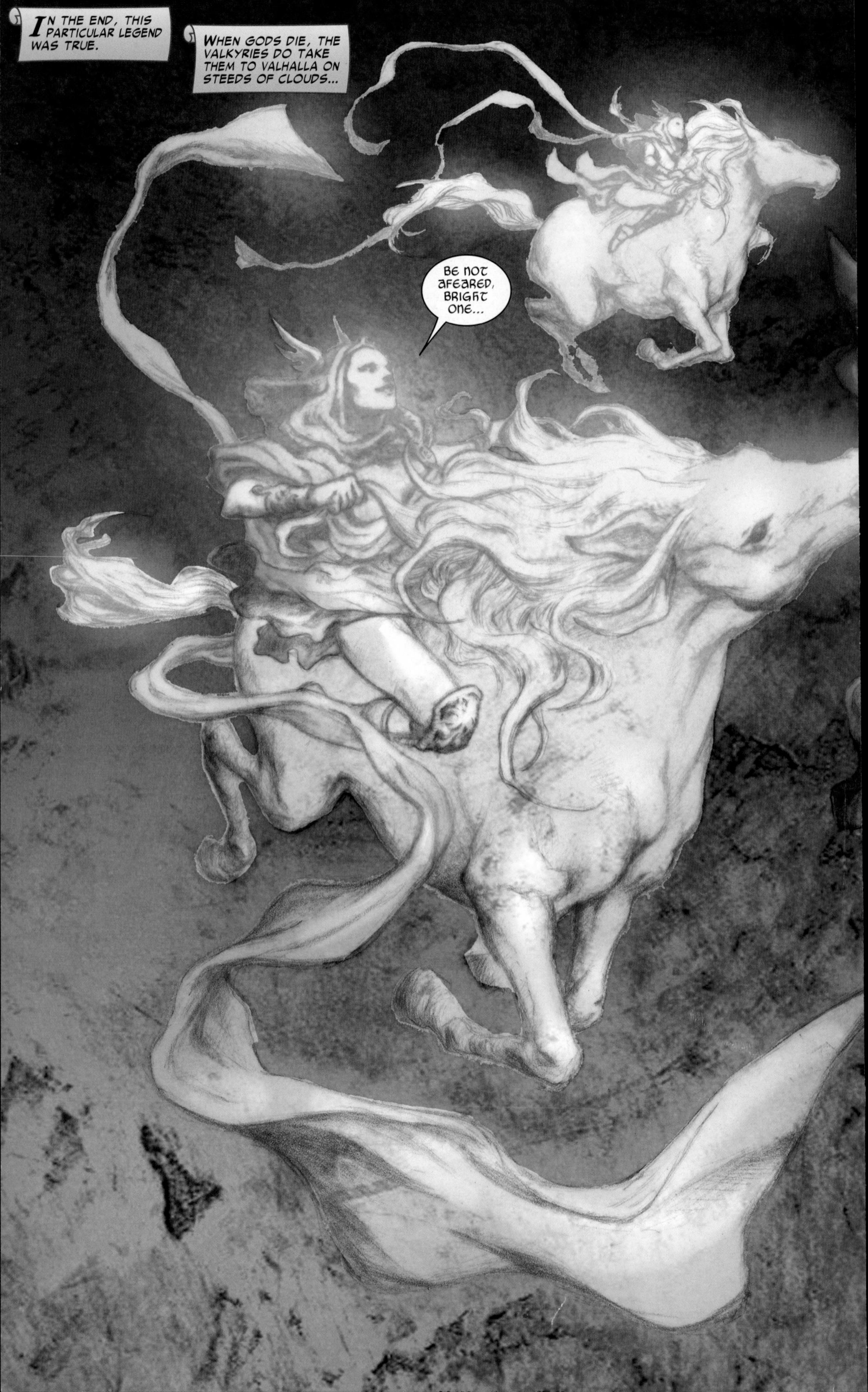
IN THE END, THIS PARTICULAR LEGEND WAS TRUE.
WHEN GODS DIE, THE VALKYRIES DO TAKE THEM TO VALHALLA ON STEEDS OF CLOUDS...
BE NOT AFEARED, BRIGHT ONE...

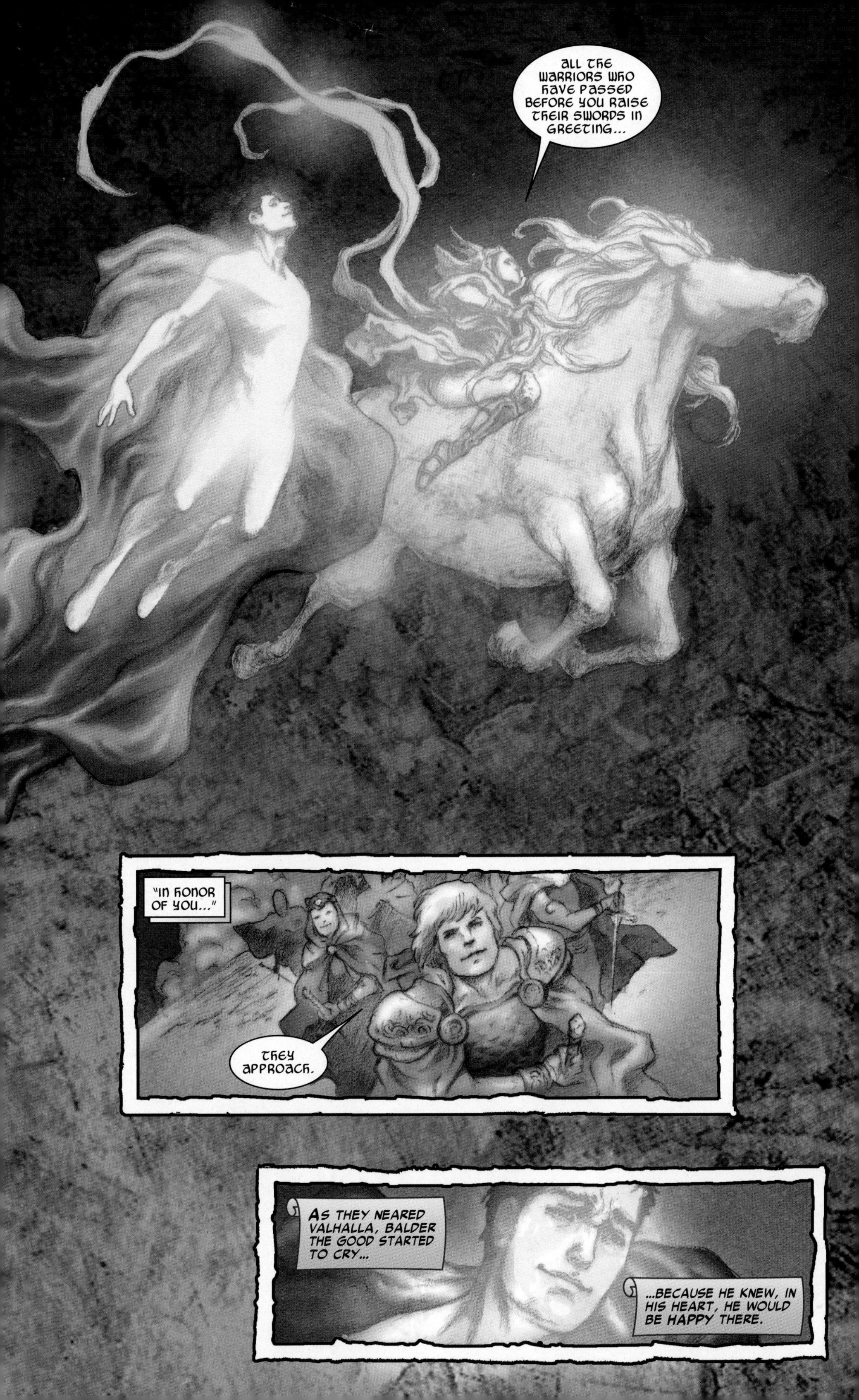
ALL THE WARRIORS WHO HAVE PASSED BEFORE YOU RAISE THEIR SWORDS IN GREETING...
"IN HONOR OF YOU..."
THEY APPROACH.
AS THEY NEARED VALHALLA, BALDER THE GOOD STARTED TO CRY...
...BECAUSE HE KNEW, IN HIS HEART, HE WOULD BE HAPPY THERE.

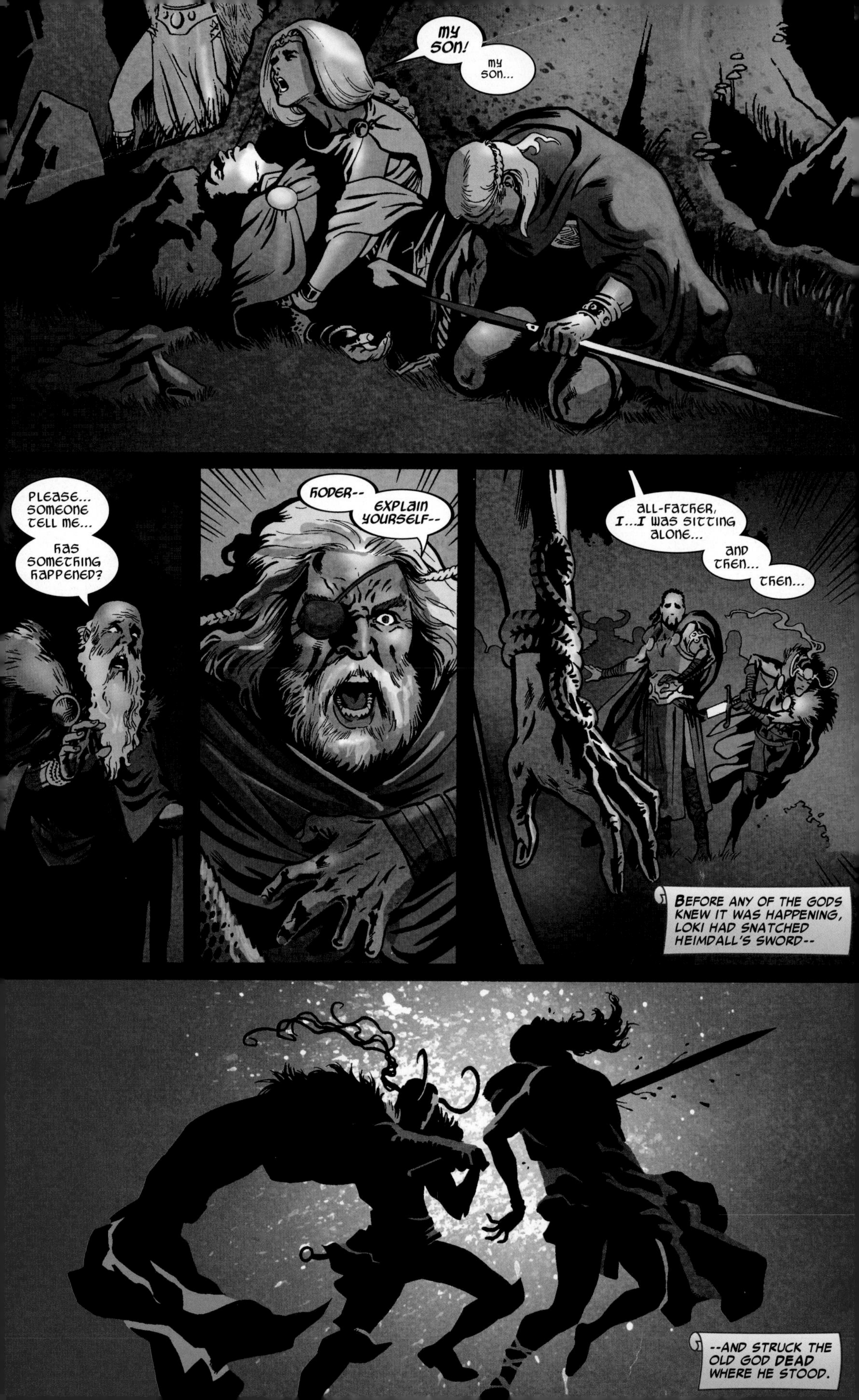
MY SON!
MY SON...
PLEASE... SOMEONE TELL ME...
HAS SOMETHING HAPPENED?
HODER--
EXPLAIN YOURSELF--
ALL-FATHER, I...I WAS SITTING ALONE...
AND THEN...
THEN...
BEFORE ANY OF THE GODS KNEW IT WAS HAPPENING, LOKI HAD SNATCHED HEIMDALL'S SWORD--
--AND STRUCK THE OLD GOD DEAD WHERE HE STOOD.

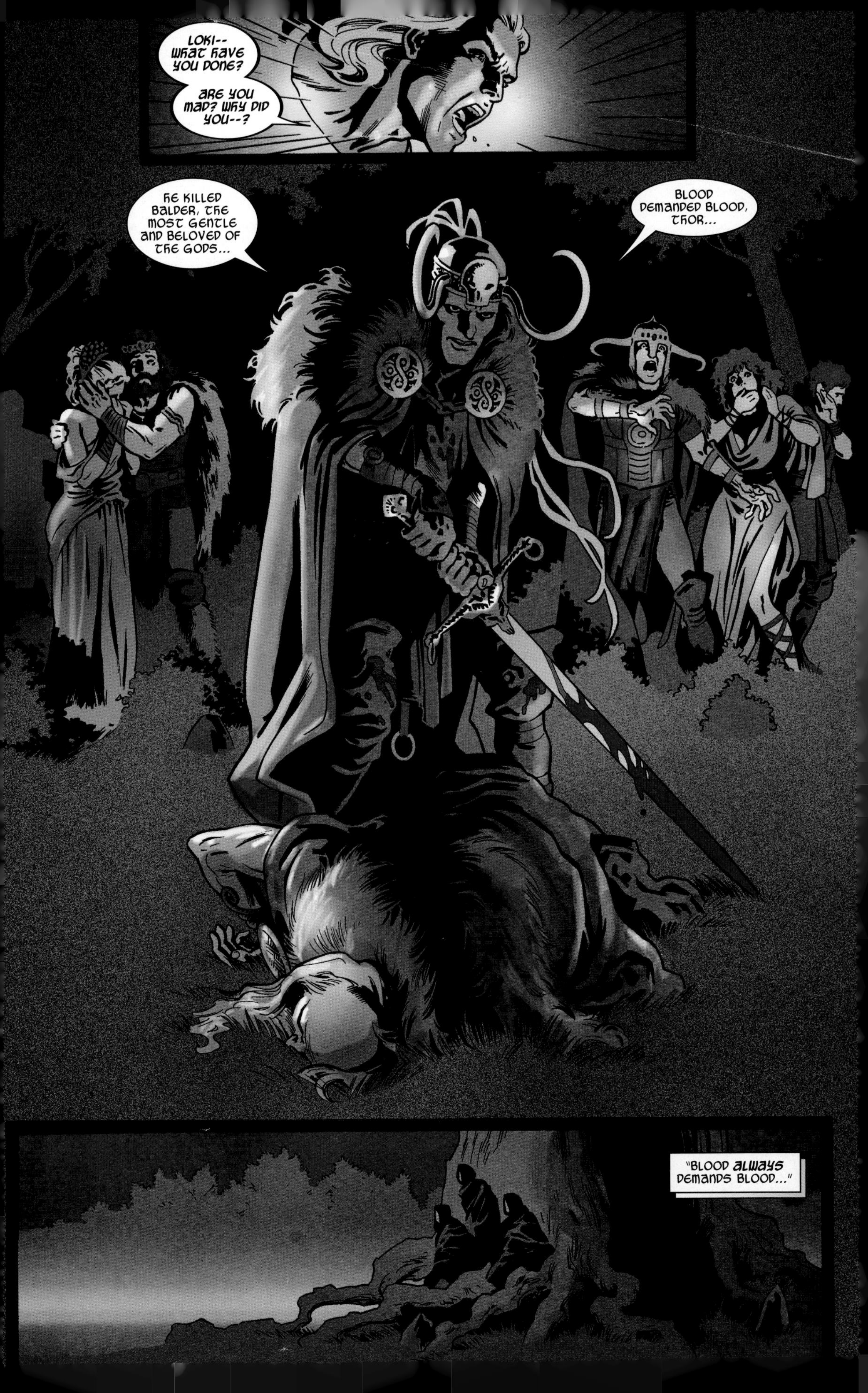
LOKI-- WHAT HAVE YOU DONE?
ARE YOU MAD? WHY DID YOU--?
HE KILLED BALDER, THE MOST GENTLE AND BELOVED OF THE GODS...
BLOOD DEMANDED BLOOD, THOR...
"BLOOD ALWAYS DEMANDS BLOOD..."

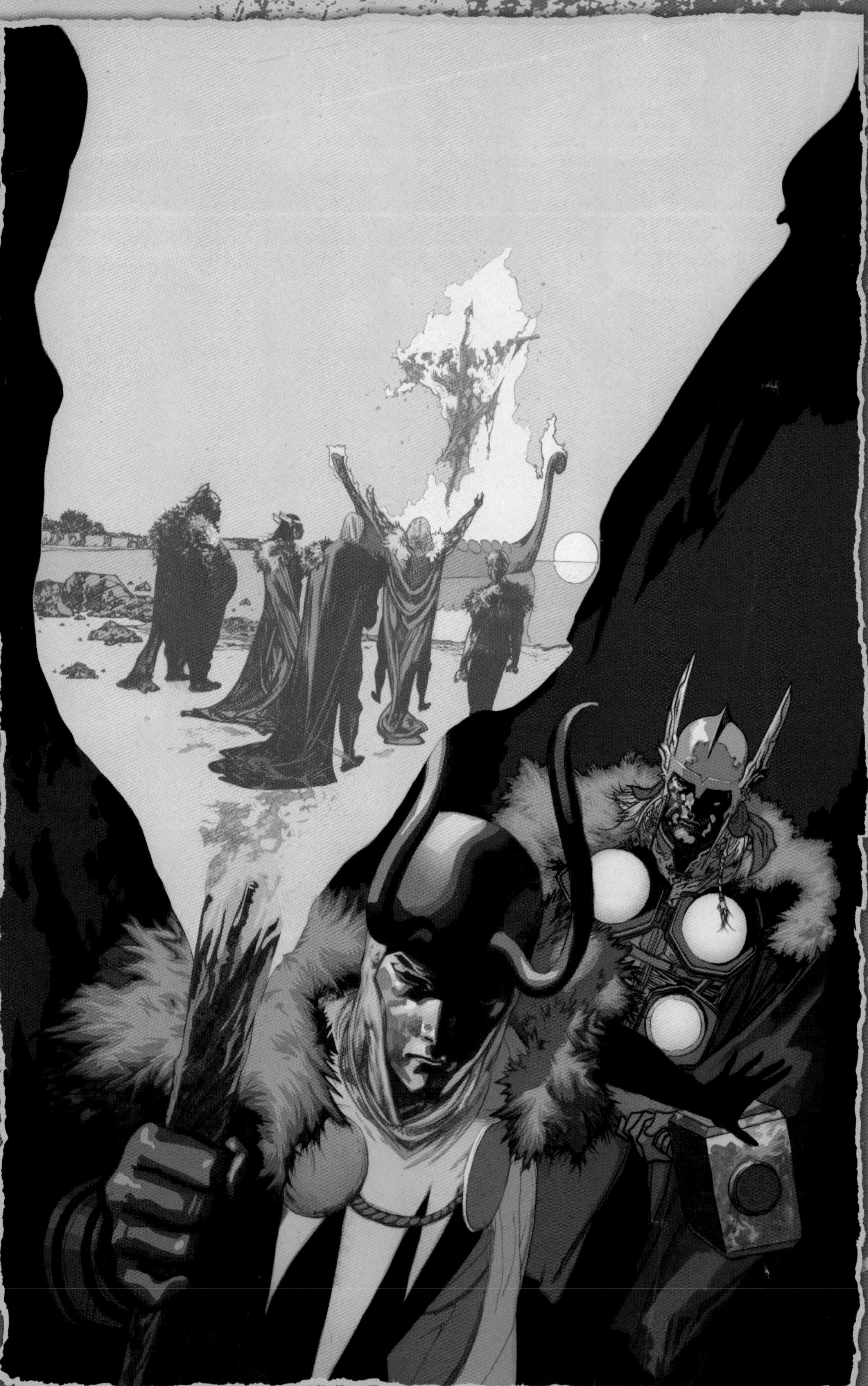

PART THREE
FUNERAL FOR A GOD

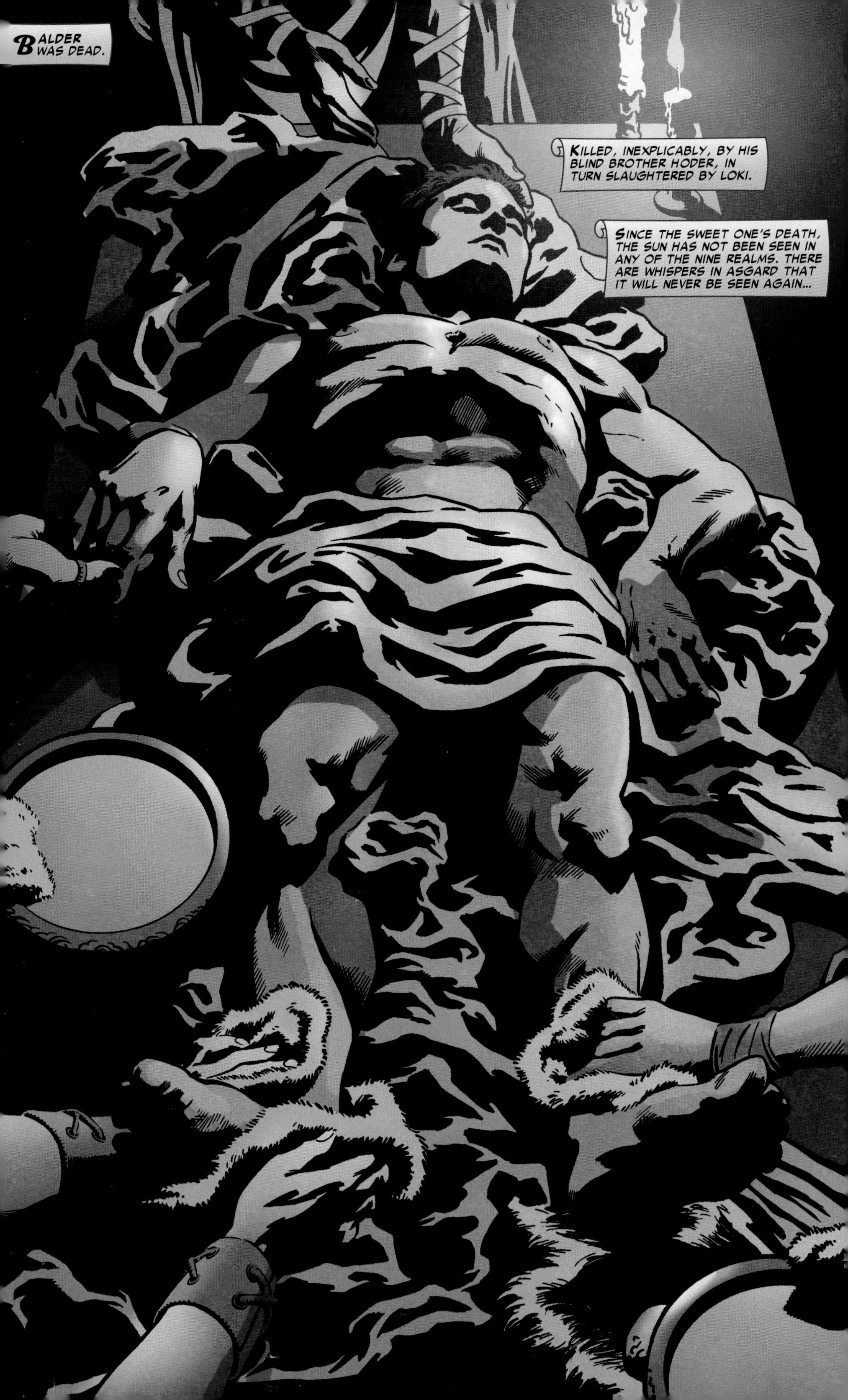
BALDER WAS DEAD.
KILLED, INEXPLICABLY, BY HIS BLIND BROTHER HODER, IN TURN SLAUGHTERED BY LOKI.
SINCE THE SWEET ONE'S DEATH, THE SUN HAS NOT BEEN SEEN IN ANY OF THE NINE REALMS. THERE ARE WHISPERS IN ASGARD THAT IT WILL NEVER BE SEEN AGAIN...

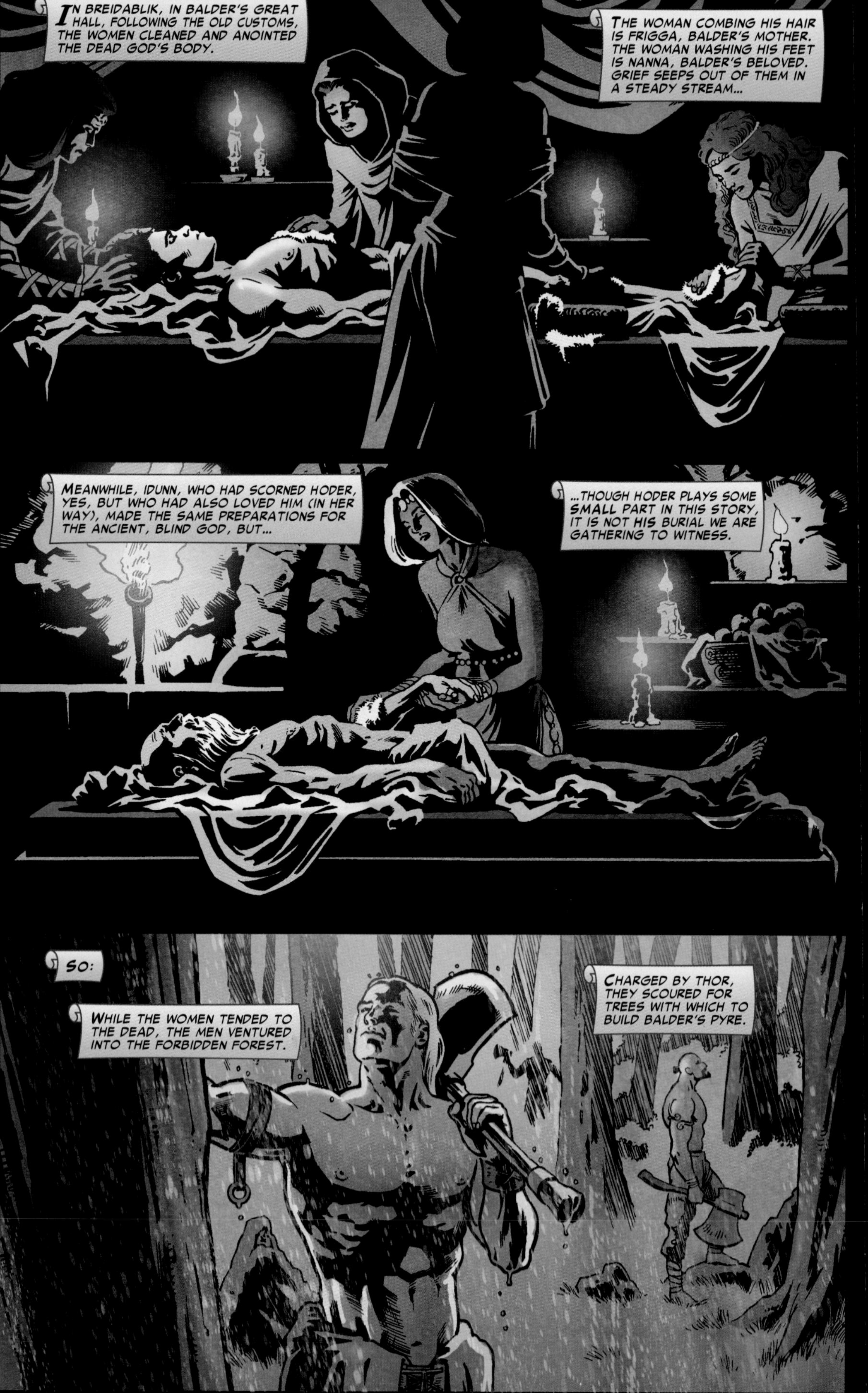
In Breidablik, in Balder's great hall, following the old customs, the women cleaned and anointed the dead god's body.
The woman combing his hair is Frigga, Balder's mother. The woman washing his feet is Nanna, Balder's beloved. Grief seeps out of them in a steady stream...
Meanwhile, Idunn, who had scorned Hoder, yes, but who had also loved him (in her way), made the same preparations for the ancient, blind god, but...
...though Hoder plays some small part in this story, it is not his burial we are gathering to witness.
So:
While the women tended to the dead, the men ventured into the forbidden forest.
Charged by Thor, they scoured for trees with which to build Balder's pyre.

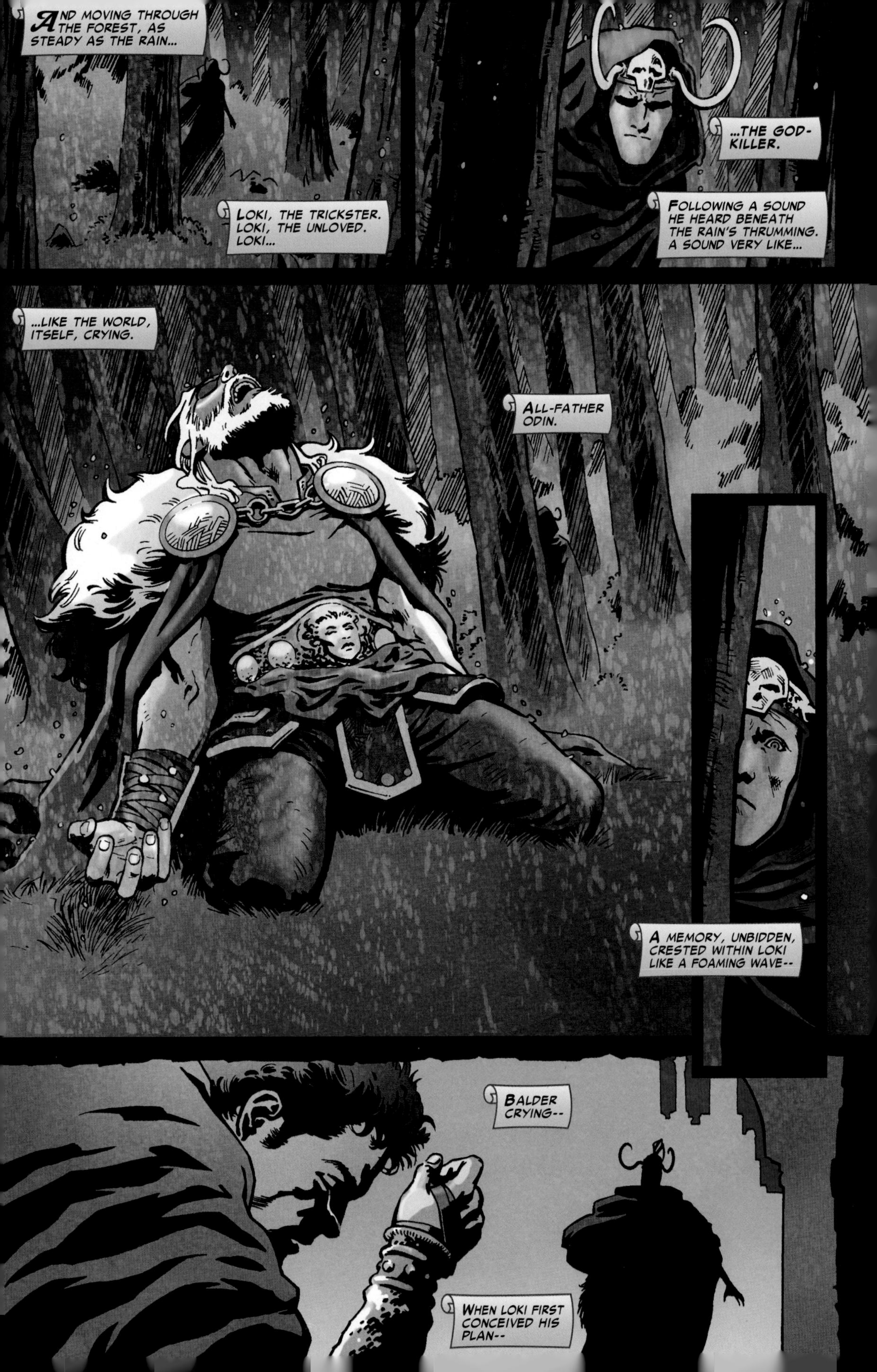
And moving through the forest, as steady as the rain...
Loki, the trickster. Loki, the unloved. Loki...
...the god-killer.
Following a sound he heard beneath the rain's thrumming. A sound very like...
...like the world, itself, crying.
All-father Odin.
A memory, unbidden, crested within Loki like a foaming wave--
Balder crying--
When Loki first conceived his plan--

LOKI SMOTHERED IT. THE PAST WAS DONE.

NOW, HE WOULD COMFORT ODIN.

FROM THIS MOMENT ON, HE WOULD--

FATHER...

MY SON...

MY ONLY SON NOW...

ODIN SAID OTHER WORDS, BUT THEY WERE LOST IN THE RAIN...

NO MORE REGRETS, THOUGHT LOKI.

THEY ARE NOT MY FAMILY...

THESE PEOPLE MEAN NOTHING TO ME...

THEY DETEST ME...

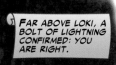

FAR ABOVE LOKI, A BOLT OF LIGHTNING CONFIRMED: YOU ARE RIGHT.

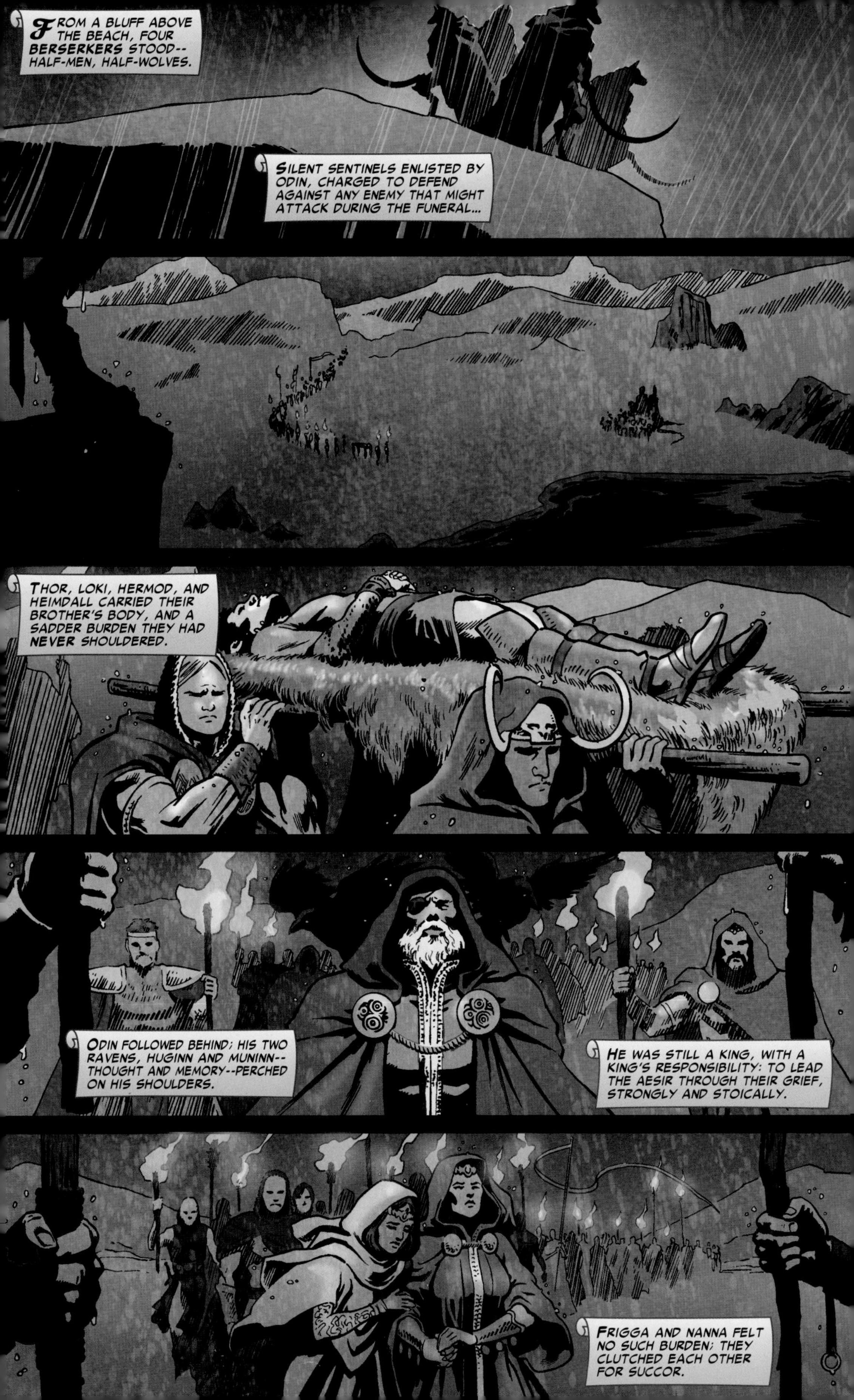
FROM A BLUFF ABOVE THE BEACH, FOUR BERSERKERS STOOD-- HALF-MEN, HALF-WOLVES.
SILENT SENTINELS ENLISTED BY ODIN, CHARGED TO DEFEND AGAINST ANY ENEMY THAT MIGHT ATTACK DURING THE FUNERAL...
THOR, LOKI, HERMOD, AND HEIMDALL CARRIED THEIR BROTHER'S BODY, AND A SADDER BURDEN THEY HAD NEVER SHOULDERED.
ODIN FOLLOWED BEHIND; HIS TWO RAVENS, HUGINN AND MUNINN-- THOUGHT AND MEMORY--PERCHED ON HIS SHOULDERS.
HE WAS STILL A KING, WITH A KING'S RESPONSIBILITY: TO LEAD THE AESIR THROUGH THEIR GRIEF, STRONGLY AND STOICALLY.
FRIGGA AND NANNA FELT NO SUCH BURDEN; THEY CLUTCHED EACH OTHER FOR SUCCOR.

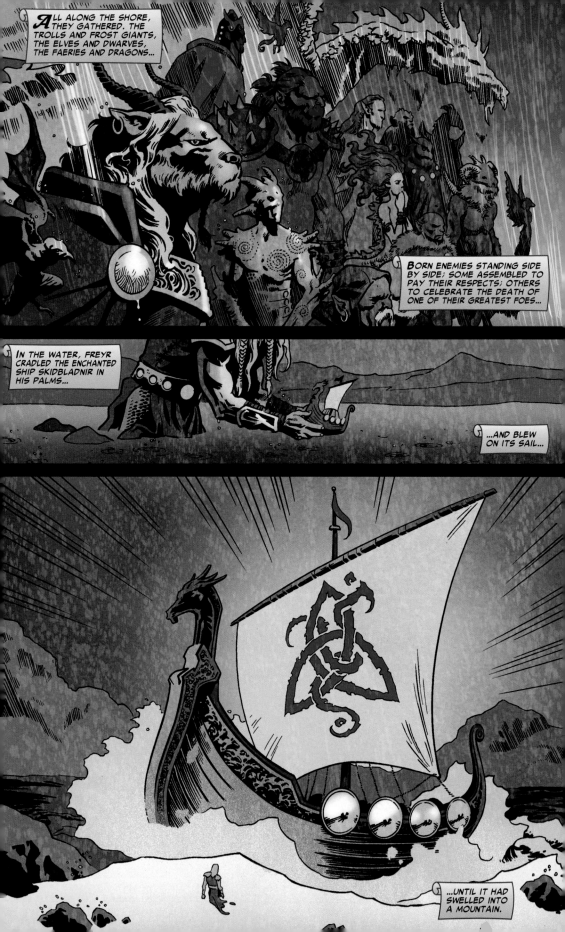

ALL ALONG THE SHORE, THEY GATHERED. THE TROLLS AND FROST GIANTS, THE ELVES AND DWARVES, THE FAERIES AND DRAGONS...

BORN ENEMIES STANDING SIDE BY SIDE; SOME ASSEMBLED TO PAY THEIR RESPECTS; OTHERS TO CELEBRATE THE DEATH OF ONE OF THEIR GREATEST FOES...

IN THE WATER, FREYR CRADLED THE ENCHANTED SHIP SKIDBLADNIR IN HIS PALMS...

...AND BLEW ON ITS SAIL...

...UNTIL IT HAD SWELLED INTO A MOUNTAIN.

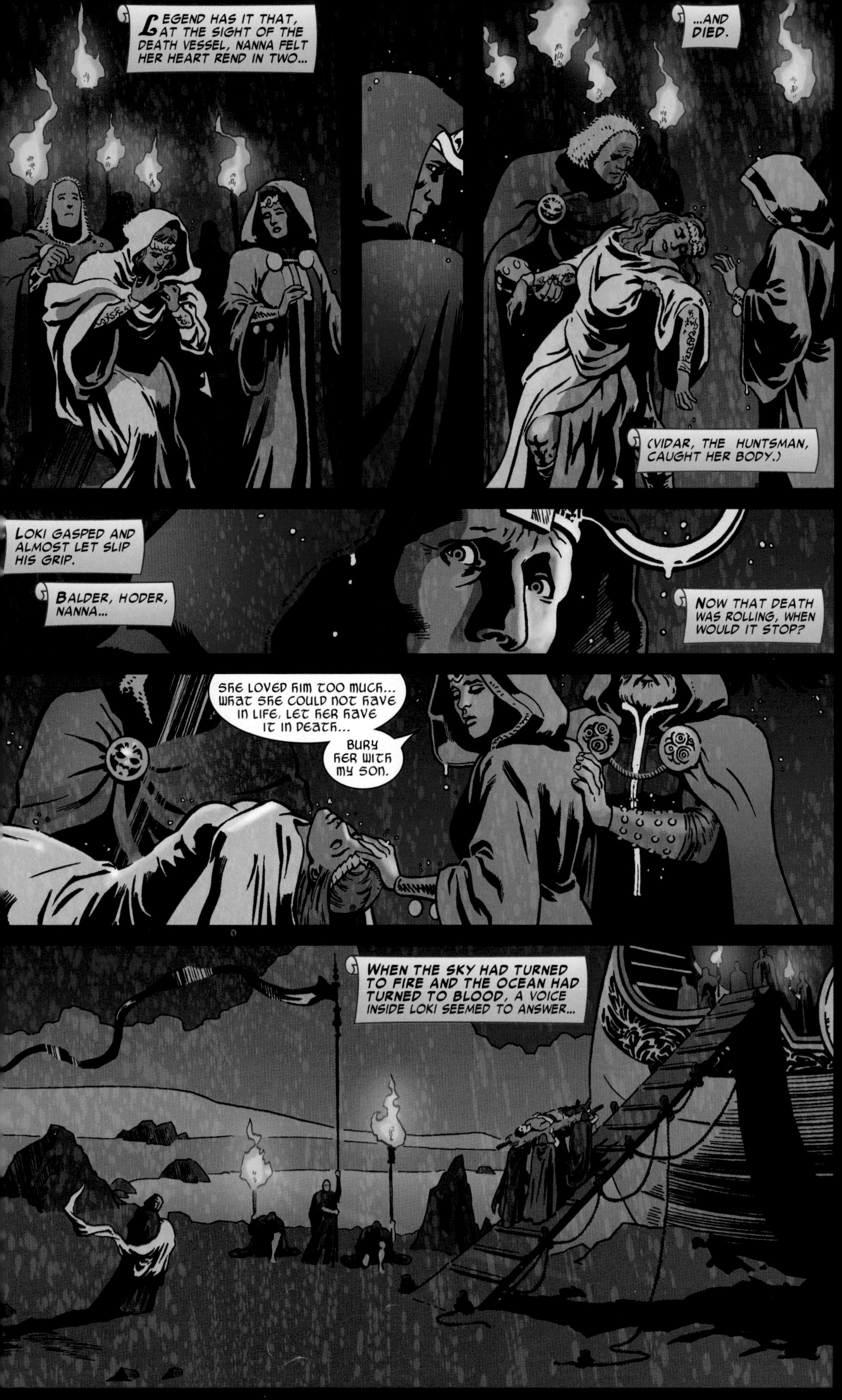
LEGEND HAS IT THAT, AT THE SIGHT OF THE DEATH VESSEL, NANNA FELT HER HEART REND IN TWO...
...AND DIED.
(VIDAR, THE HUNTSMAN, CAUGHT HER BODY.)
LOKI GASPED AND ALMOST LET SLIP HIS GRIP.
BALDER, HODER, NANNA...
NOW THAT DEATH WAS ROLLING, WHEN WOULD IT STOP?
SHE LOVED HIM TOO MUCH... WHAT SHE COULD NOT HAVE IN LIFE, LET HER HAVE IT IN DEATH...
BURY HER WITH MY SON.
WHEN THE SKY HAD TURNED TO FIRE AND THE OCEAN HAD TURNED TO BLOOD, A VOICE INSIDE LOKI SEEMED TO ANSWER...

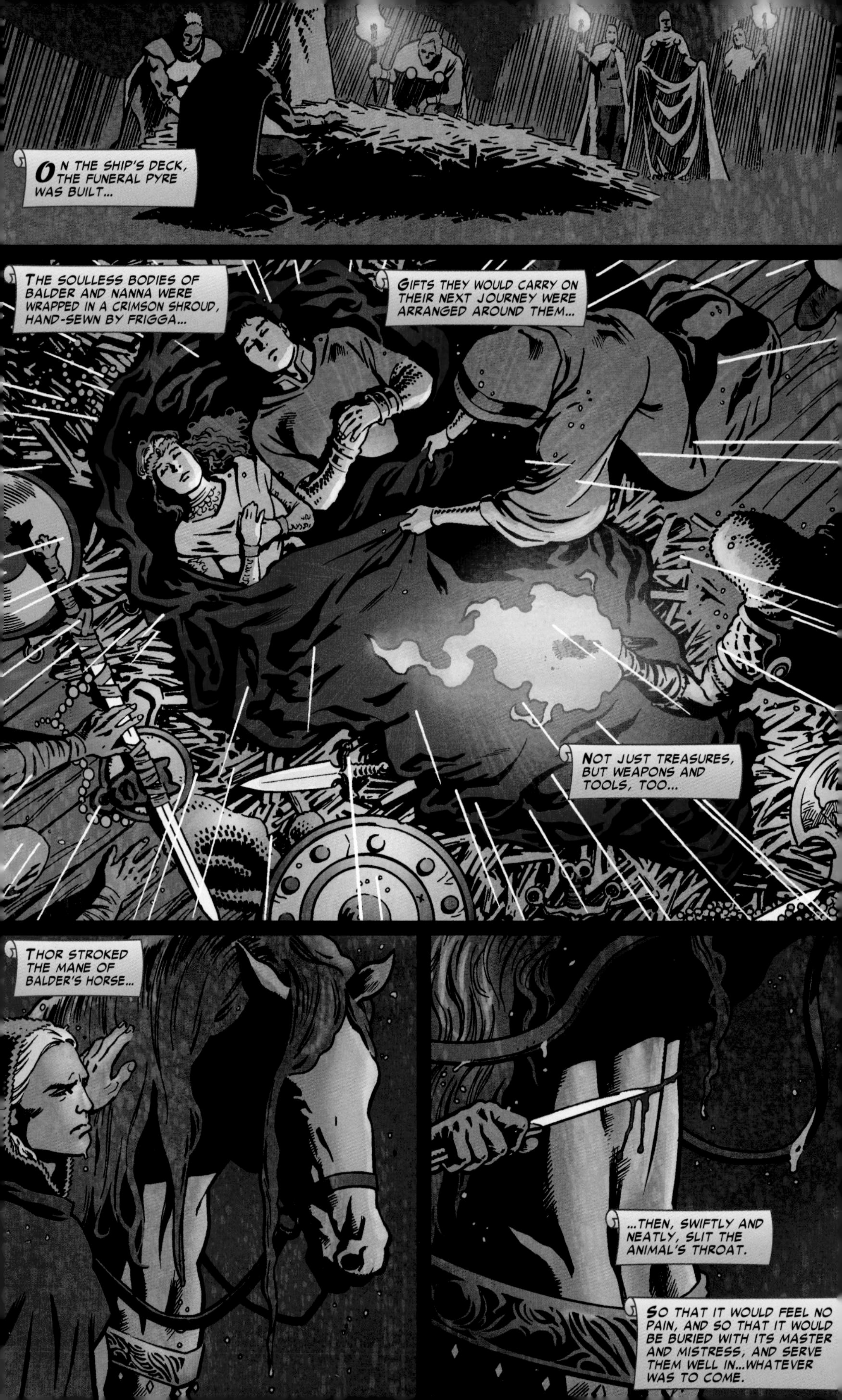
ON THE SHIP'S DECK, THE FUNERAL PYRE WAS BUILT...
THE SOULLESS BODIES OF BALDER AND NANNA WERE WRAPPED IN A CRIMSON SHROUD, HAND-SEWN BY FRIGGA...
GIFTS THEY WOULD CARRY ON THEIR NEXT JOURNEY WERE ARRANGED AROUND THEM...
NOT JUST TREASURES, BUT WEAPONS AND TOOLS, TOO...
THOR STROKED THE MANE OF BALDER'S HORSE...
...THEN, SWIFTLY AND NEATLY, SLIT THE ANIMAL'S THROAT.
SO THAT IT WOULD FEEL NO PAIN, AND SO THAT IT WOULD BE BURIED WITH ITS MASTER AND MISTRESS, AND SERVE THEM WELL IN...WHATEVER WAS TO COME.

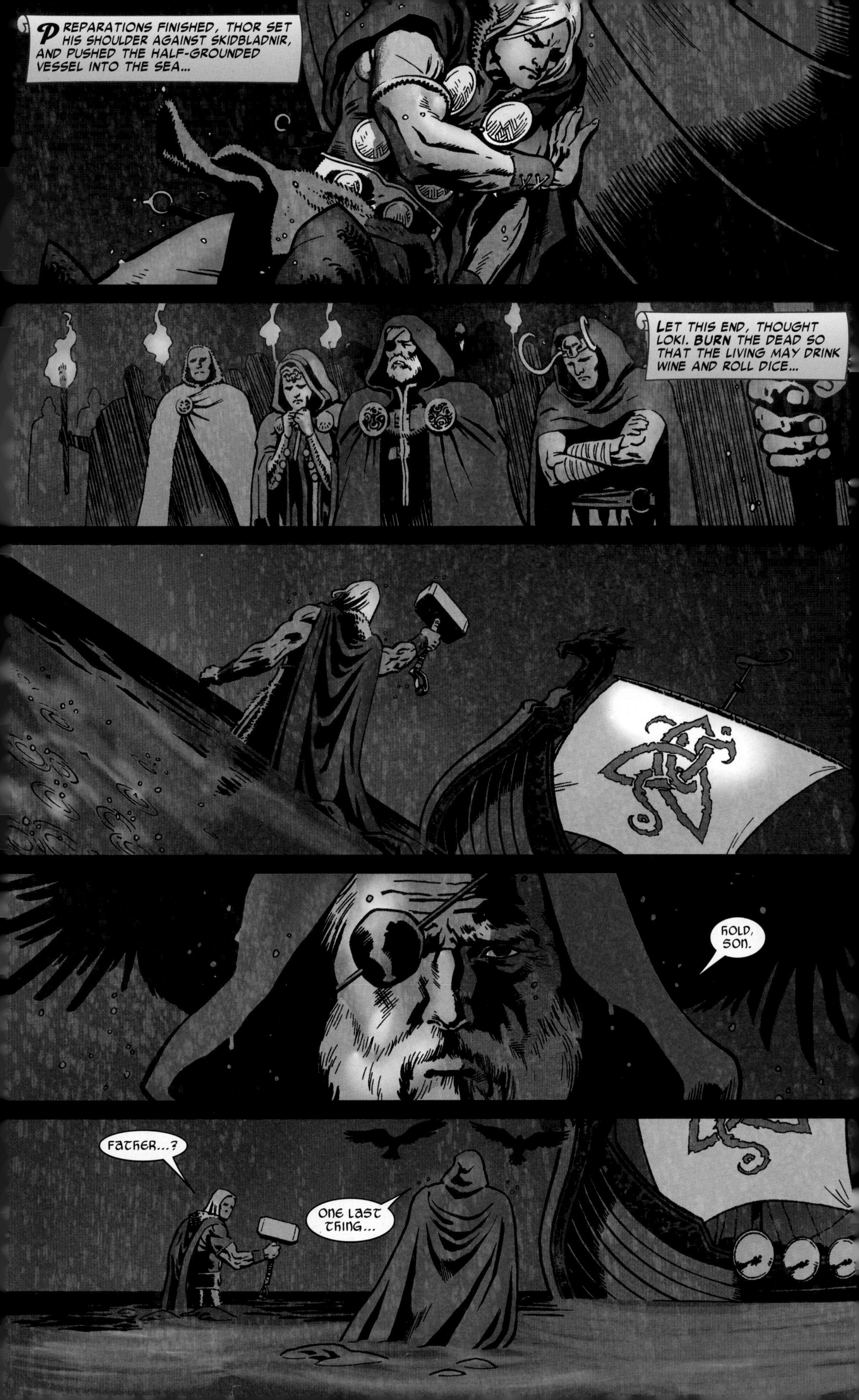
PREPARATIONS FINISHED, THOR SET HIS SHOULDER AGAINST SKIDBLADNIR, AND PUSHED THE HALF-GROUNDED VESSEL INTO THE SEA...
LET THIS END, THOUGHT LOKI. BURN THE DEAD SO THAT THE LIVING MAY DRINK WINE AND ROLL DICE...
HOLD, SON.
FATHER...?
ONE LAST THING...

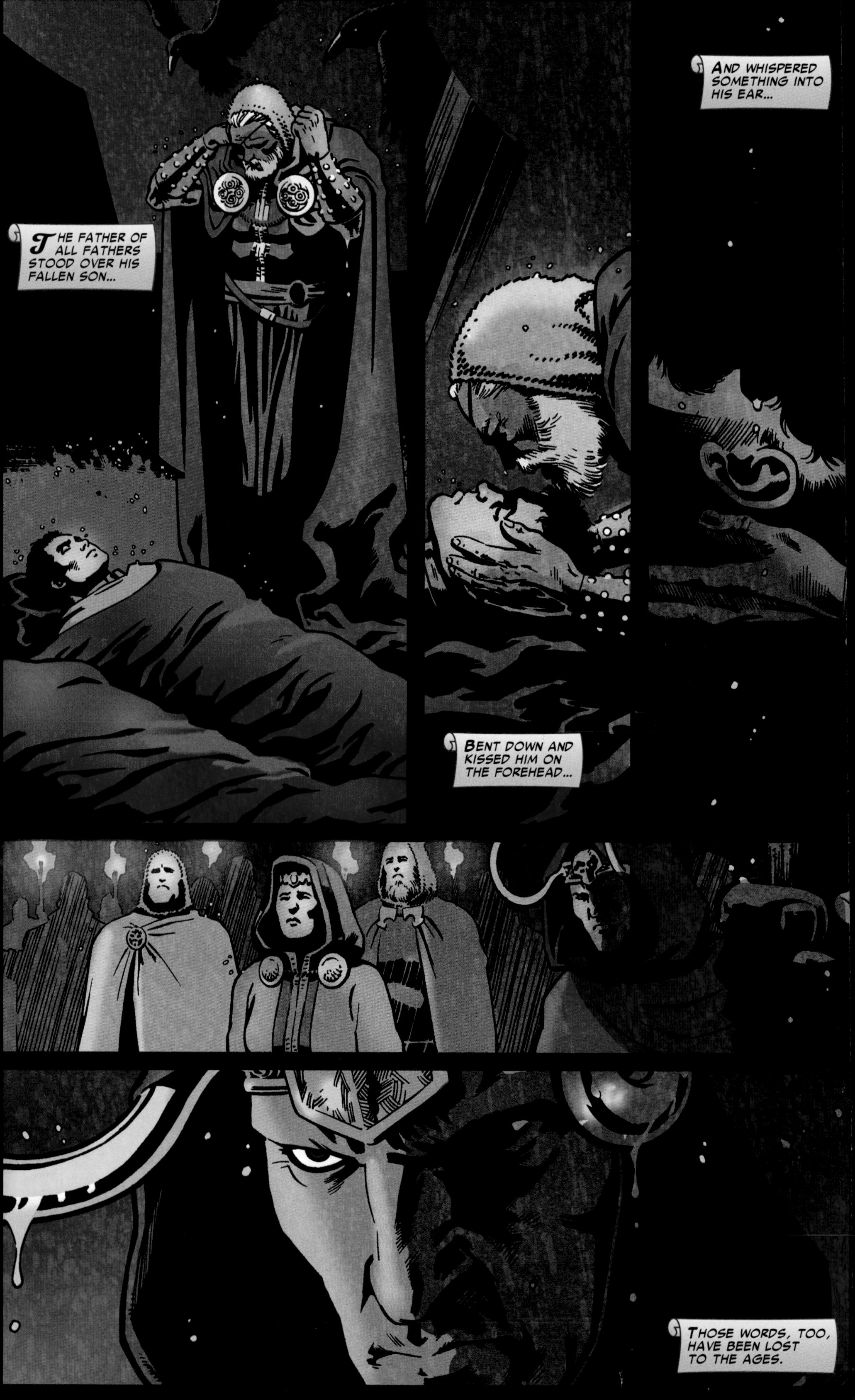
THE FATHER OF ALL FATHERS STOOD OVER HIS FALLEN SON...
BENT DOWN AND KISSED HIM ON THE FOREHEAD...
AND WHISPERED SOMETHING INTO HIS EAR...
THOSE WORDS, TOO, HAVE BEEN LOST TO THE AGES.

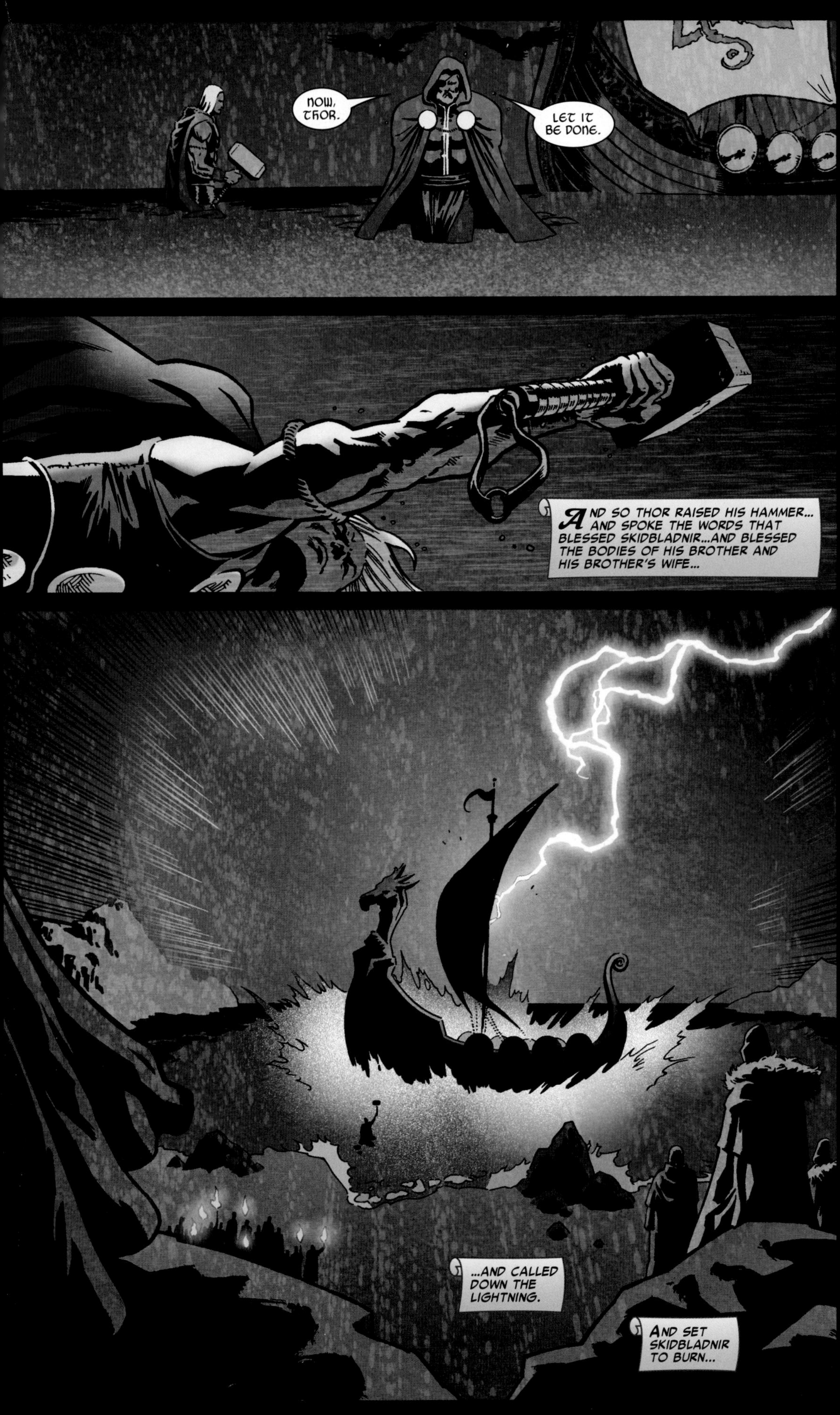
NOW, THOR.
LET IT BE DONE.
AND SO THOR RAISED HIS HAMMER... AND SPOKE THE WORDS THAT BLESSED SKIDBLADNIR...AND BLESSED THE BODIES OF HIS BROTHER AND HIS BROTHER'S WIFE...
...AND CALLED DOWN THE LIGHTNING.
AND SET SKIDBLADNIR TO BURN...

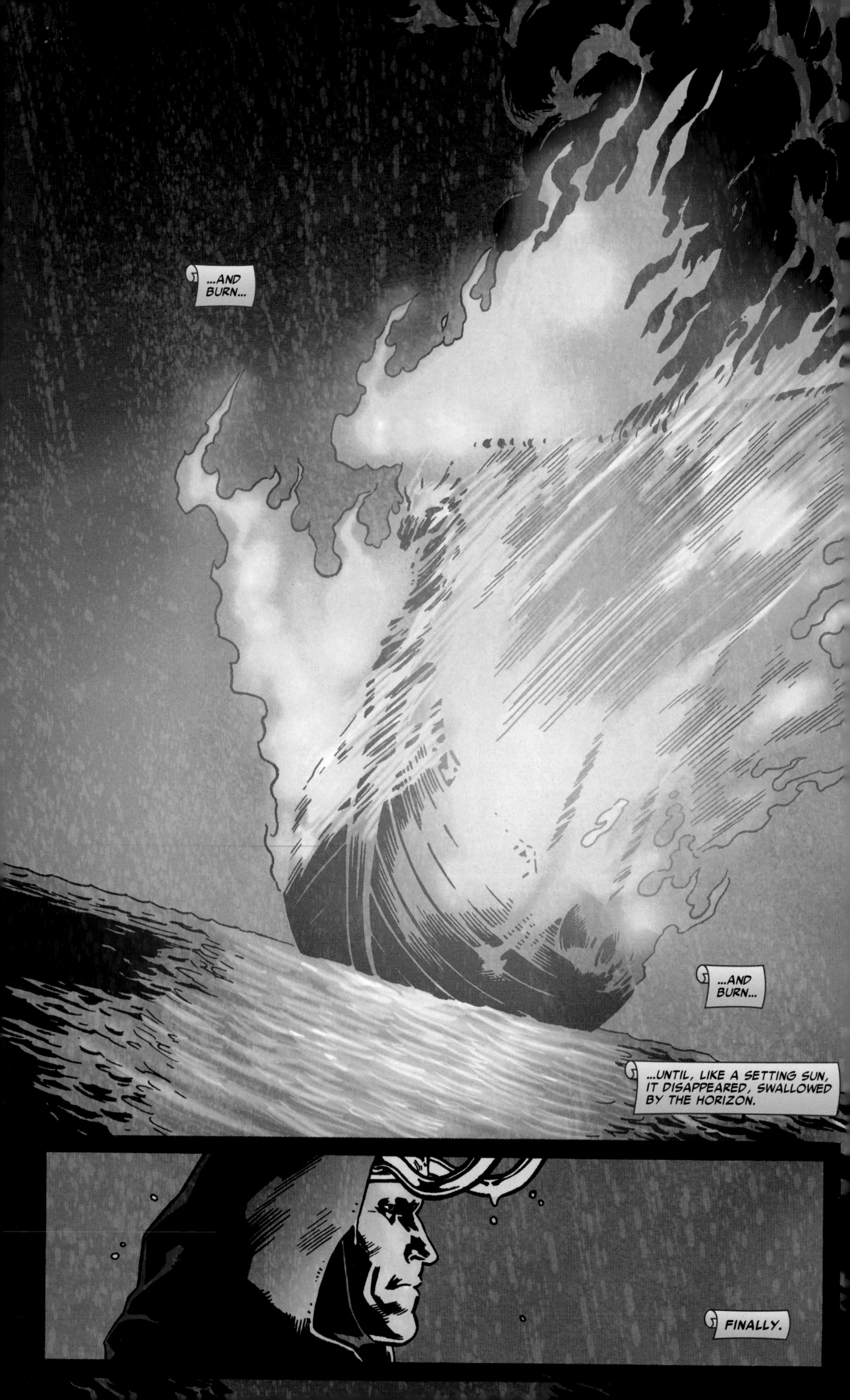
...AND BURN...
...AND BURN...
...UNTIL, LIKE A SETTING SUN, IT DISAPPEARED, SWALLOWED BY THE HORIZON.
FINALLY.

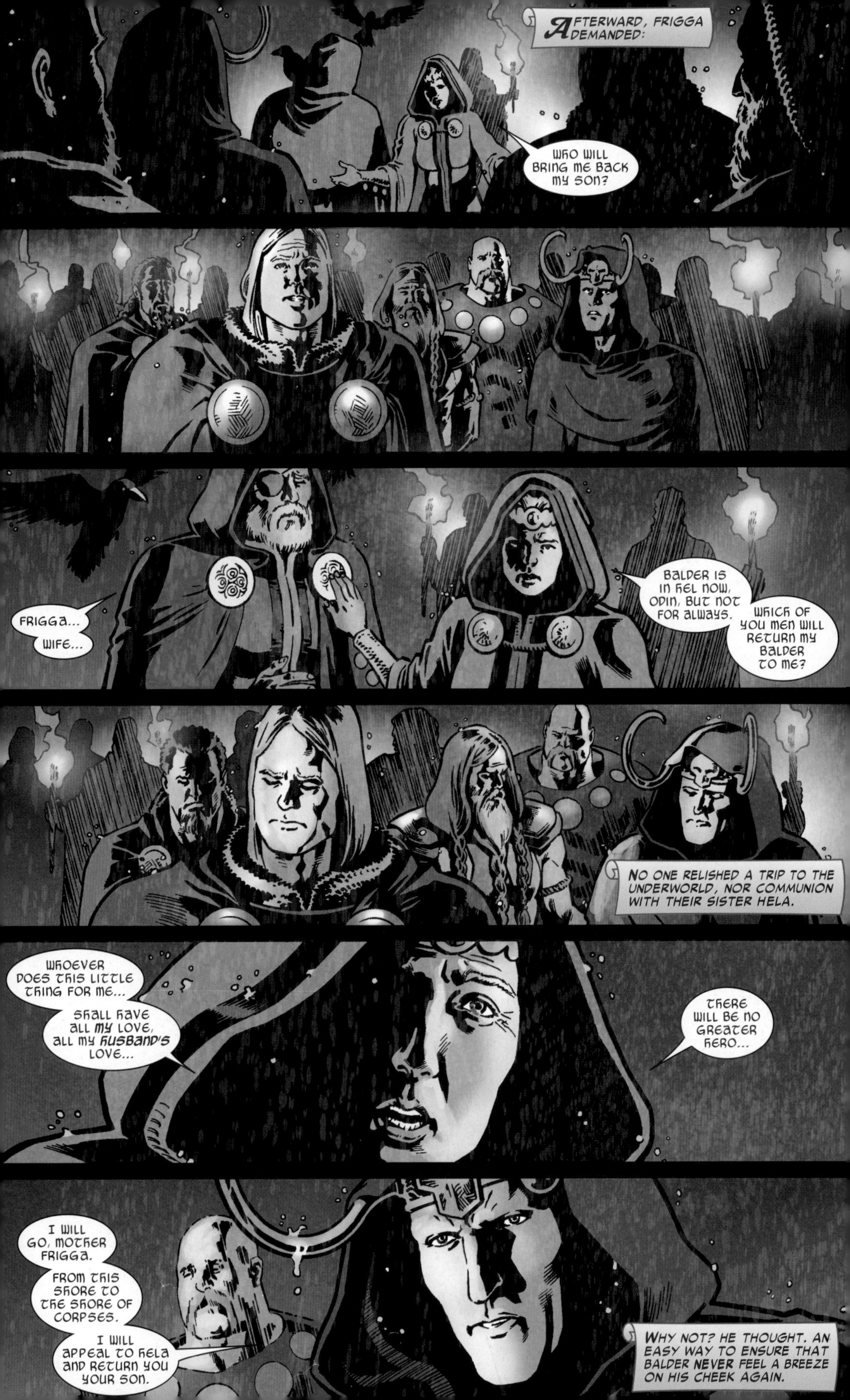
AFTERWARD, FRIGGA DEMANDED:
WHO WILL BRING ME BACK MY SON?
FRIGGA... WIFE...
BALDER IS IN HEL NOW, ODIN, BUT NOT FOR ALWAYS.
WHICH OF YOU MEN WILL RETURN MY BALDER TO ME?
NO ONE RELISHED A TRIP TO THE UNDERWORLD, NOR COMMUNION WITH THEIR SISTER HELA.
WHOEVER DOES THIS LITTLE THING FOR ME...
SHALL HAVE ALL MY LOVE, ALL MY HUSBAND'S LOVE...
THERE WILL BE NO GREATER HERO...
I WILL GO, MOTHER FRIGGA.
FROM THIS SHORE TO THE SHORE OF CORPSES.
I WILL APPEAL TO HELA AND RETURN YOU YOUR SON.
WHY NOT? HE THOUGHT. AN EASY WAY TO ENSURE THAT BALDER NEVER FEEL A BREEZE ON HIS CHEEK AGAIN.

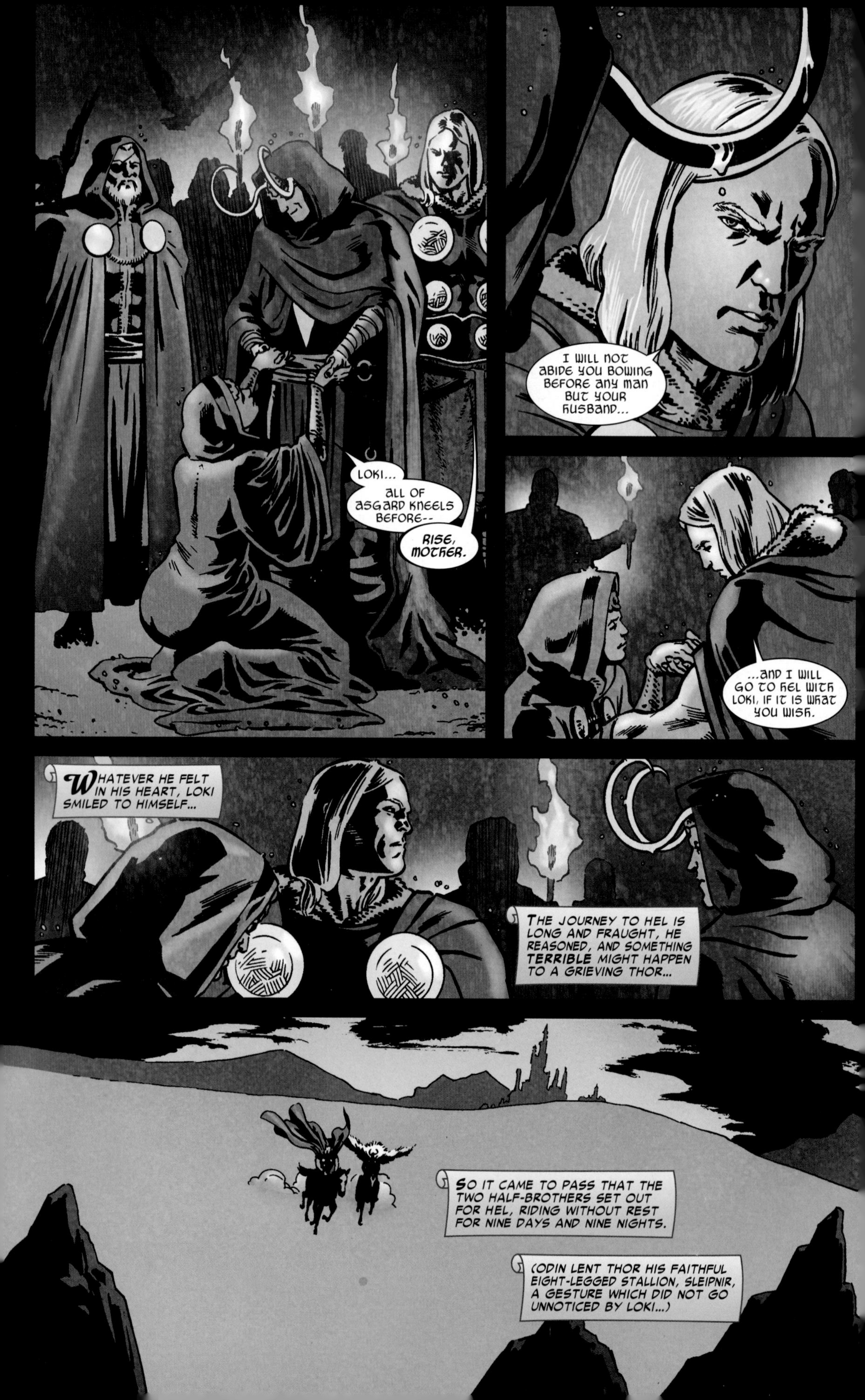
LOKI... ALL OF ASGARD KNEELS BEFORE--
RISE, MOTHER.
I WILL NOT ABIDE YOU BOWING BEFORE ANY MAN BUT YOUR HUSBAND...
...AND I WILL GO TO HEL WITH LOKI, IF IT IS WHAT YOU WISH.
WHATEVER HE FELT IN HIS HEART, LOKI SMILED TO HIMSELF...
THE JOURNEY TO HEL IS LONG AND FRAUGHT, HE REASONED, AND SOMETHING TERRIBLE MIGHT HAPPEN TO A GRIEVING THOR...
SO IT CAME TO PASS THAT THE TWO HALF-BROTHERS SET OUT FOR HEL, RIDING WITHOUT REST FOR NINE DAYS AND NINE NIGHTS.
(ODIN LENT THOR HIS FAITHFUL EIGHT-LEGGED STALLION, SLEIPNIR, A GESTURE WHICH DID NOT GO UNNOTICED BY LOKI...)

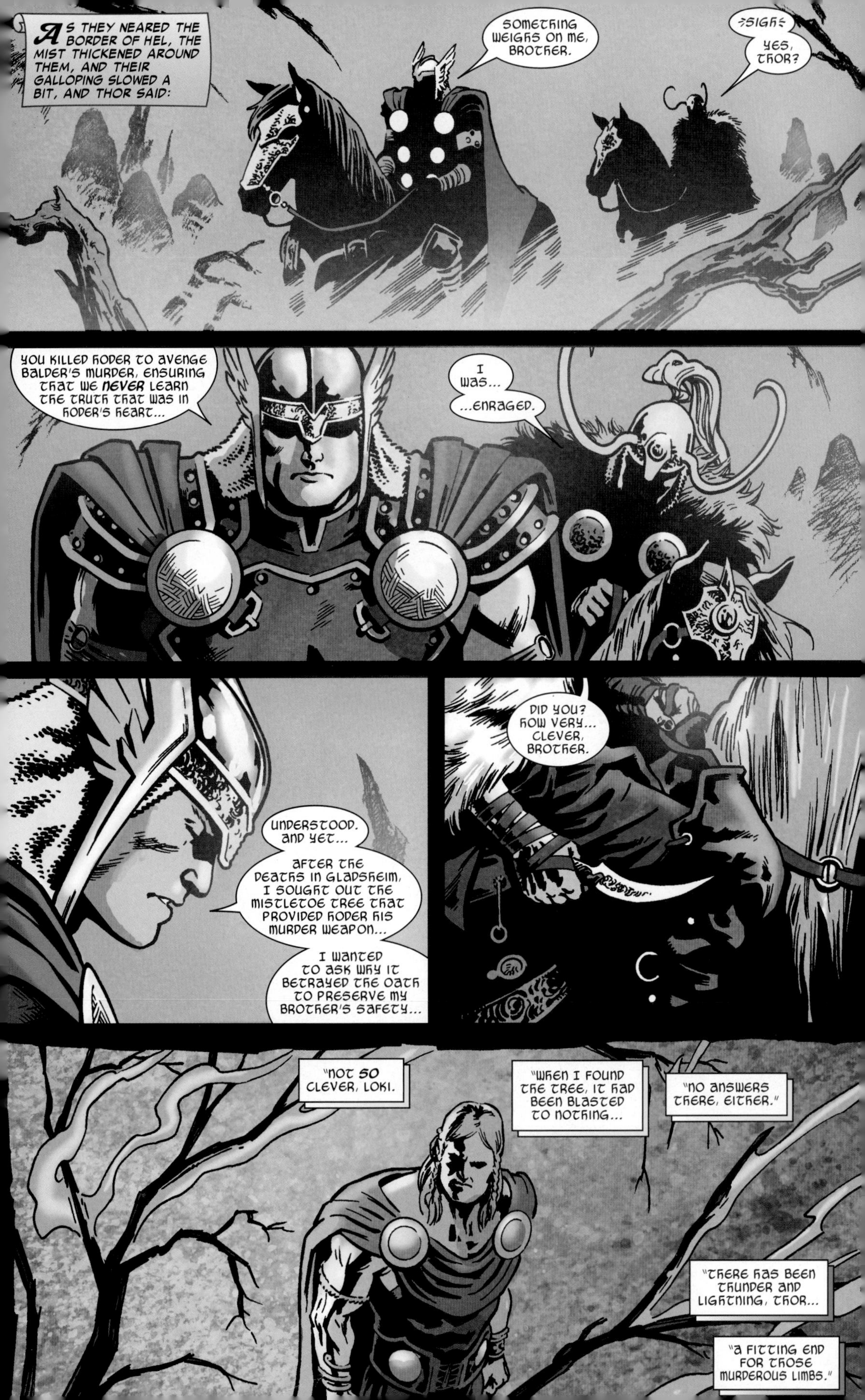

AS THEY NEARED THE BORDER OF HEL, THE MIST THICKENED AROUND THEM, AND THEIR GALLOPING SLOWED A BIT, AND THOR SAID:
SOMETHING WEIGHS ON ME, BROTHER.
SIGH
YES, THOR?
YOU KILLED HODER TO AVENGE BALDER'S MURDER, ENSURING THAT WE NEVER LEARN THE TRUTH THAT WAS IN HODER'S HEART...
I WAS...
...ENRAGED.
UNDERSTOOD. AND YET...
AFTER THE DEATHS IN GLADSHEIM, I SOUGHT OUT THE MISTLETOE TREE THAT PROVIDED HODER HIS MURDER WEAPON...
I WANTED TO ASK WHY IT BETRAYED THE OATH TO PRESERVE MY BROTHER'S SAFETY...
DID YOU? HOW VERY... CLEVER, BROTHER.
"NOT SO CLEVER, LOKI.
"WHEN I FOUND THE TREE, IT HAD BEEN BLASTED TO NOTHING...
"NO ANSWERS THERE, EITHER."
"THERE HAS BEEN THUNDER AND LIGHTNING, THOR...
"A FITTING END FOR THOSE MURDEROUS LIMBS."

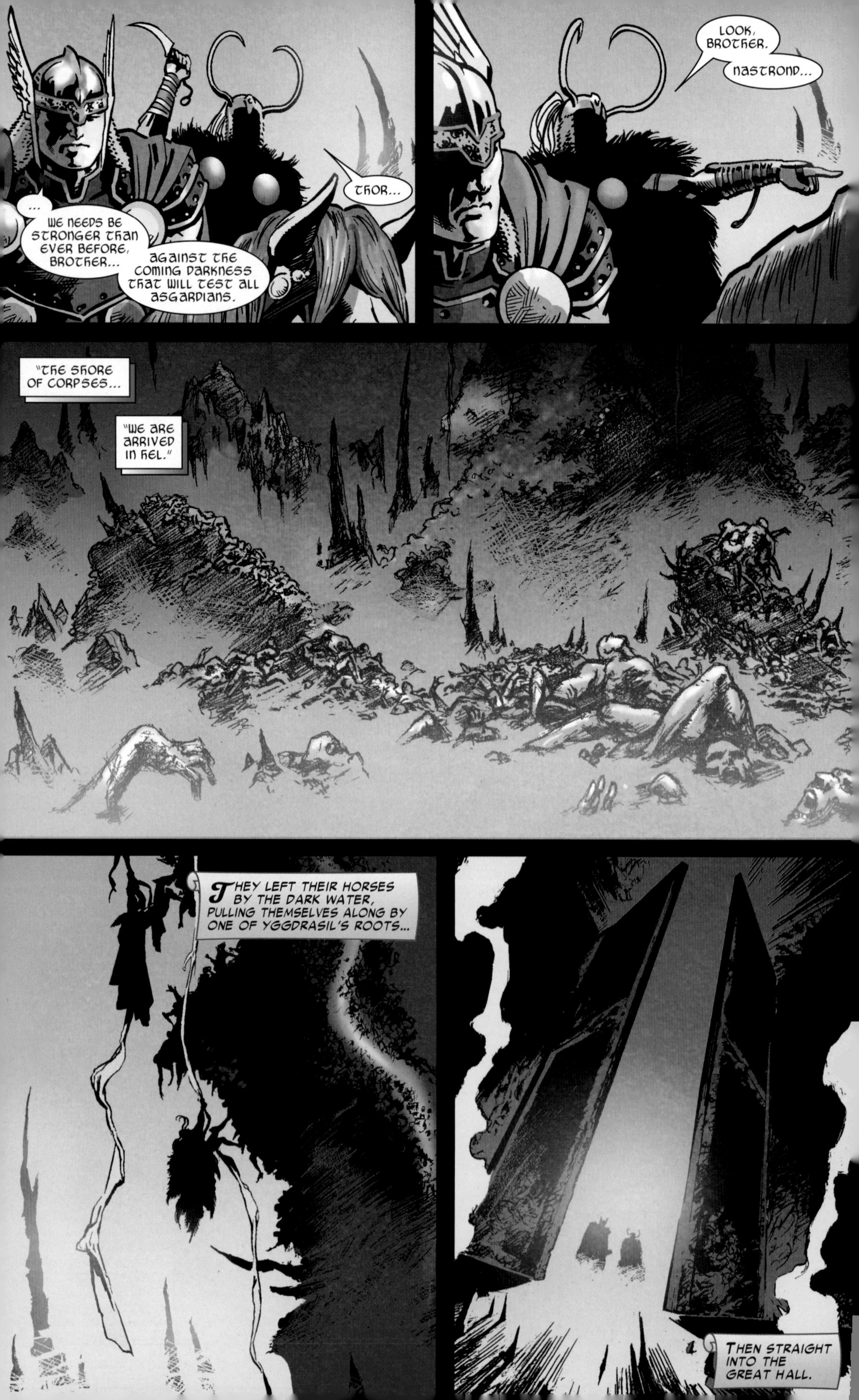
...
WE NEEDS BE STRONGER THAN EVER BEFORE, BROTHER...
AGAINST THE COMING DARKNESS THAT WILL TEST ALL ASGARDIANS.
THOR...
LOOK, BROTHER.
NASTROND...
"THE SHORE OF CORPSES...
"WE ARE ARRIVED IN HEL."
THEY LEFT THEIR HORSES BY THE DARK WATER, PULLING THEMSELVES ALONG BY ONE OF YGGDRASIL'S ROOTS...
THEN STRAIGHT INTO THE GREAT HALL.

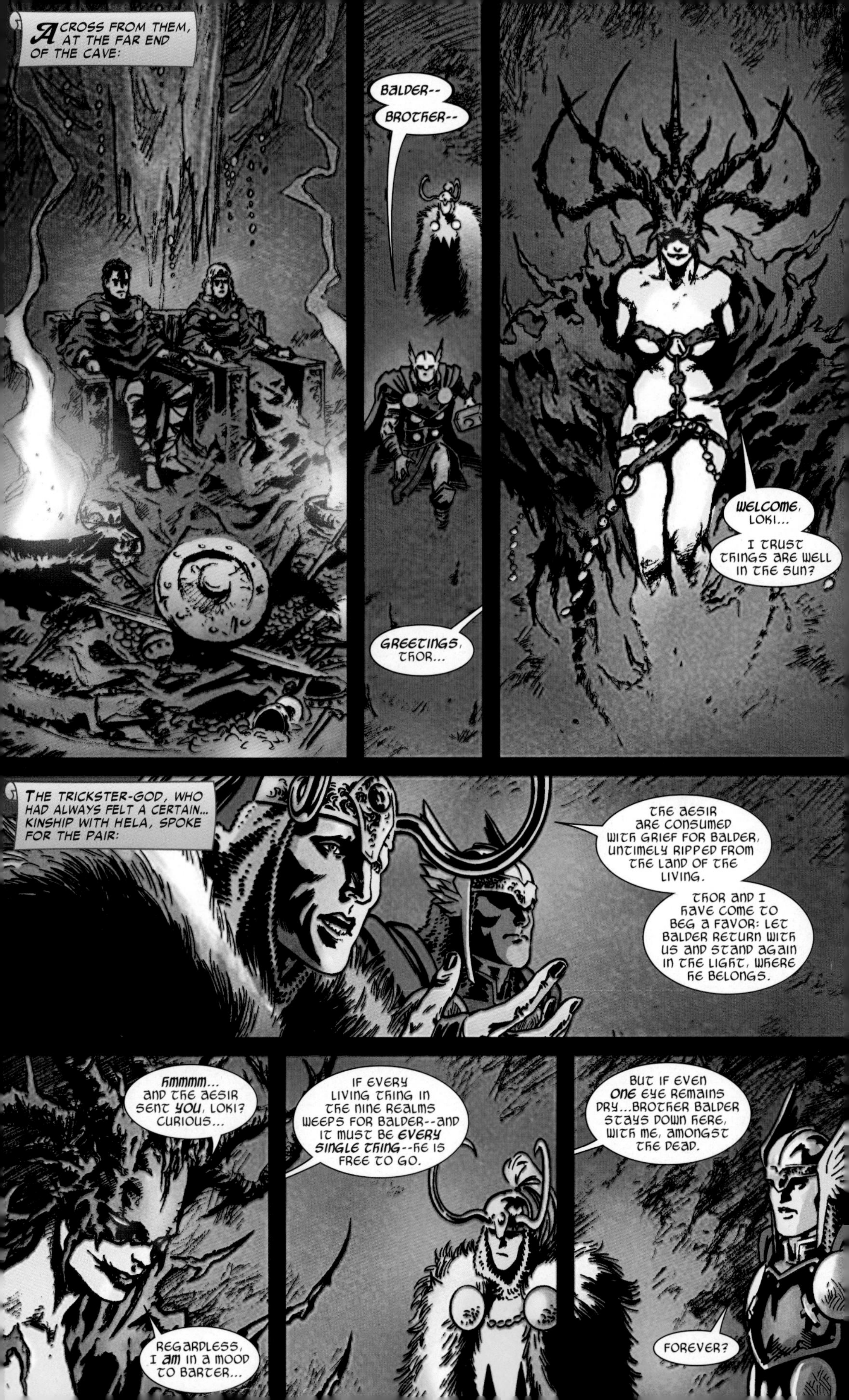
ACROSS FROM THEM, AT THE FAR END OF THE CAVE:
BALDER--
BROTHER--
GREETINGS, THOR...
WELCOME, LOKI...
I TRUST THINGS ARE WELL IN THE SUN?
THE TRICKSTER-GOD, WHO HAD ALWAYS FELT A CERTAIN... KINSHIP WITH HELA, SPOKE FOR THE PAIR:
THE AESIR ARE CONSUMED WITH GRIEF FOR BALDER, UNTIMELY RIPPED FROM THE LAND OF THE LIVING.
THOR AND I HAVE COME TO BEG A FAVOR: LET BALDER RETURN WITH US AND STAND AGAIN IN THE LIGHT, WHERE HE BELONGS.
HMMMM... AND THE AESIR SENT YOU, LOKI? CURIOUS...
REGARDLESS, I AM IN A MOOD TO BARTER...
IF EVERY LIVING THING IN THE NINE REALMS WEEPS FOR BALDER--AND IT MUST BE EVERY SINGLE THING--HE IS FREE TO GO.
BUT IF EVEN ONE EYE REMAINS DRY...BROTHER BALDER STAYS DOWN HERE, WITH ME, AMONGST THE DEAD.
FOREVER?

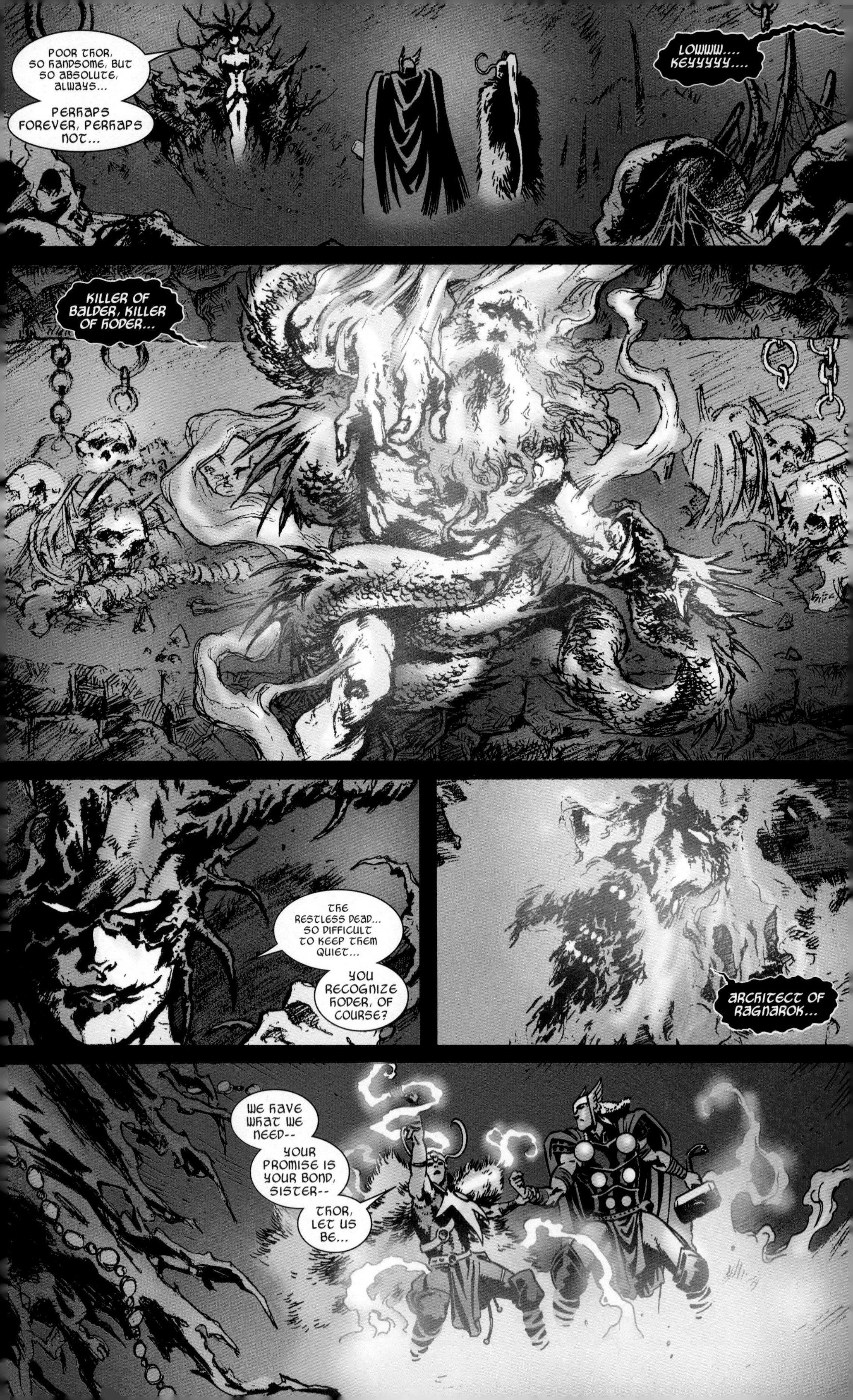
POOR THOR, SO HANDSOME, BUT SO ABSOLUTE, ALWAYS...
PERHAPS FOREVER, PERHAPS NOT...
LOWWW.... KEYYYYY....
KILLER OF BALDER, KILLER OF HODER...
THE RESTLESS DEAD... SO DIFFICULT TO KEEP THEM QUIET...
YOU RECOGNIZE HODER, OF COURSE?
ARCHITECT OF RAGNAROK...
WE HAVE WHAT WE NEED--
YOUR PROMISE IS YOUR BOND, SISTER--
THOR, LET US BE...

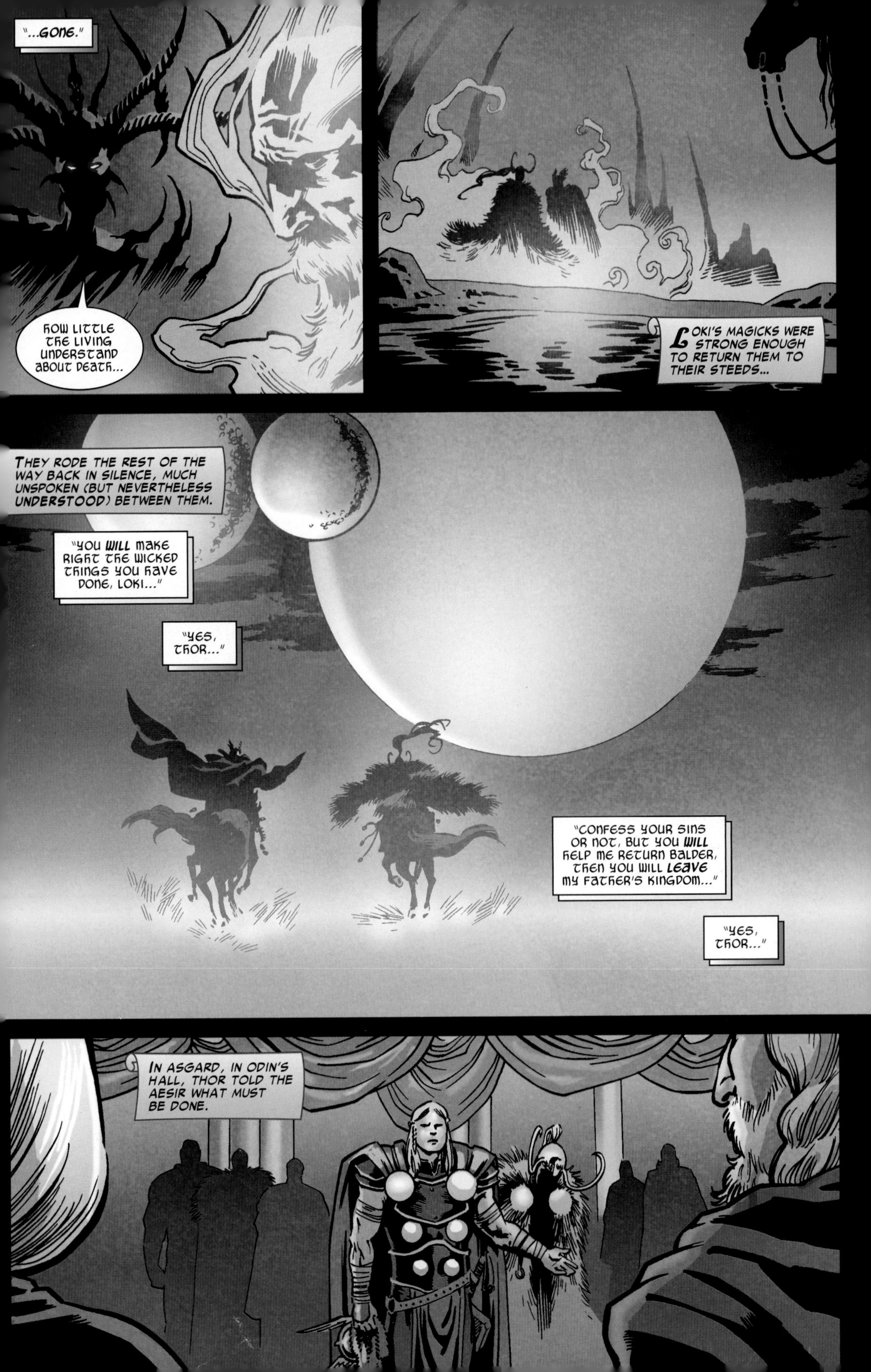
"...GONE."
HOW LITTLE THE LIVING UNDERSTAND ABOUT DEATH...
LOKI'S MAGICKS WERE STRONG ENOUGH TO RETURN THEM TO THEIR STEEDS...
THEY RODE THE REST OF THE WAY BACK IN SILENCE, MUCH UNSPOKEN (BUT NEVERTHELESS UNDERSTOOD) BETWEEN THEM.
"YOU WILL MAKE RIGHT THE WICKED THINGS YOU HAVE DONE, LOKI..."
"YES, THOR..."
"CONFESS YOUR SINS OR NOT, BUT YOU WILL HELP ME RETURN BALDER, THEN YOU WILL LEAVE MY FATHER'S KINGDOM..."
"YES, THOR..."
IN ASGARD, IN ODIN'S HALL, THOR TOLD THE AESIR WHAT MUST BE DONE.

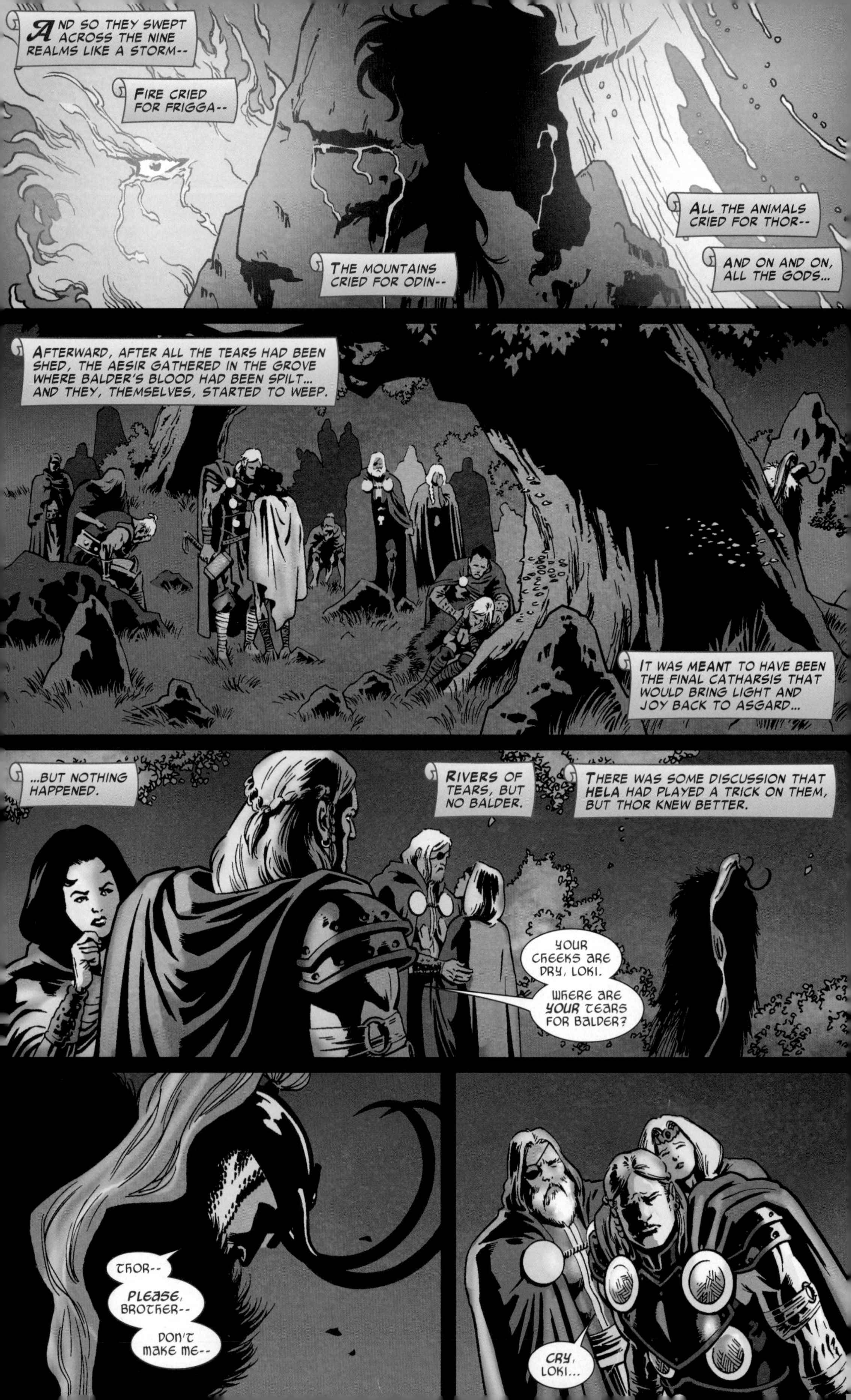

AND SO THEY SWEPT ACROSS THE NINE REALMS LIKE A STORM--
FIRE CRIED FOR FRIGGA--
THE MOUNTAINS CRIED FOR ODIN--
ALL THE ANIMALS CRIED FOR THOR--
AND ON AND ON, ALL THE GODS...
AFTERWARD, AFTER ALL THE TEARS HAD BEEN SHED, THE AESIR GATHERED IN THE GROVE WHERE BALDER'S BLOOD HAD BEEN SPILT... AND THEY, THEMSELVES, STARTED TO WEEP.
IT WAS MEANT TO HAVE BEEN THE FINAL CATHARSIS THAT WOULD BRING LIGHT AND JOY BACK TO ASGARD...
...BUT NOTHING HAPPENED.
RIVERS OF TEARS, BUT NO BALDER.
THERE WAS SOME DISCUSSION THAT HELA HAD PLAYED A TRICK ON THEM, BUT THOR KNEW BETTER.
YOUR CHEEKS ARE DRY, LOKI.
WHERE ARE YOUR TEARS FOR BALDER?
THOR--
PLEASE, BROTHER--
DON'T MAKE ME--
CRY, LOKI...

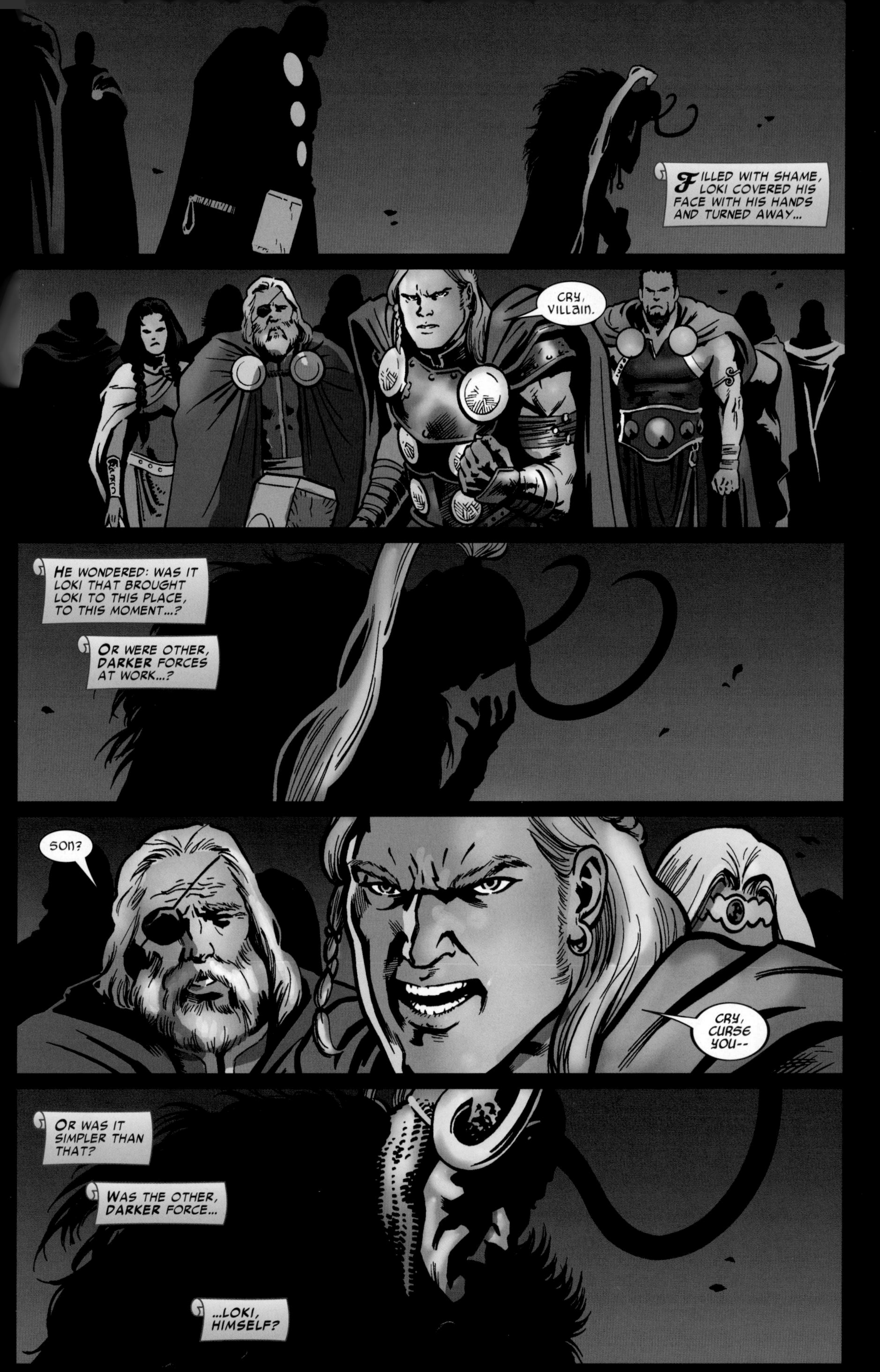
FILLED WITH SHAME, LOKI COVERED HIS FACE WITH HIS HANDS AND TURNED AWAY...
CRY, VILLAIN.
HE WONDERED: WAS IT LOKI THAT BROUGHT LOKI TO THIS PLACE, TO THIS MOMENT...?
OR WERE OTHER, DARKER FORCES AT WORK...?
SON?
CRY, CURSE YOU--
OR WAS IT SIMPLER THAN THAT?
WAS THE OTHER, DARKER FORCE...
...LOKI, HIMSELF?

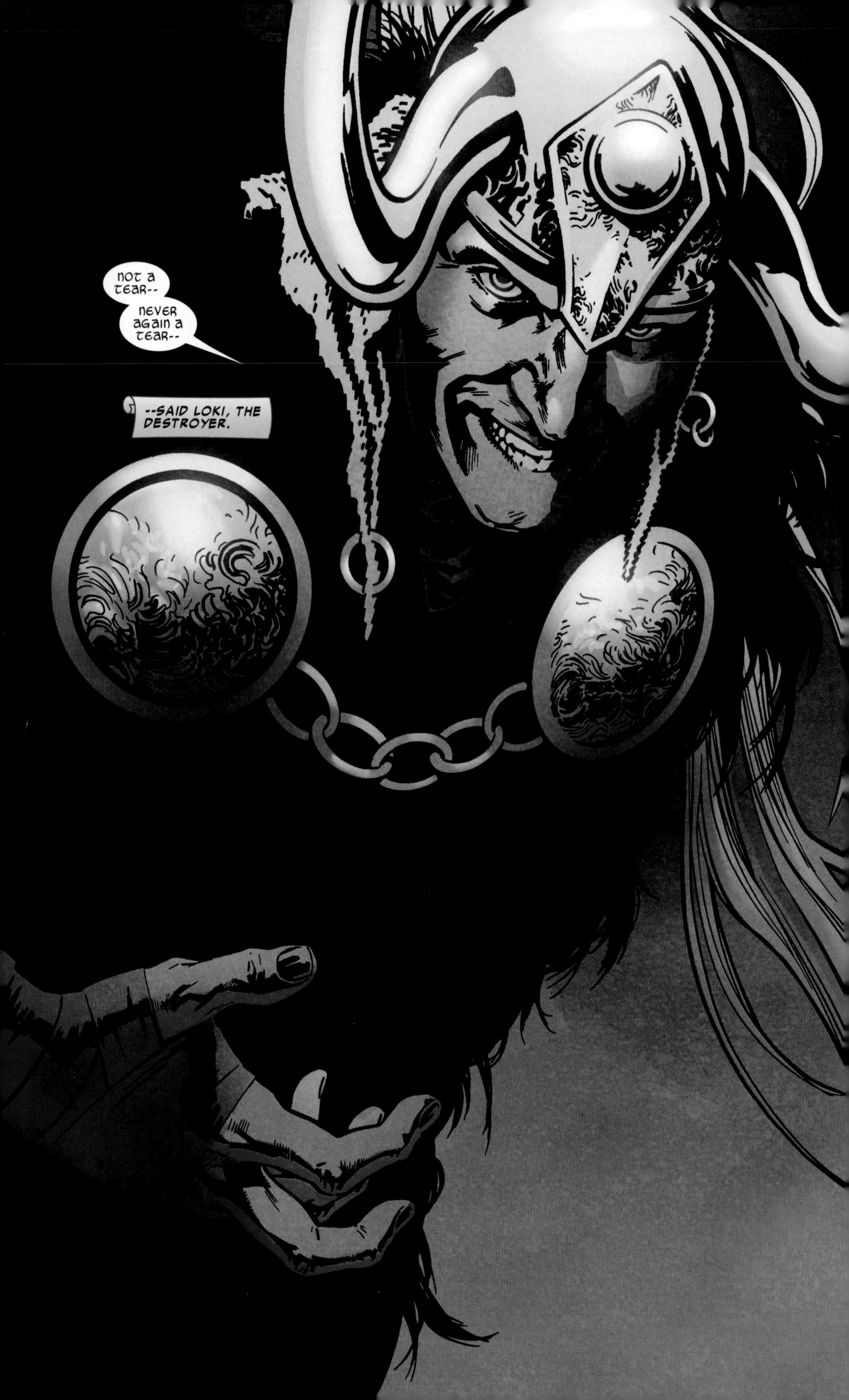
NOT A TEAR--
NEVER AGAIN A TEAR--
--SAID LOKI, THE DESTROYER.

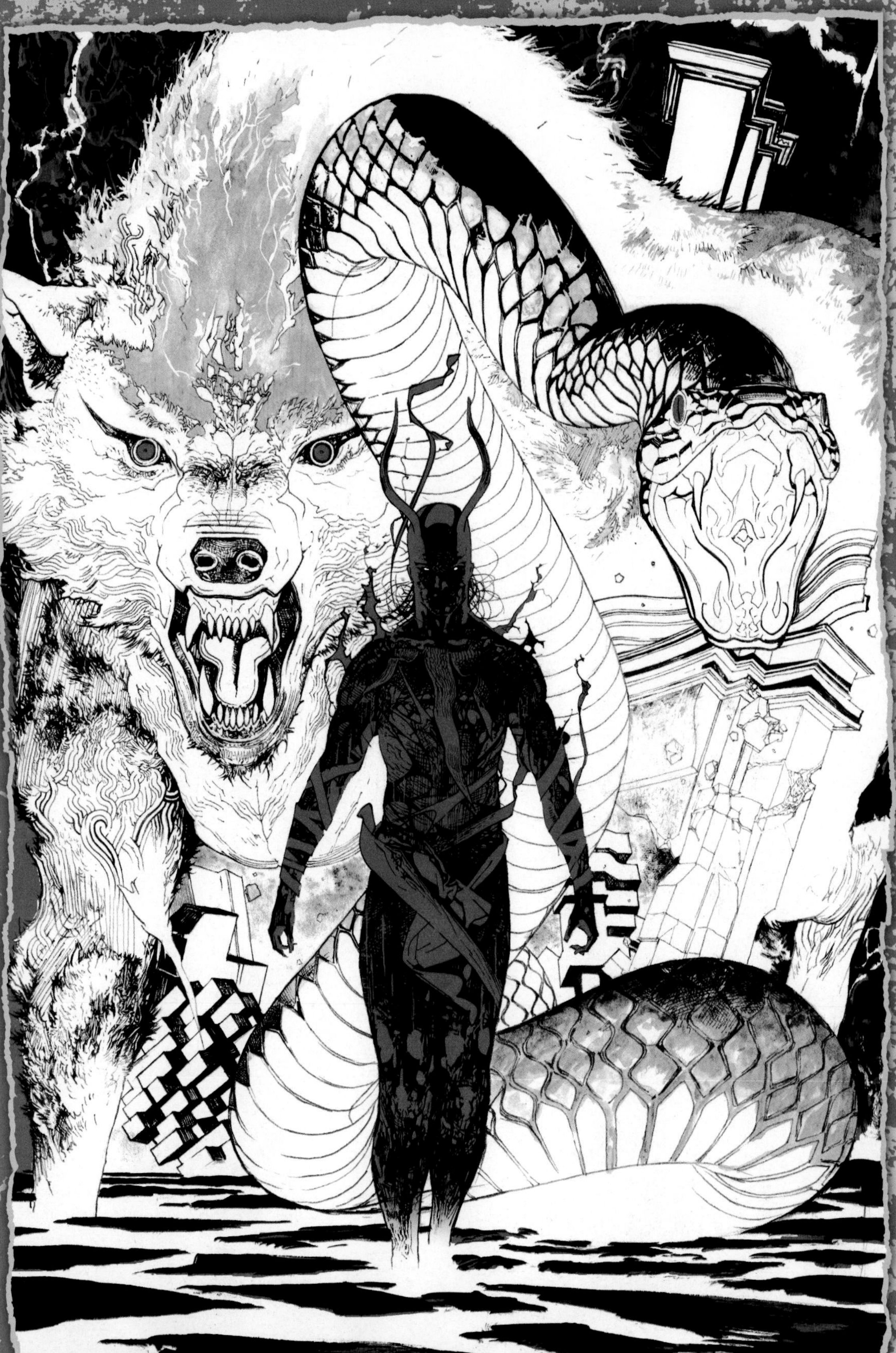

PART FOUR
THE CROOKED PATH

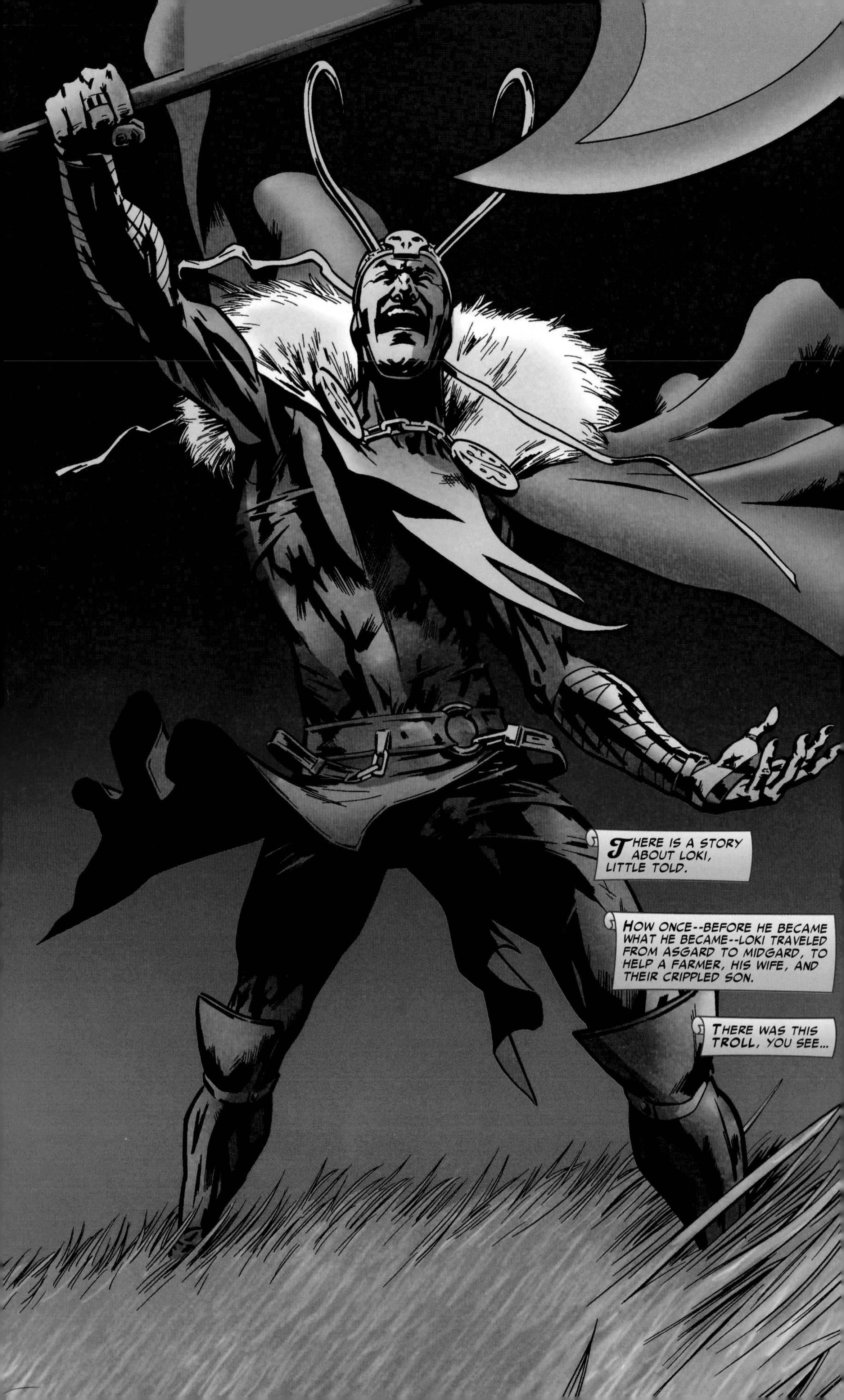
THERE IS A STORY ABOUT LOKI, LITTLE TOLD.
HOW ONCE--BEFORE HE BECAME WHAT HE BECAME--LOKI TRAVELED FROM ASGARD TO MIDGARD, TO HELP A FARMER, HIS WIFE, AND THEIR CRIPPLED SON.
THERE WAS THIS TROLL, YOU SEE...

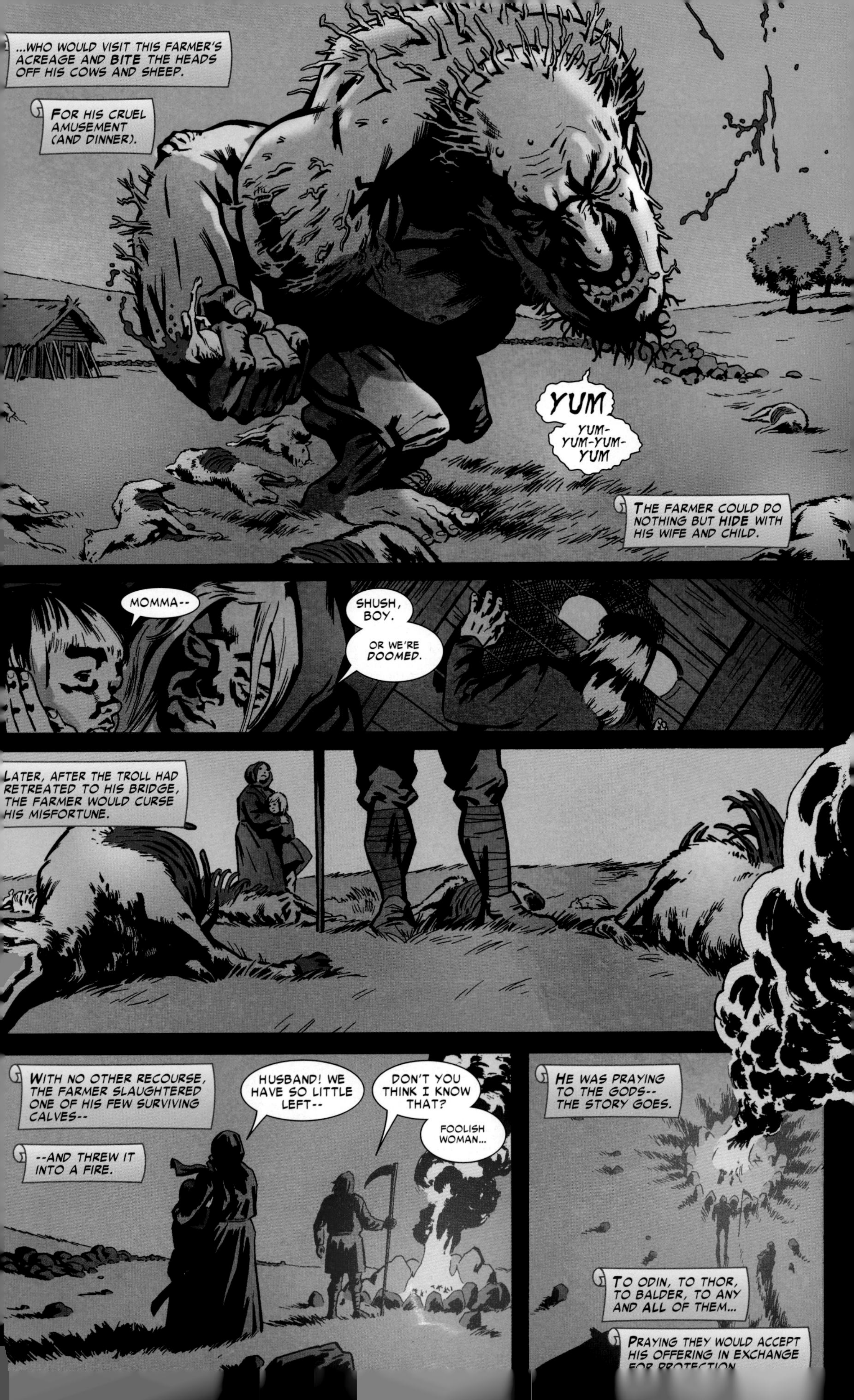
...WHO WOULD VISIT THIS FARMER'S ACREAGE AND BITE THE HEADS OFF HIS COWS AND SHEEP.
FOR HIS CRUEL AMUSEMENT (AND DINNER).
YUM
YUM-YUM-YUM-YUM
THE FARMER COULD DO NOTHING BUT HIDE WITH HIS WIFE AND CHILD.
MOMMA--
SHUSH, BOY.
OR WE'RE DOOMED.
LATER, AFTER THE TROLL HAD RETREATED TO HIS BRIDGE, THE FARMER WOULD CURSE HIS MISFORTUNE.
WITH NO OTHER RECOURSE, THE FARMER SLAUGHTERED ONE OF HIS FEW SURVIVING CALVES--
--AND THREW IT INTO A FIRE.
HUSBAND! WE HAVE SO LITTLE LEFT--
DON'T YOU THINK I KNOW THAT?
FOOLISH WOMAN...
HE WAS PRAYING TO THE GODS-- THE STORY GOES.
TO ODIN, TO THOR, TO BALDER, TO ANY AND ALL OF THEM...
PRAYING THEY WOULD ACCEPT HIS OFFERING IN EXCHANGE

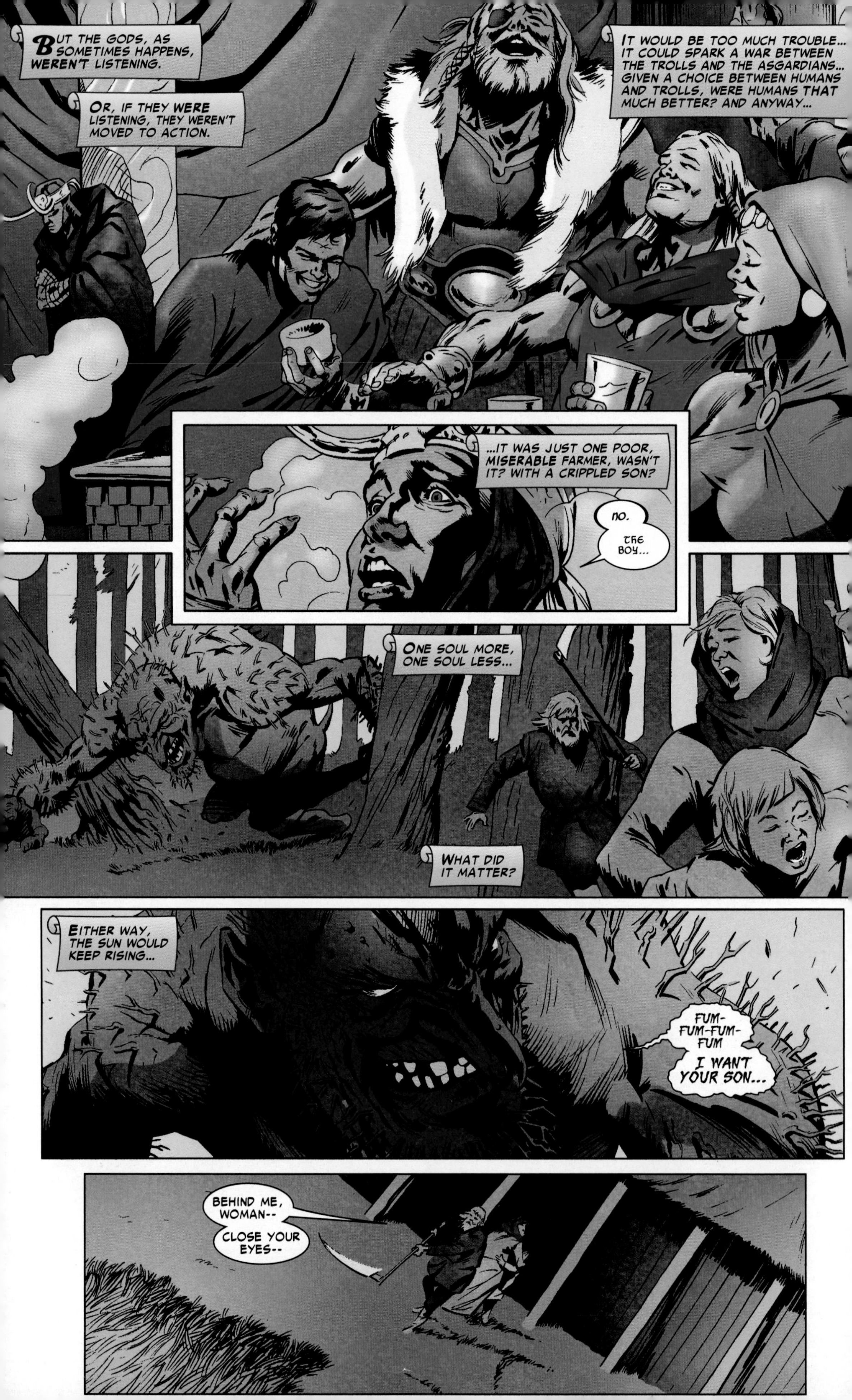
BUT THE GODS, AS SOMETIMES HAPPENS, WEREN'T LISTENING.
OR, IF THEY WERE LISTENING, THEY WEREN'T MOVED TO ACTION.
IT WOULD BE TOO MUCH TROUBLE... IT COULD SPARK A WAR BETWEEN THE TROLLS AND THE ASGARDIANS... GIVEN A CHOICE BETWEEN HUMANS AND TROLLS, WERE HUMANS THAT MUCH BETTER? AND ANYWAY...
...IT WAS JUST ONE POOR, MISERABLE FARMER, WASN'T IT? WITH A CRIPPLED SON?
NO.
THE BOY...
ONE SOUL MORE, ONE SOUL LESS...
WHAT DID IT MATTER?
EITHER WAY, THE SUN WOULD KEEP RISING...
FUM-FUM-FUM-FUM
I WANT YOUR SON...
BEHIND ME, WOMAN--
CLOSE YOUR EYES--

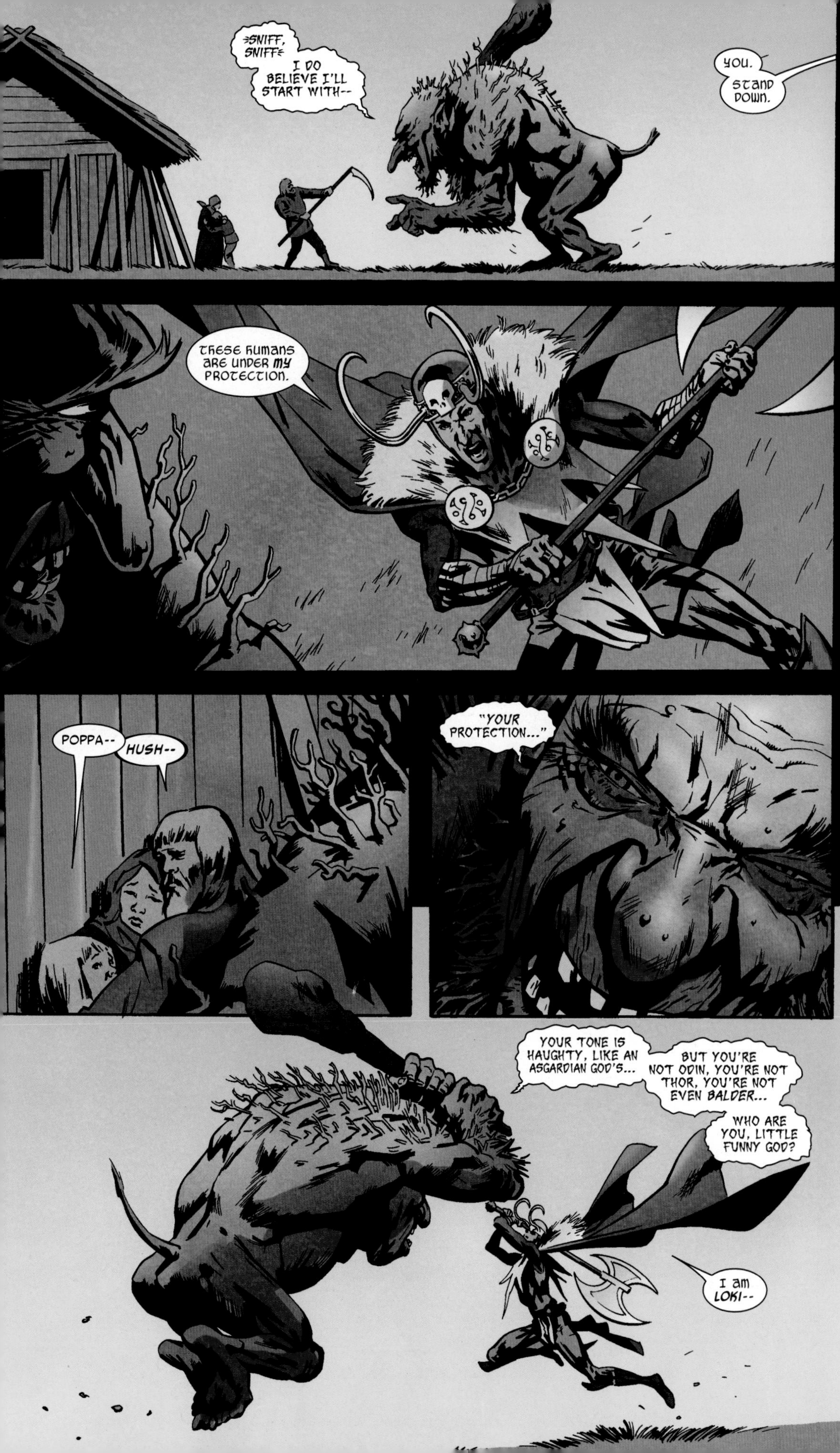

SNIFF, SNIFF
I DO BELIEVE I'LL START WITH--
YOU. STAND DOWN.
THESE HUMANS ARE UNDER MY PROTECTION.
POPPA--
HUSH--
"YOUR PROTECTION..."
YOUR TONE IS HAUGHTY, LIKE AN ASGARDIAN GOD'S...
BUT YOU'RE NOT ODIN, YOU'RE NOT THOR, YOU'RE NOT EVEN BALDER...
WHO ARE YOU, LITTLE FUNNY GOD?
I AM LOKI--

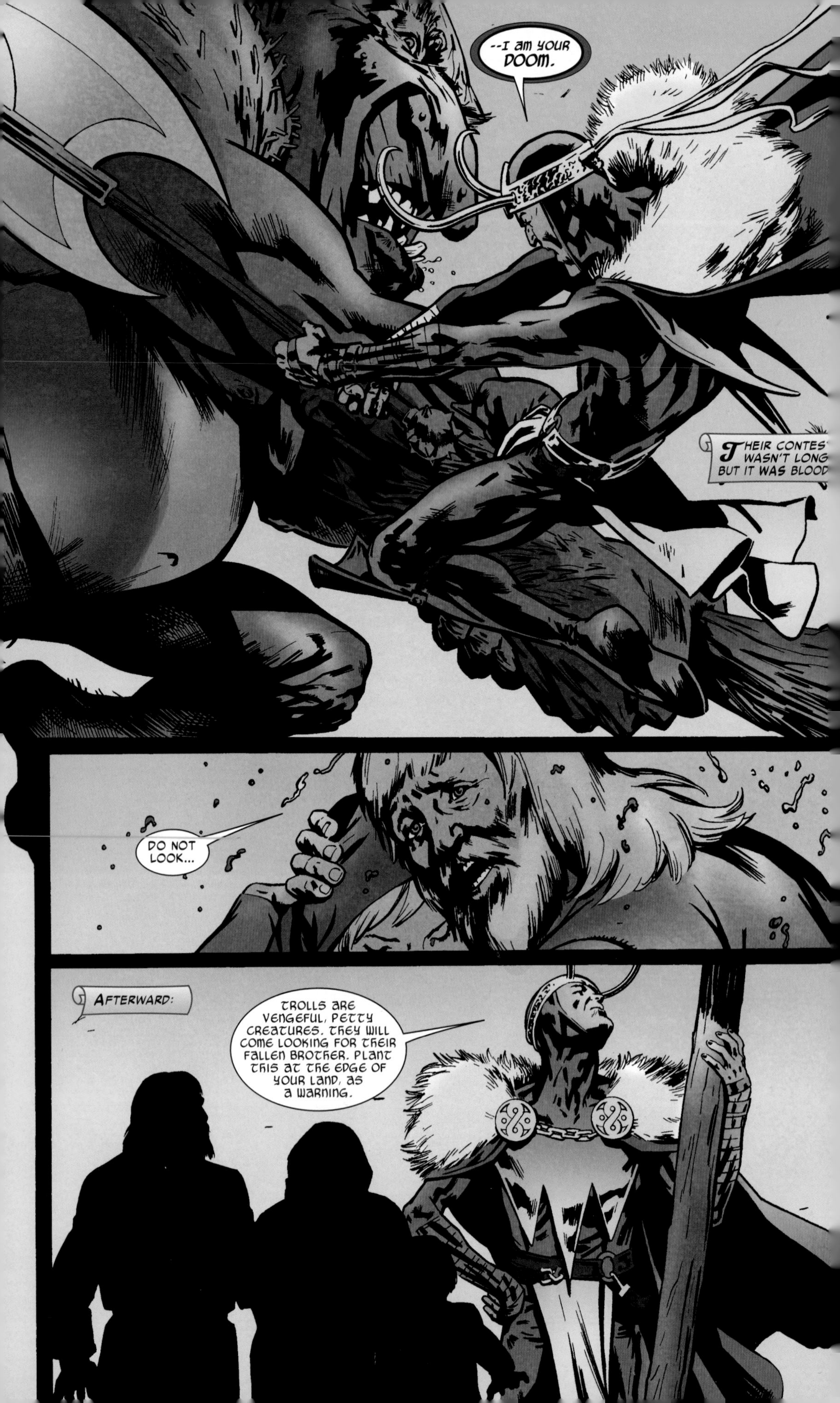
--I am your DOOM.
THEIR CONTES
WASN'T LONG
BUT IT WAS BLOOD
DO NOT LOOK...
AFTERWARD:
TROLLS ARE VENGEFUL, PETTY CREATURES. THEY WILL COME LOOKING FOR THEIR FALLEN BROTHER. PLANT THIS AT THE EDGE OF YOUR LAND, AS A WARNING.

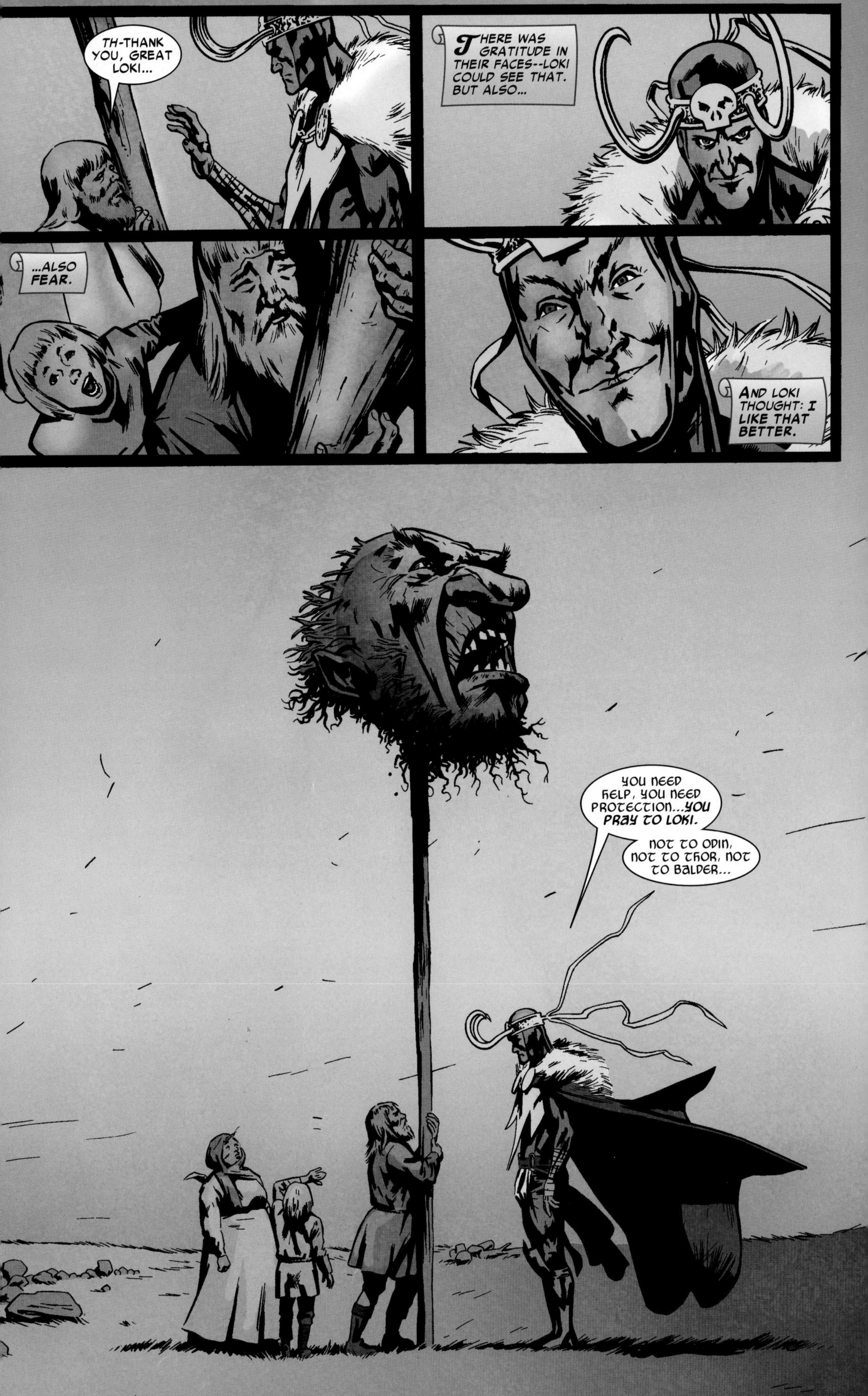
TH-THANK YOU, GREAT LOKI...
THERE WAS GRATITUDE IN THEIR FACES--LOKI COULD SEE THAT. BUT ALSO...
...ALSO FEAR.
AND LOKI THOUGHT: I LIKE THAT BETTER.
YOU NEED HELP, YOU NEED PROTECTION...YOU PRAY TO LOKI.
NOT TO ODIN, NOT TO THOR, NOT TO BALDER...

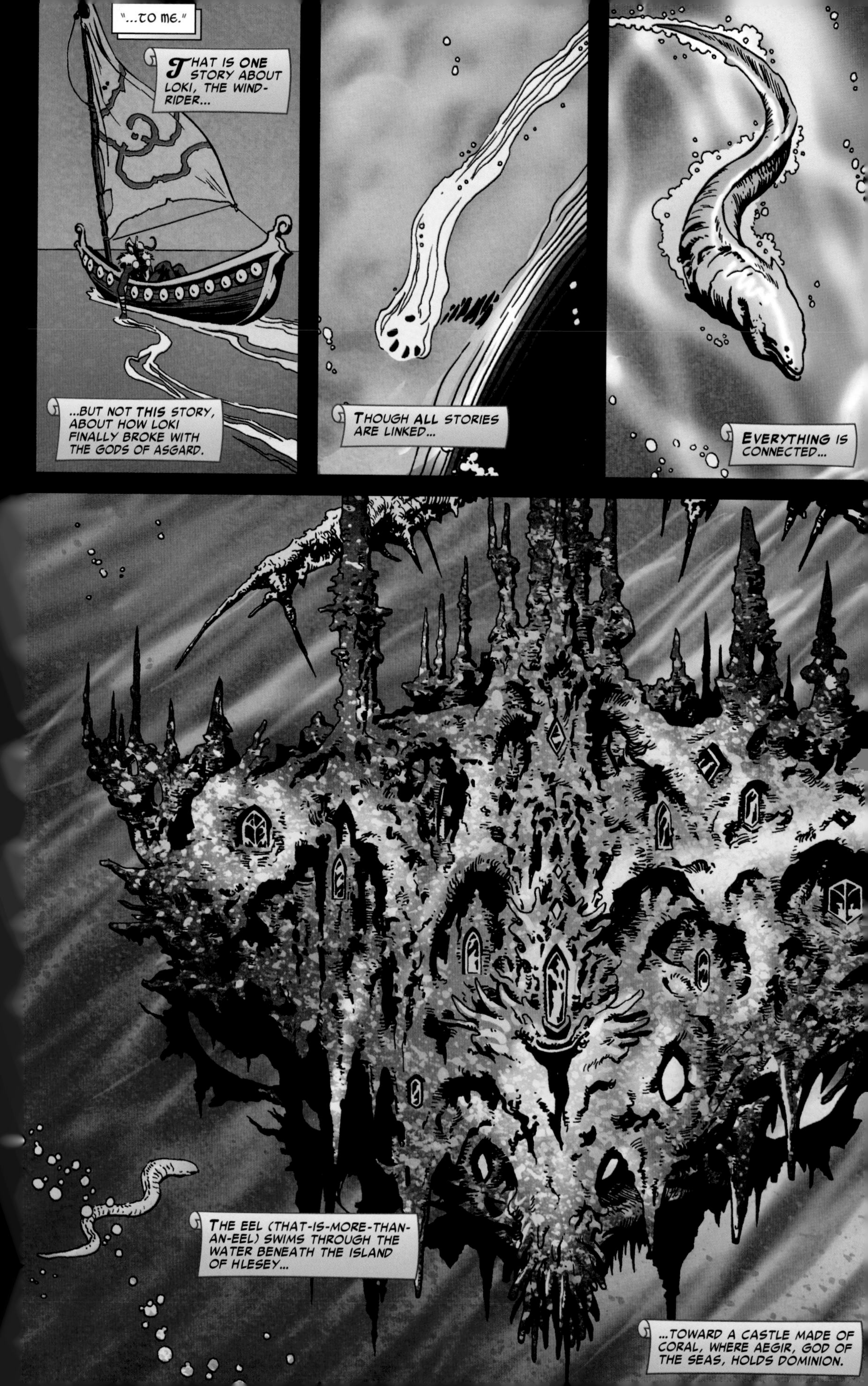
"...TO ME."
THAT IS ONE STORY ABOUT LOKI, THE WIND-RIDER...
...BUT NOT THIS STORY, ABOUT HOW LOKI FINALLY BROKE WITH THE GODS OF ASGARD.
THOUGH ALL STORIES ARE LINKED...
EVERYTHING IS CONNECTED...
THE EEL (THAT-IS-MORE-THAN-AN-EEL) SWIMS THROUGH THE WATER BENEATH THE ISLAND OF HLESEY...
...TOWARD A CASTLE MADE OF CORAL, WHERE AEGIR, GOD OF THE SEAS, HOLDS DOMINION.

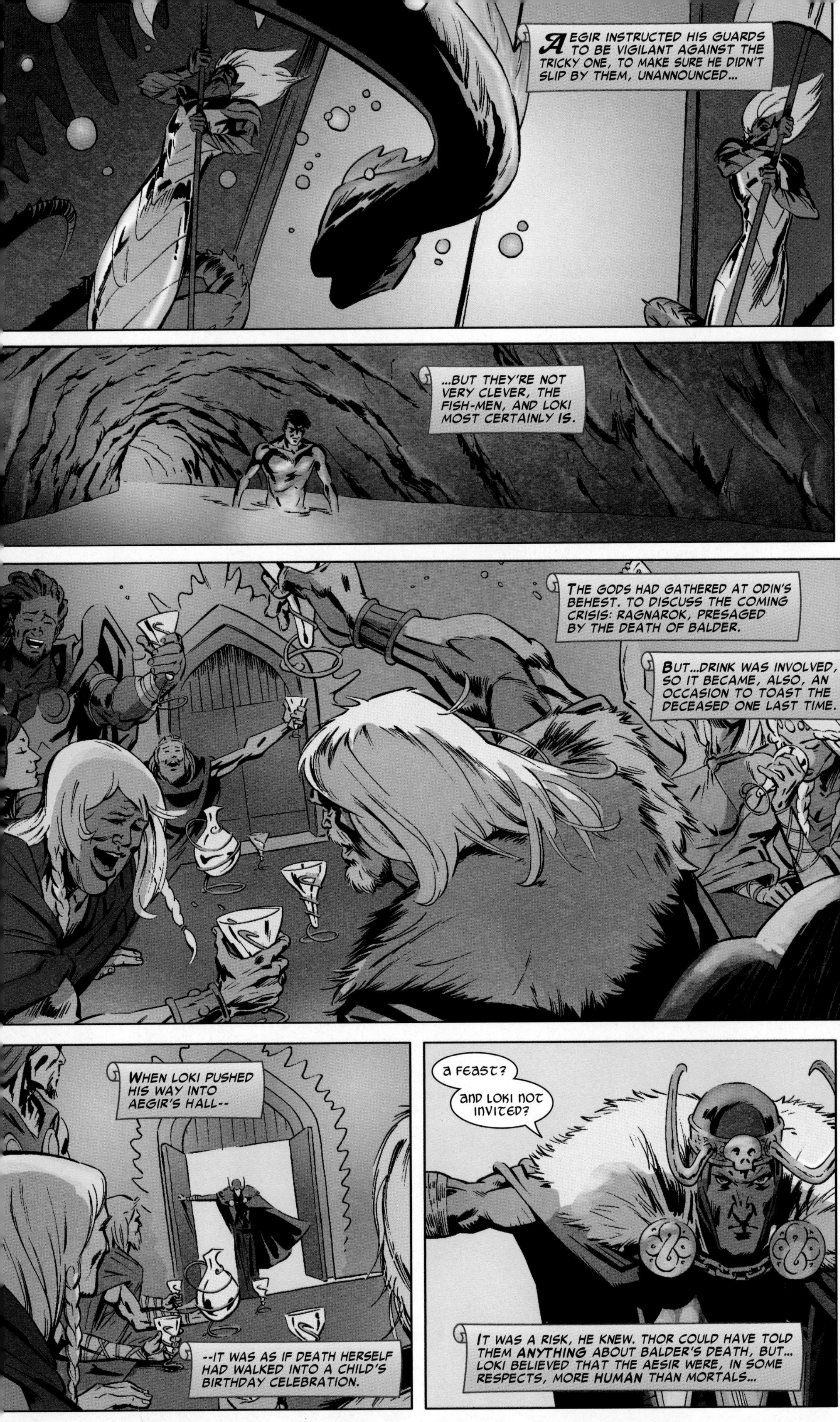
AEGIR INSTRUCTED HIS GUARDS TO BE VIGILANT AGAINST THE TRICKY ONE, TO MAKE SURE HE DIDN'T SLIP BY THEM, UNANNOUNCED...
...BUT THEY'RE NOT VERY CLEVER, THE FISH-MEN, AND LOKI MOST CERTAINLY IS.
THE GODS HAD GATHERED AT ODIN'S BEHEST. TO DISCUSS THE COMING CRISIS: RAGNAROK, PRESAGED BY THE DEATH OF BALDER.
BUT...DRINK WAS INVOLVED, SO IT BECAME, ALSO, AN OCCASION TO TOAST THE DECEASED ONE LAST TIME.
WHEN LOKI PUSHED HIS WAY INTO AEGIR'S HALL--
--IT WAS AS IF DEATH HERSELF HAD WALKED INTO A CHILD'S BIRTHDAY CELEBRATION.
A FEAST?
AND LOKI NOT INVITED?
IT WAS A RISK, HE KNEW. THOR COULD HAVE TOLD THEM ANYTHING ABOUT BALDER'S DEATH, BUT... LOKI BELIEVED THAT THE AESIR WERE, IN SOME RESPECTS, MORE HUMAN THAN MORTALS...

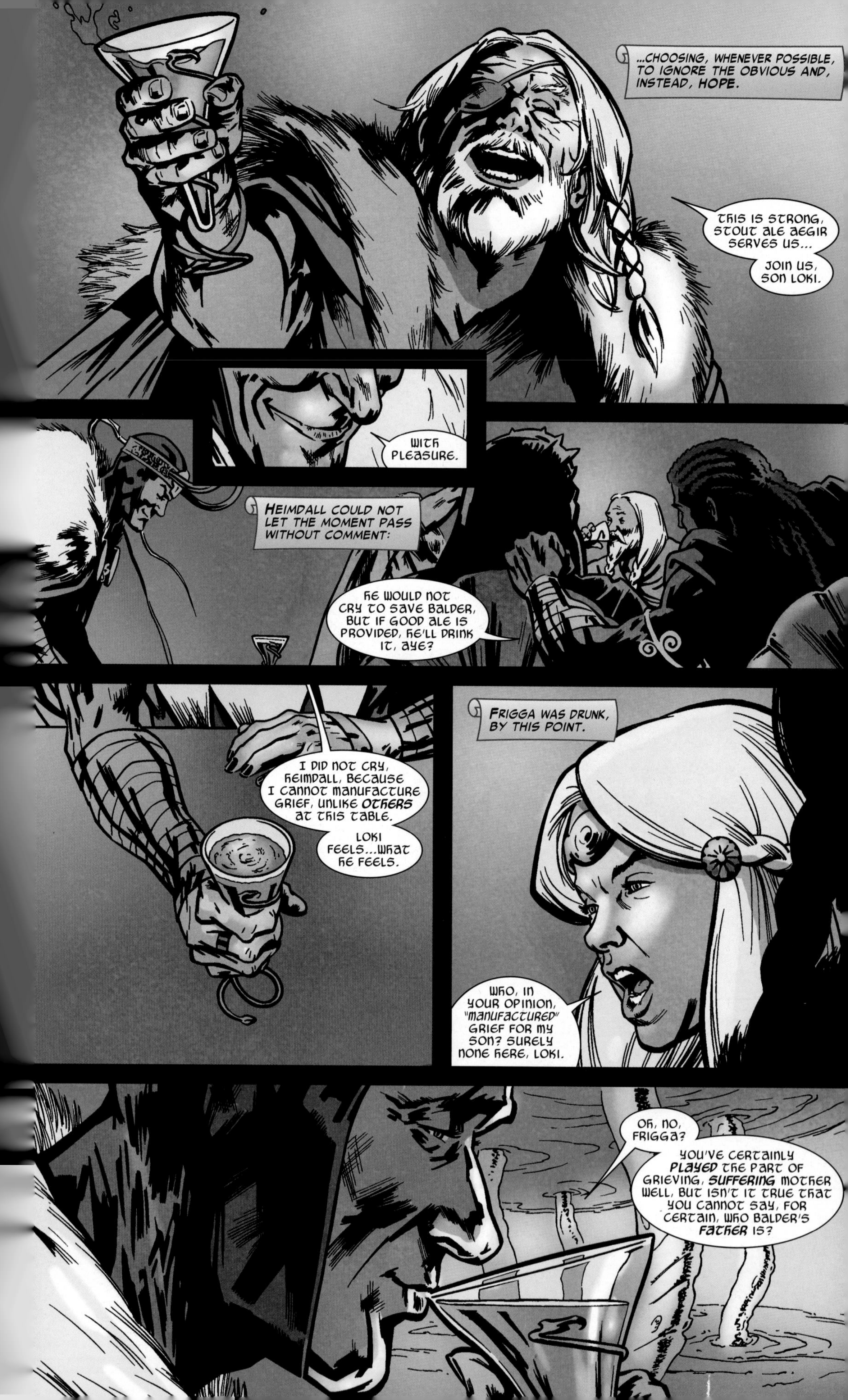
...CHOOSING, WHENEVER POSSIBLE, TO IGNORE THE OBVIOUS AND, INSTEAD, HOPE.
THIS IS STRONG, STOUT ALE AEGIR SERVES US...
JOIN US, SON LOKI.
WITH PLEASURE.
HEIMDALL COULD NOT LET THE MOMENT PASS WITHOUT COMMENT:
HE WOULD NOT CRY TO SAVE BALDER, BUT IF GOOD ALE IS PROVIDED, HE'LL DRINK IT, AYE?
I DID NOT CRY, HEIMDALL, BECAUSE I CANNOT MANUFACTURE GRIEF, UNLIKE OTHERS AT THIS TABLE.
LOKI FEELS...WHAT HE FEELS.
FRIGGA WAS DRUNK, BY THIS POINT.
WHO, IN YOUR OPINION, "MANUFACTURED" GRIEF FOR MY SON? SURELY NONE HERE, LOKI.
OH, NO, FRIGGA?
YOU'VE CERTAINLY PLAYED THE PART OF GRIEVING, SUFFERING MOTHER WELL, BUT ISN'T IT TRUE THAT YOU CANNOT SAY, FOR CERTAIN, WHO BALDER'S FATHER IS?

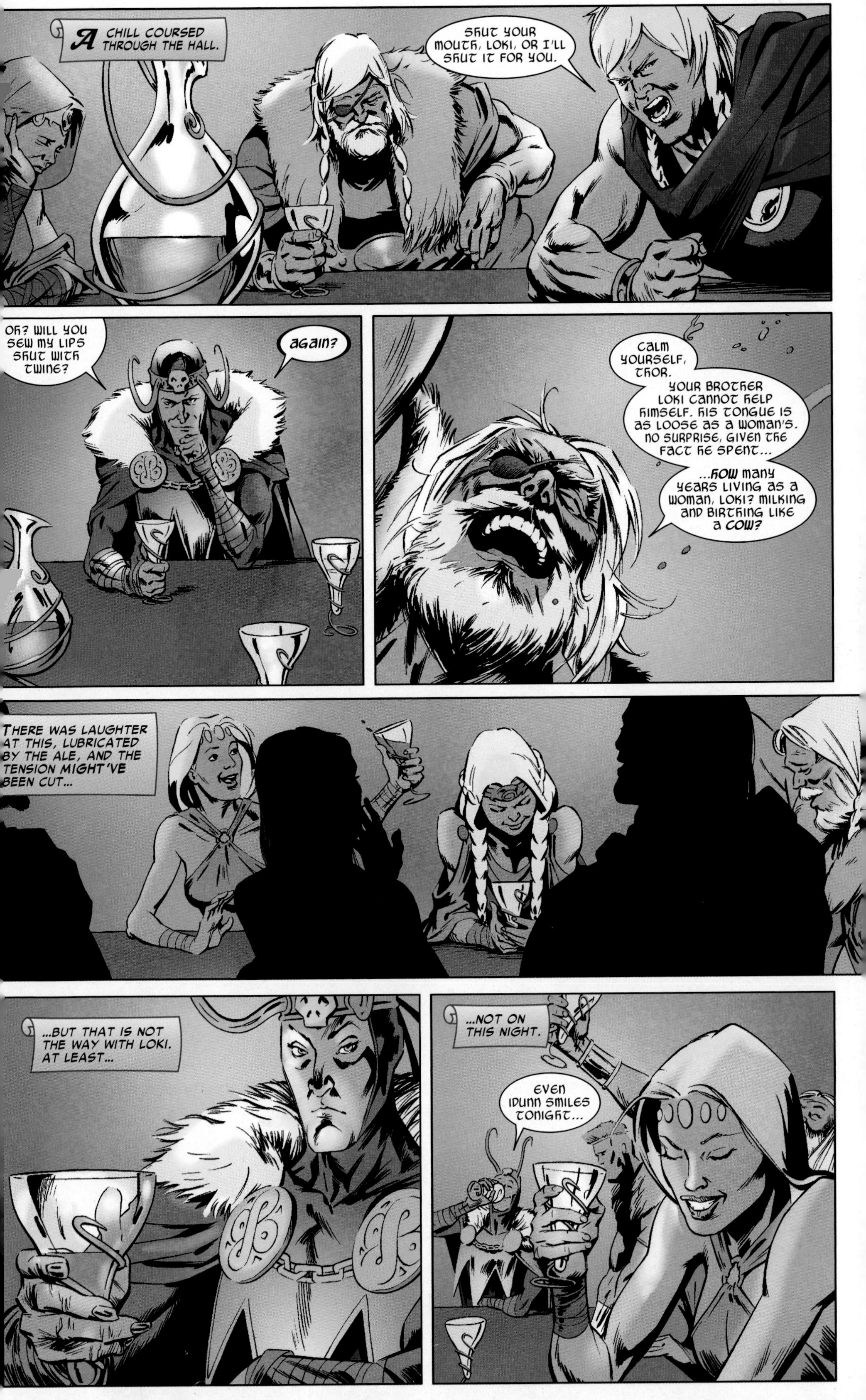
A CHILL COURSED THROUGH THE HALL.
SHUT YOUR MOUTH, LOKI, OR I'LL SHUT IT FOR YOU.
OH? WILL YOU SEW MY LIPS SHUT WITH TWINE?
AGAIN?
CALM YOURSELF, THOR.
YOUR BROTHER LOKI CANNOT HELP HIMSELF. HIS TONGUE IS AS LOOSE AS A WOMAN'S. NO SURPRISE, GIVEN THE FACT HE SPENT...
...HOW MANY YEARS LIVING AS A WOMAN, LOKI? MILKING AND BIRTHING LIKE A COW?
THERE WAS LAUGHTER AT THIS, LUBRICATED BY THE ALE, AND THE TENSION MIGHT'VE BEEN CUT...
...BUT THAT IS NOT THE WAY WITH LOKI. AT LEAST...
...NOT ON THIS NIGHT.
EVEN IDUNN SMILES TONIGHT...

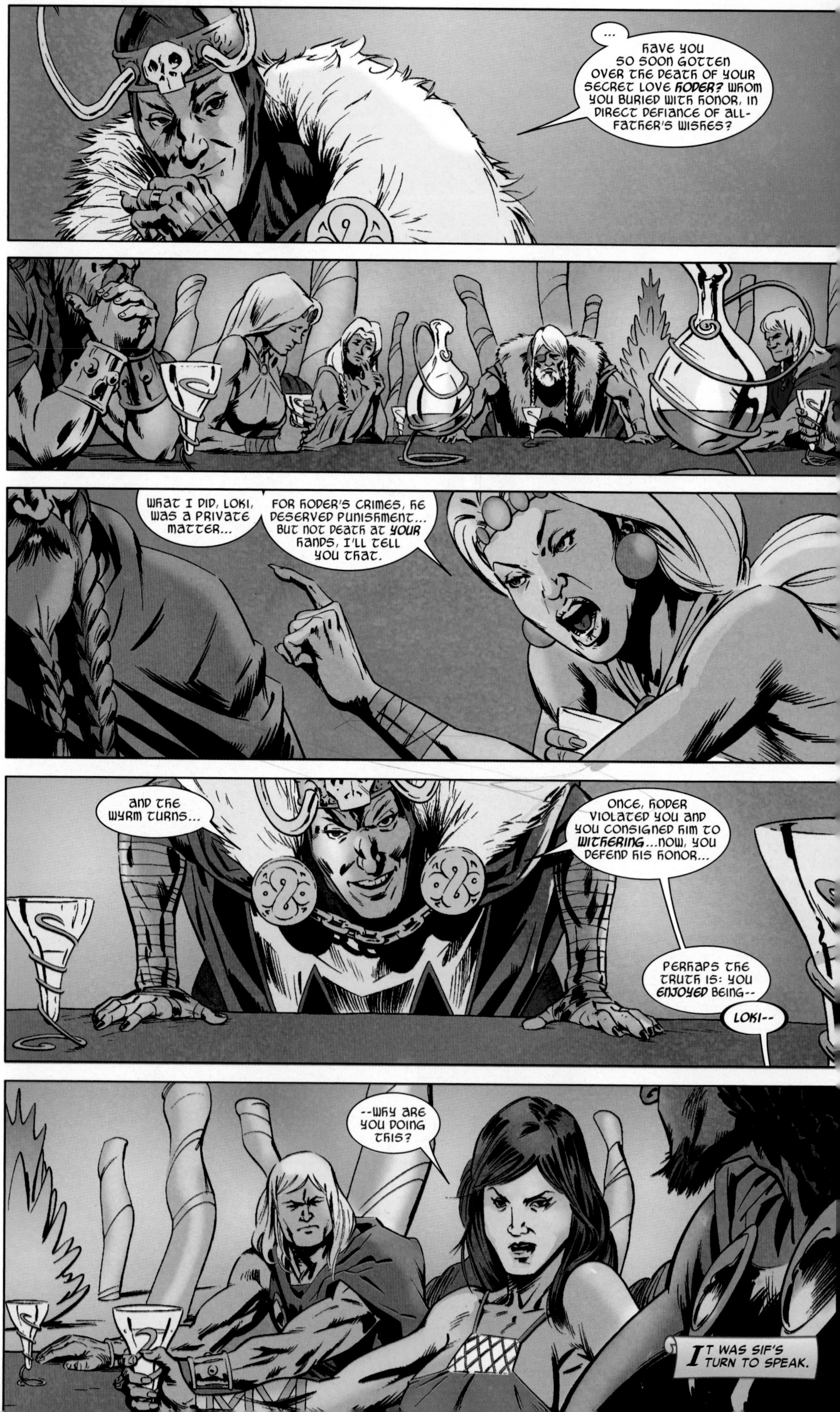
...
HAVE YOU SO SOON GOTTEN OVER THE DEATH OF YOUR SECRET LOVE HODER? WHOM YOU BURIED WITH HONOR, IN DIRECT DEFIANCE OF ALL-FATHER'S WISHES?
WHAT I DID, LOKI, WAS A PRIVATE MATTER...
FOR HODER'S CRIMES, HE DESERVED PUNISHMENT... BUT NOT DEATH AT YOUR HANDS, I'LL TELL YOU THAT.
AND THE WYRM TURNS...
ONCE, HODER VIOLATED YOU AND YOU CONSIGNED HIM TO WITHERING...NOW, YOU DEFEND HIS HONOR...
PERHAPS THE TRUTH IS: YOU ENJOYED BEING--
LOKI--
--WHY ARE YOU DOING THIS?
IT WAS SIF'S TURN TO SPEAK.

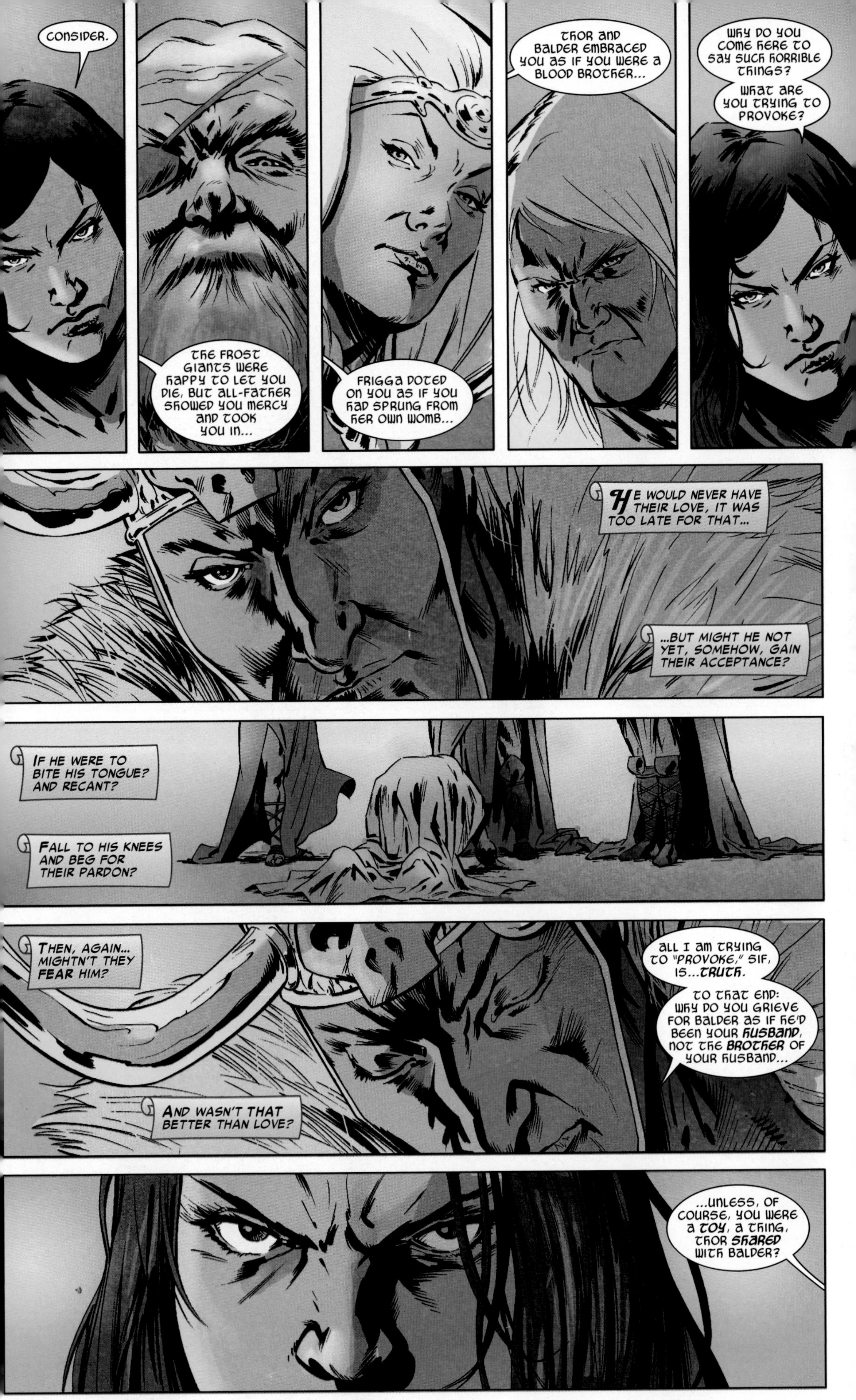
CONSIDER.
THE FROST GIANTS WERE HAPPY TO LET YOU DIE, BUT ALL-FATHER SHOWED YOU MERCY AND TOOK YOU IN...
FRIGGA DOTED ON YOU AS IF YOU HAD SPRUNG FROM HER OWN WOMB...
THOR AND BALDER EMBRACED YOU AS IF YOU WERE A BLOOD BROTHER...
WHY DO YOU COME HERE TO SAY SUCH HORRIBLE THINGS?
WHAT ARE YOU TRYING TO PROVOKE?
HE WOULD NEVER HAVE THEIR LOVE, IT WAS TOO LATE FOR THAT...
...BUT MIGHT HE NOT YET, SOMEHOW, GAIN THEIR ACCEPTANCE?
IF HE WERE TO BITE HIS TONGUE? AND RECANT?
FALL TO HIS KNEES AND BEG FOR THEIR PARDON?
THEN, AGAIN... MIGHTN'T THEY FEAR HIM?
AND WASN'T THAT BETTER THAN LOVE?
ALL I AM TRYING TO "PROVOKE," SIF, IS...TRUTH.
TO THAT END: WHY DO YOU GRIEVE FOR BALDER AS IF HE'D BEEN YOUR HUSBAND, NOT THE BROTHER OF YOUR HUSBAND...
...UNLESS, OF COURSE, YOU WERE A TOY, A THING, THOR SHARED WITH BALDER?

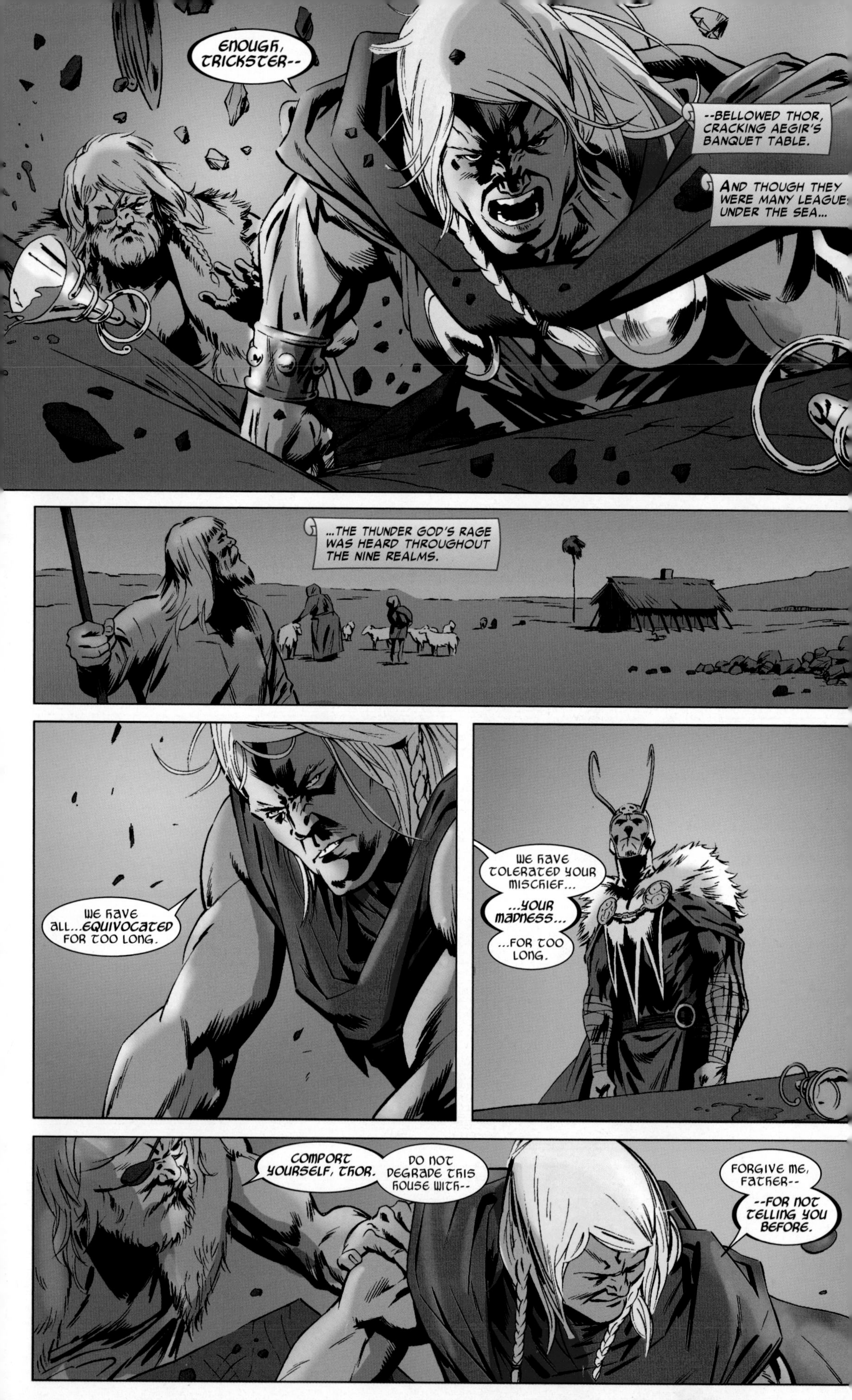
ENOUGH, TRICKSTER--
--BELLOWED THOR, CRACKING AEGIR'S BANQUET TABLE.
AND THOUGH THEY WERE MANY LEAGUES UNDER THE SEA...
...THE THUNDER GOD'S RAGE WAS HEARD THROUGHOUT THE NINE REALMS.
WE HAVE ALL...EQUIVOCATED FOR TOO LONG.
WE HAVE TOLERATED YOUR MISCHIEF...
...YOUR MADNESS...
...FOR TOO LONG.
COMPORT YOURSELF, THOR.
DO NOT DEGRADE THIS HOUSE WITH--
FORGIVE ME, FATHER--
--FOR NOT TELLING YOU BEFORE.

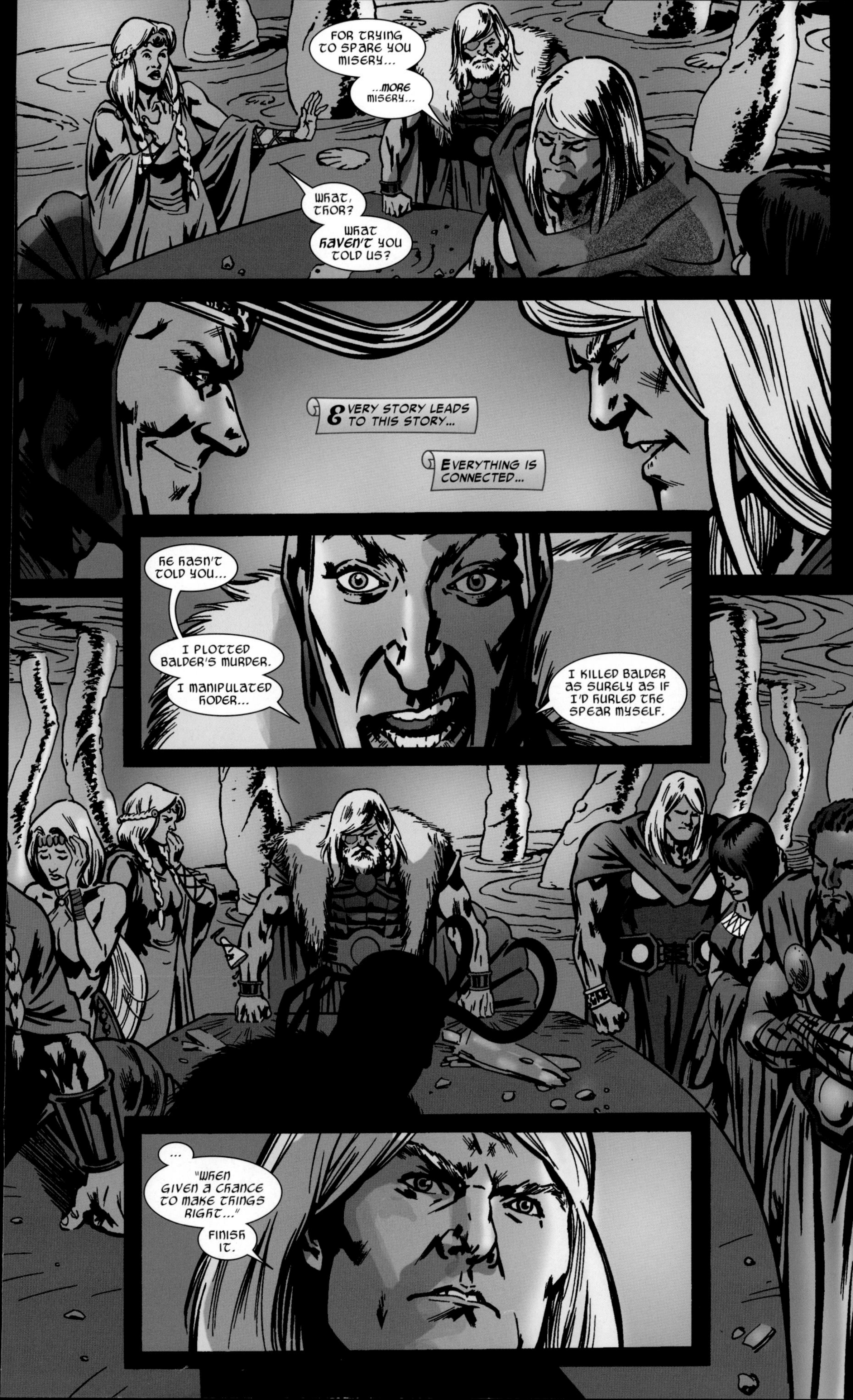
FOR TRYING TO SPARE YOU MISERY...
...MORE MISERY...
WHAT, THOR?
WHAT HAVEN'T YOU TOLD US?
EVERY STORY LEADS TO THIS STORY...
EVERYTHING IS CONNECTED...
HE HASN'T TOLD YOU...
I PLOTTED BALDER'S MURDER.
I MANIPULATED HODER...
I KILLED BALDER AS SURELY AS IF I'D HURLED THE SPEAR MYSELF.
...
"WHEN GIVEN A CHANCE TO MAKE THINGS RIGHT..."
FINISH IT.

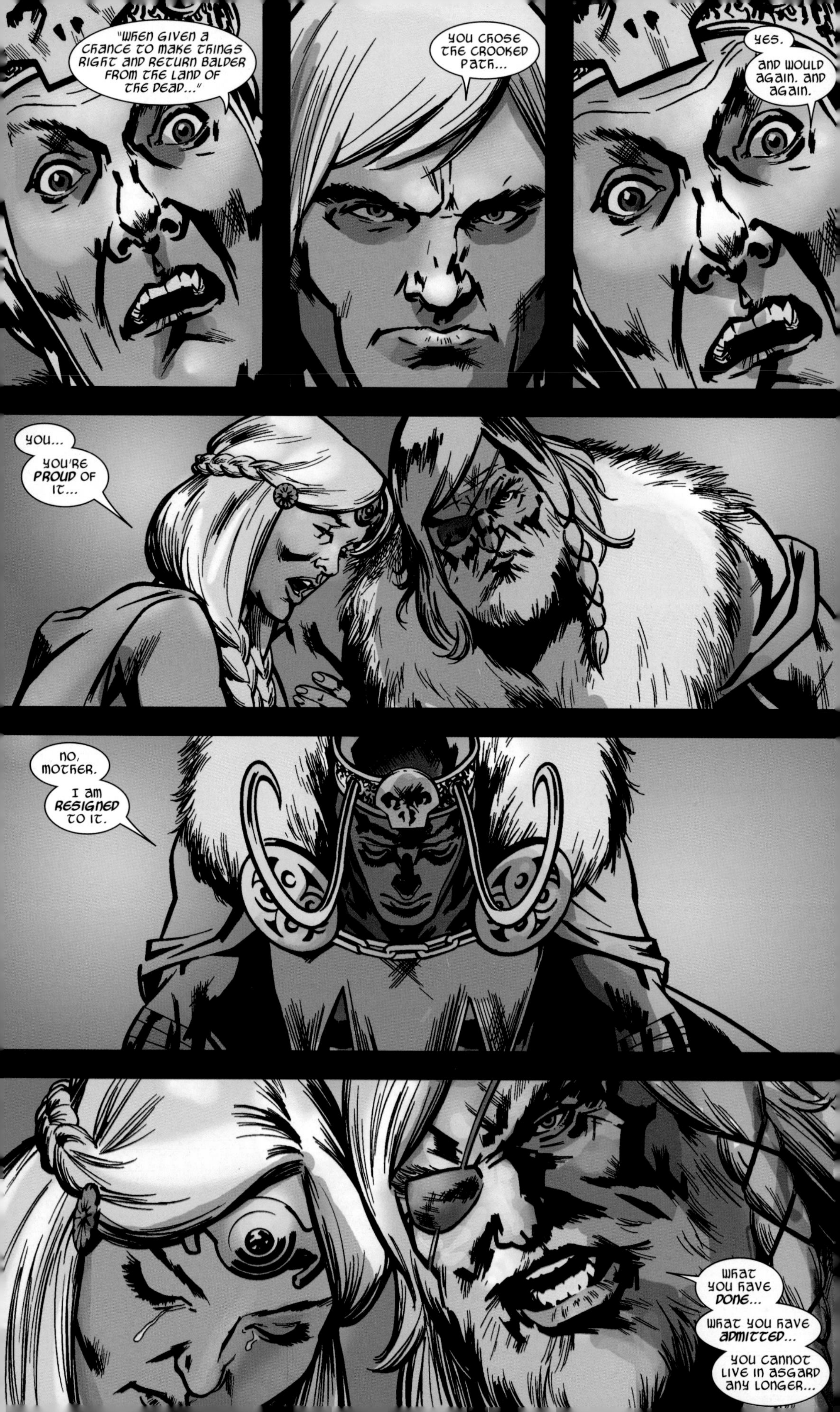
"WHEN GIVEN A CHANCE TO MAKE THINGS RIGHT AND RETURN BALDER FROM THE LAND OF THE DEAD..."
YOU CHOSE THE CROOKED PATH...
YES.
AND WOULD AGAIN. AND AGAIN.
YOU... YOU'RE **PROUD** OF IT...
NO, MOTHER.
I AM **RESIGNED** TO IT.
WHAT YOU HAVE **DONE**...
WHAT YOU HAVE **ADMITTED**...
YOU CANNOT LIVE IN ASGARD ANY LONGER...

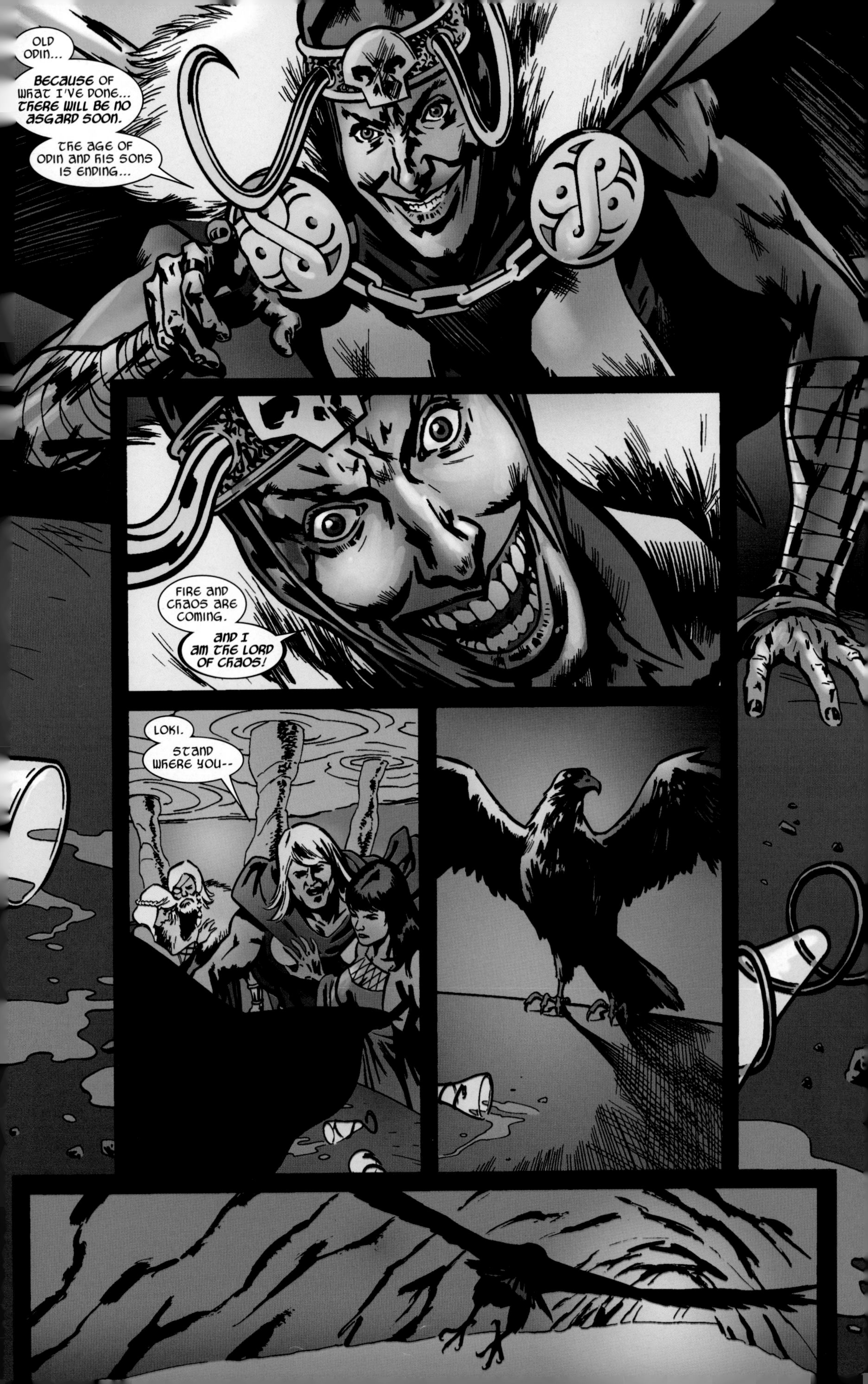
OLD ODIN...
BECAUSE OF WHAT I'VE DONE... THERE WILL BE NO ASGARD SOON.
THE AGE OF ODIN AND HIS SONS IS ENDING...
FIRE AND CHAOS ARE COMING.
AND I AM THE LORD OF CHAOS!
LOKI.
STAND WHERE YOU--

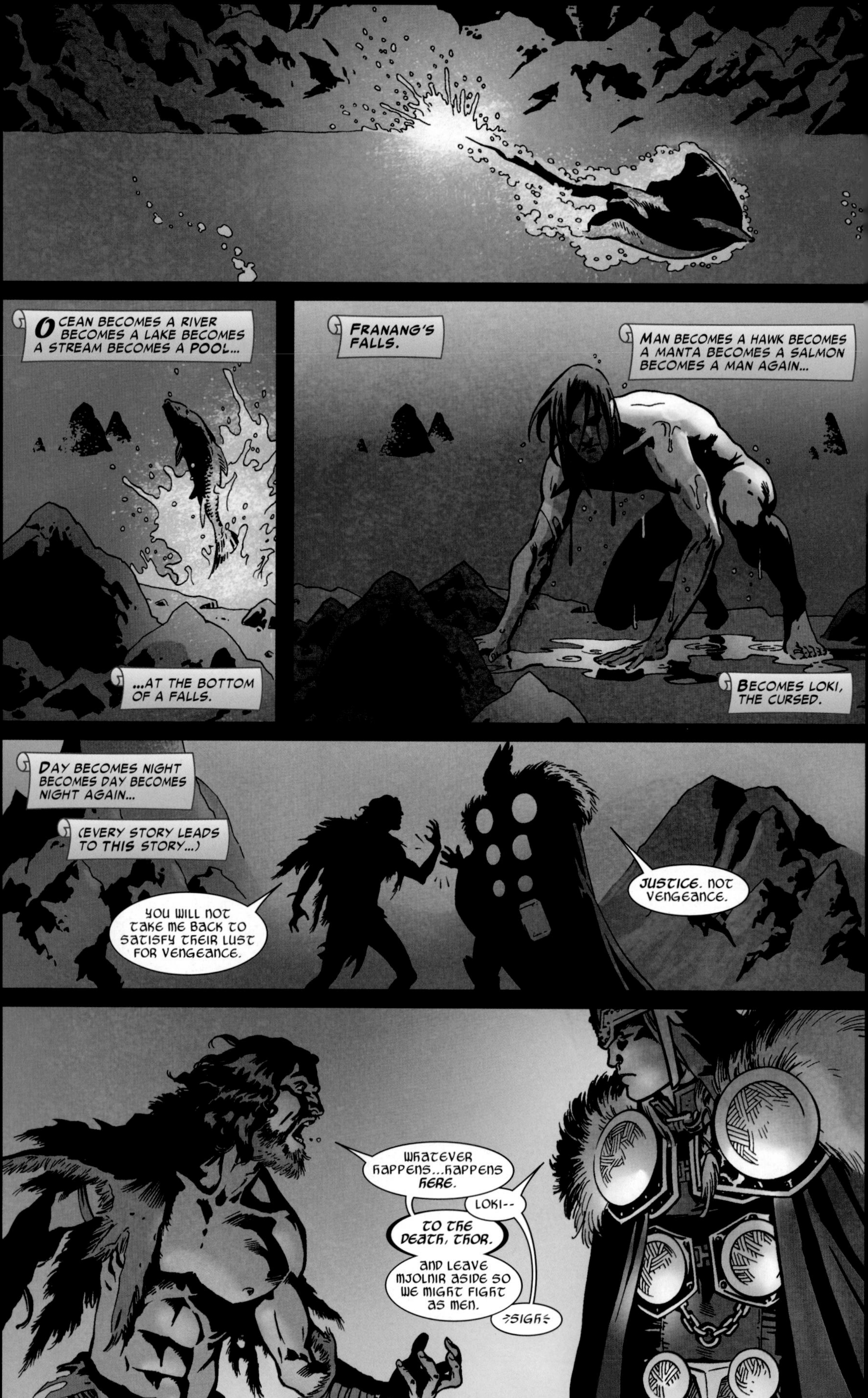
OCEAN BECOMES A RIVER BECOMES A LAKE BECOMES A STREAM BECOMES A POOL...
...AT THE BOTTOM OF A FALLS.
FRANANG'S FALLS.
MAN BECOMES A HAWK BECOMES A MANTA BECOMES A SALMON BECOMES A MAN AGAIN...
BECOMES LOKI, THE CURSED.
DAY BECOMES NIGHT BECOMES DAY BECOMES NIGHT AGAIN...
(EVERY STORY LEADS TO THIS STORY...)
YOU WILL NOT TAKE ME BACK TO SATISFY THEIR LUST FOR VENGEANCE.
JUSTICE. NOT VENGEANCE.
WHATEVER HAPPENS...HAPPENS HERE.
LOKI--
TO THE DEATH, THOR.
AND LEAVE MJOLNIR ASIDE SO WE MIGHT FIGHT AS MEN.
SIGH

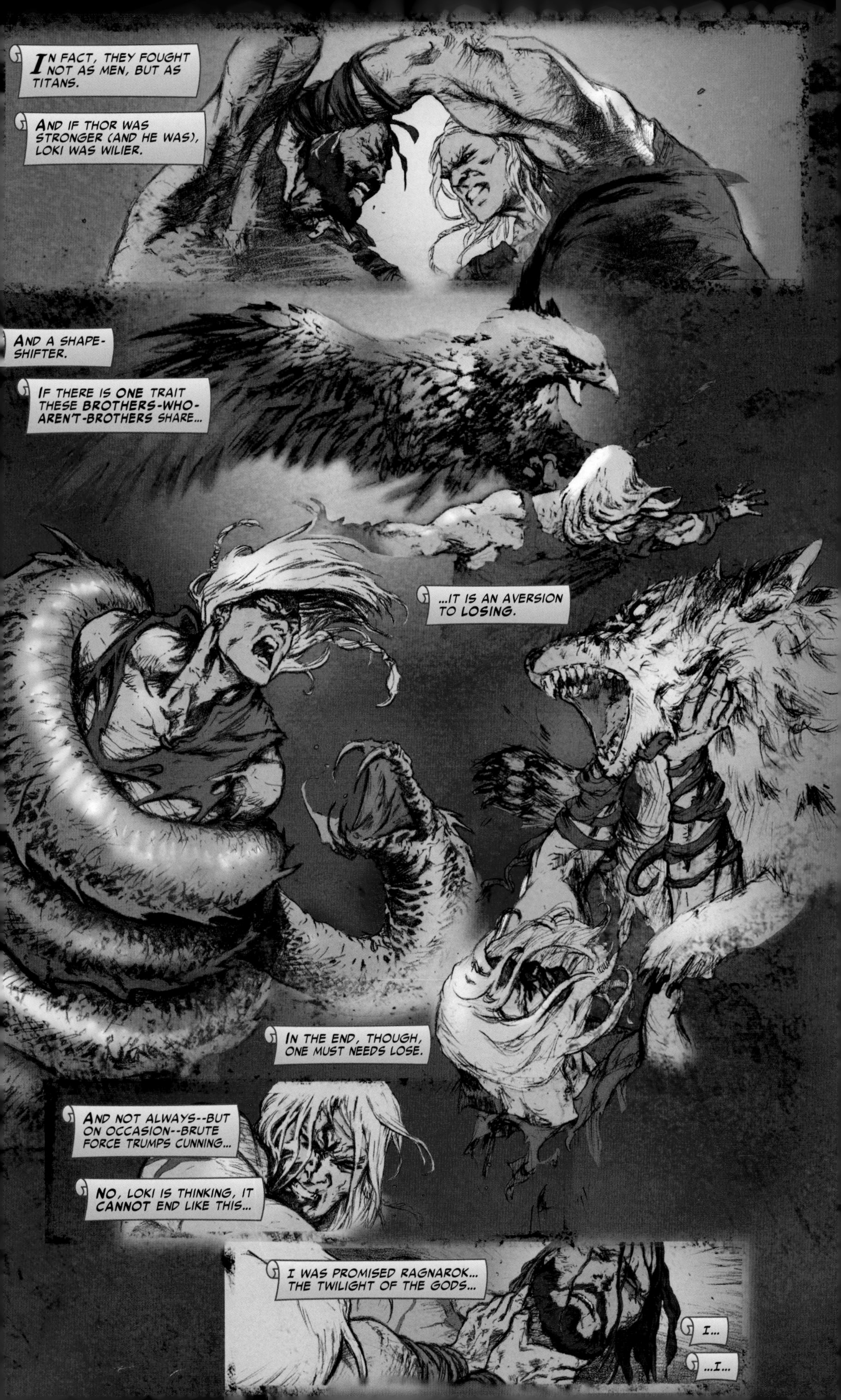
IN FACT, THEY FOUGHT NOT AS MEN, BUT AS TITANS.
AND IF THOR WAS STRONGER (AND HE WAS), LOKI WAS WILIER.
AND A SHAPE-SHIFTER.
IF THERE IS ONE TRAIT THESE BROTHERS-WHO-AREN'T-BROTHERS SHARE...
...IT IS AN AVERSION TO LOSING.
IN THE END, THOUGH, ONE MUST NEEDS LOSE.
AND NOT ALWAYS--BUT ON OCCASION--BRUTE FORCE TRUMPS CUNNING...
NO, LOKI IS THINKING, IT CANNOT END LIKE THIS...
I WAS PROMISED RAGNAROK... THE TWILIGHT OF THE GODS...
I...
...I...

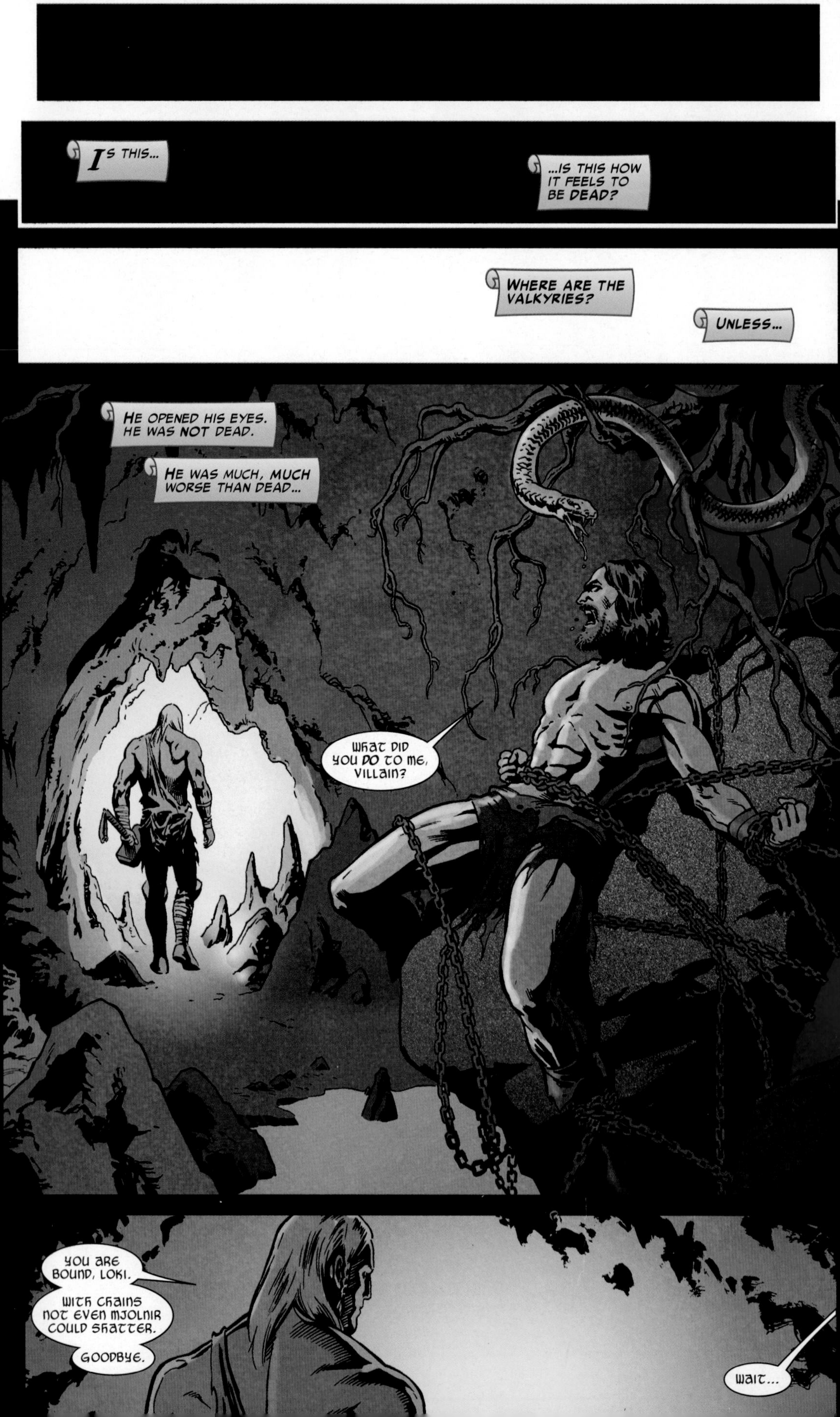

I'S THIS...
...IS THIS HOW IT FEELS TO BE DEAD?
WHERE ARE THE VALKYRIES?
UNLESS...
HE OPENED HIS EYES. HE WAS NOT DEAD.
HE WAS MUCH, MUCH WORSE THAN DEAD...
WHAT DID YOU DO TO ME, VILLAIN?
YOU ARE BOUND, LOKI.
WITH CHAINS NOT EVEN MJOLNIR COULD SHATTER.
GOODBYE.
WAIT...

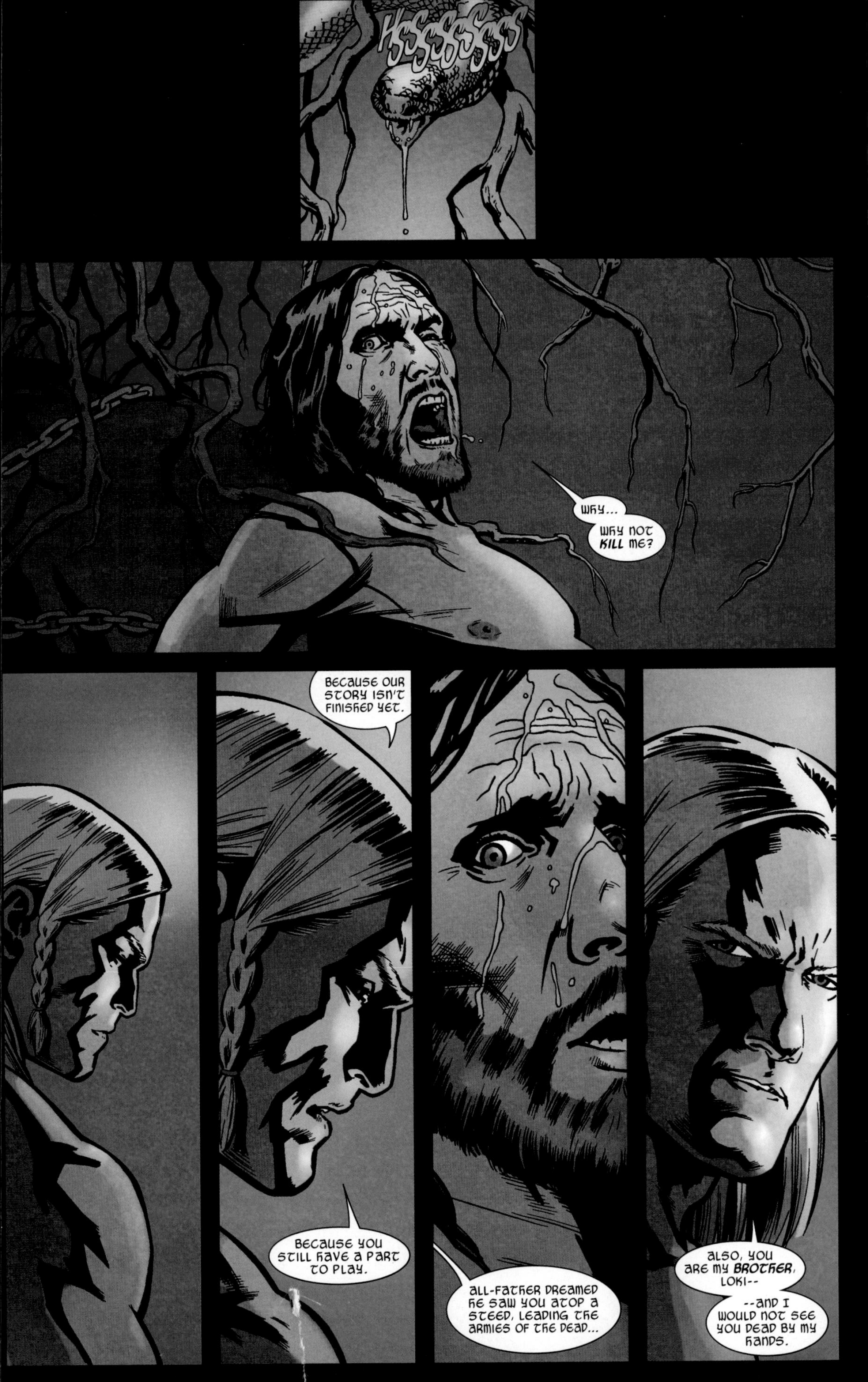
HSSSSSSSS
WHY... WHY NOT KILL ME?
BECAUSE OUR STORY ISN'T FINISHED YET.
BECAUSE YOU STILL HAVE A PART TO PLAY.
ALL-FATHER DREAMED HE SAW YOU ATOP A STEED, LEADING THE ARMIES OF THE DEAD...
ALSO, YOU ARE MY BROTHER, LOKI--
--AND I WOULD NOT SEE YOU DEAD BY MY HANDS.

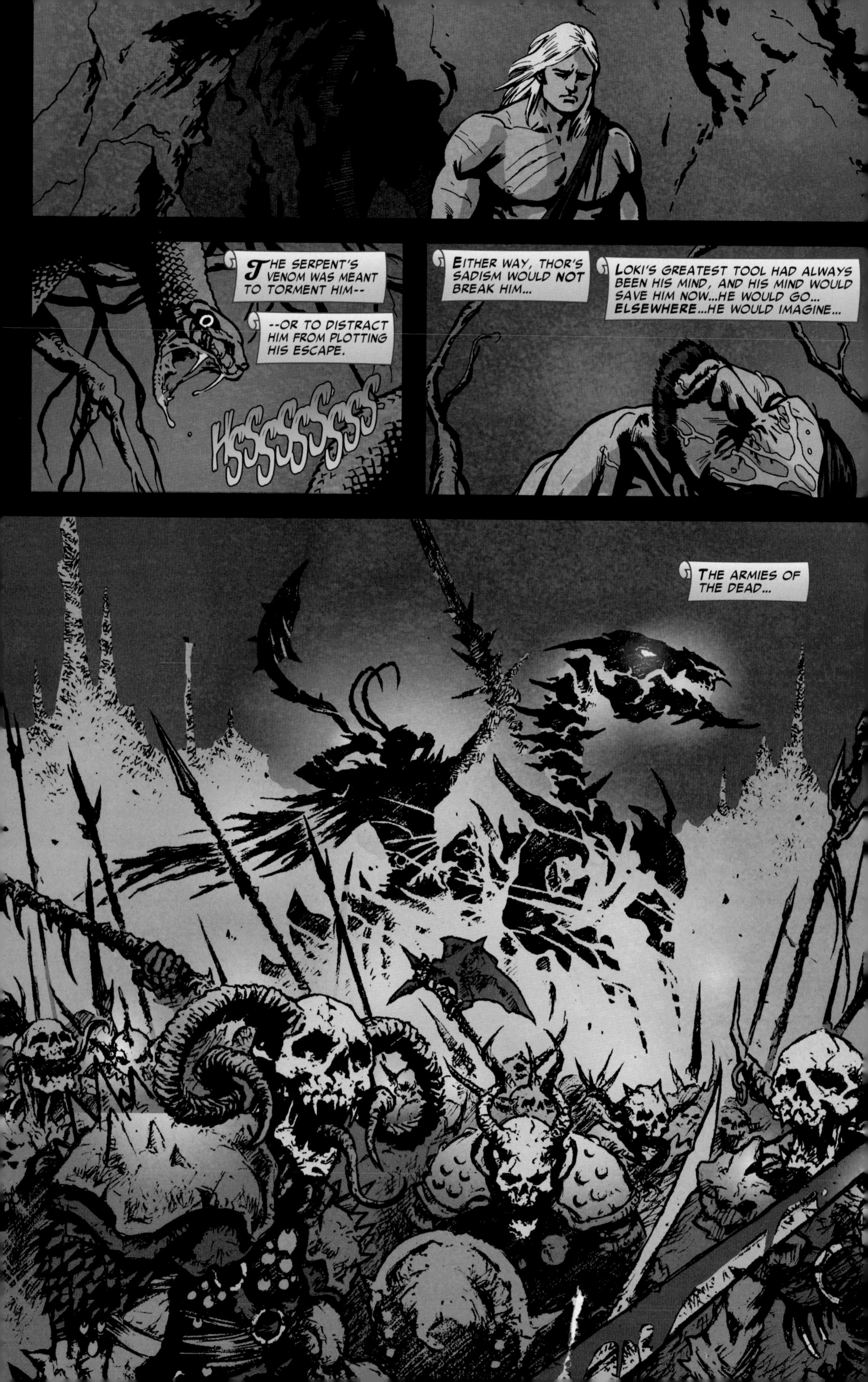
THE SERPENT'S VENOM WAS MEANT TO TORMENT HIM--
--OR TO DISTRACT HIM FROM PLOTTING HIS ESCAPE.
HSSSSSSSSSS
EITHER WAY, THOR'S SADISM WOULD NOT BREAK HIM...
LOKI'S GREATEST TOOL HAD ALWAYS BEEN HIS MIND, AND HIS MIND WOULD SAVE HIM NOW...HE WOULD GO... ELSEWHERE...HE WOULD IMAGINE...
THE ARMIES OF THE DEAD...

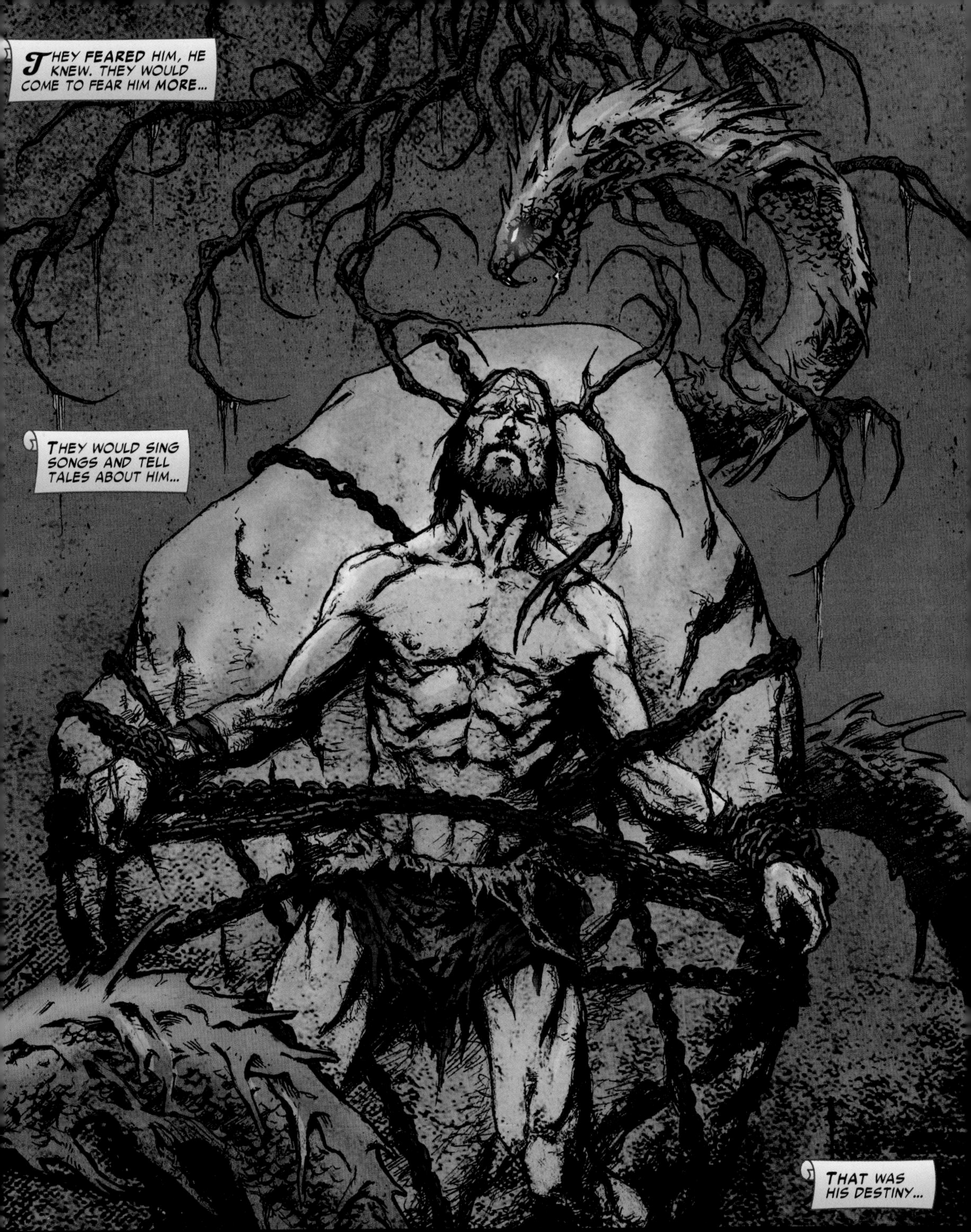
THEY FEARED HIM, HE KNEW. THEY WOULD COME TO FEAR HIM MORE...
THEY WOULD SING SONGS AND TELL TALES ABOUT HIM...
THAT WAS HIS DESTINY...

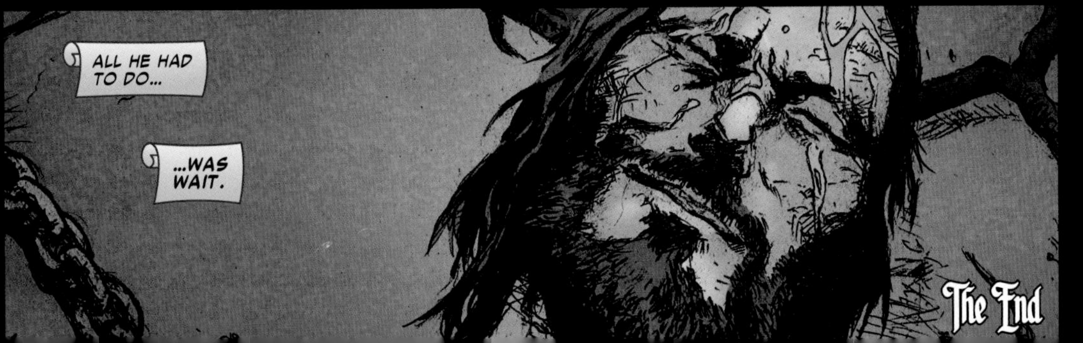
ALL HE HAD TO DO...
...WAS WAIT.
The End

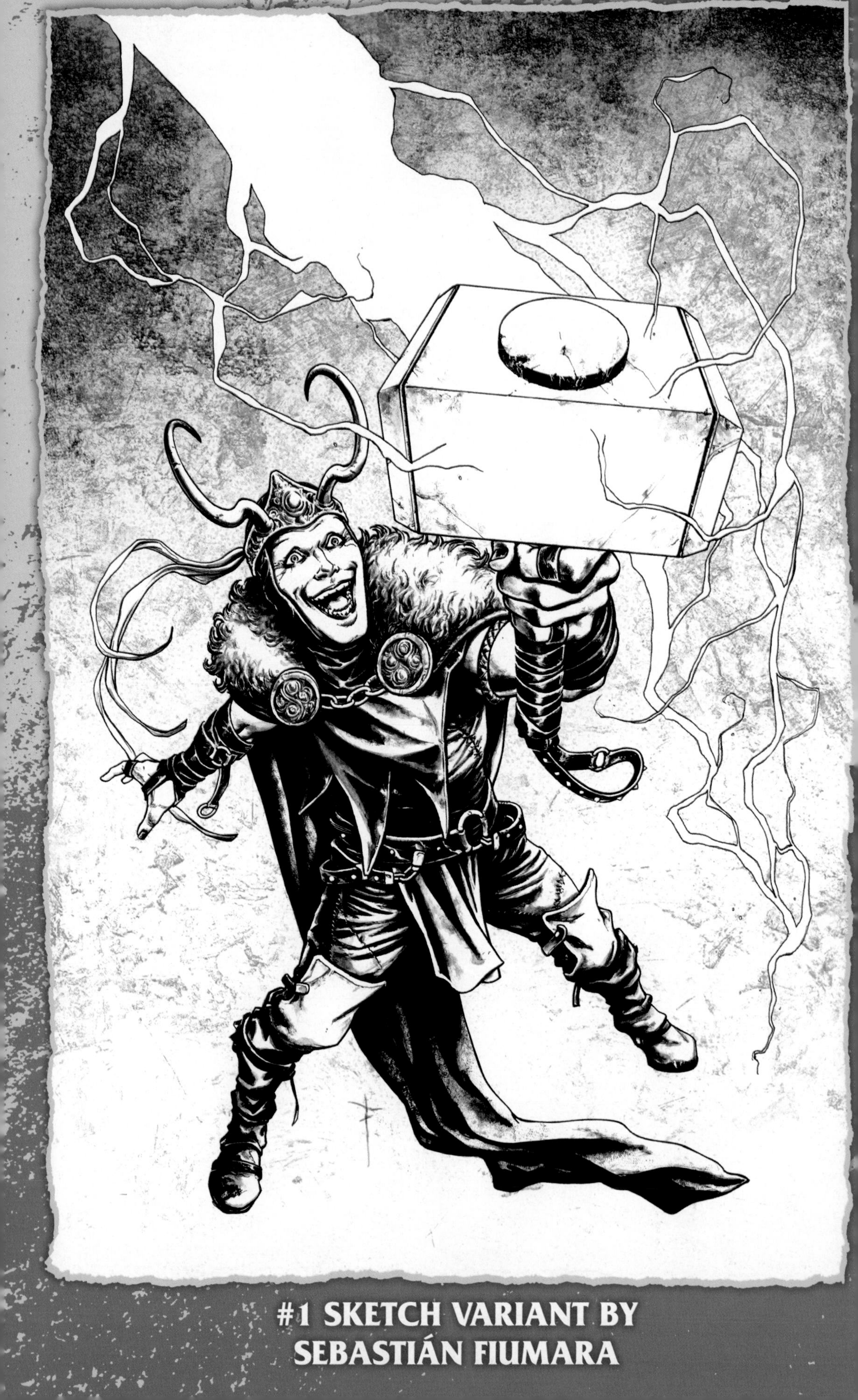

#1 SKETCH VARIANT BY
SEBASTIÁN FIUMARA

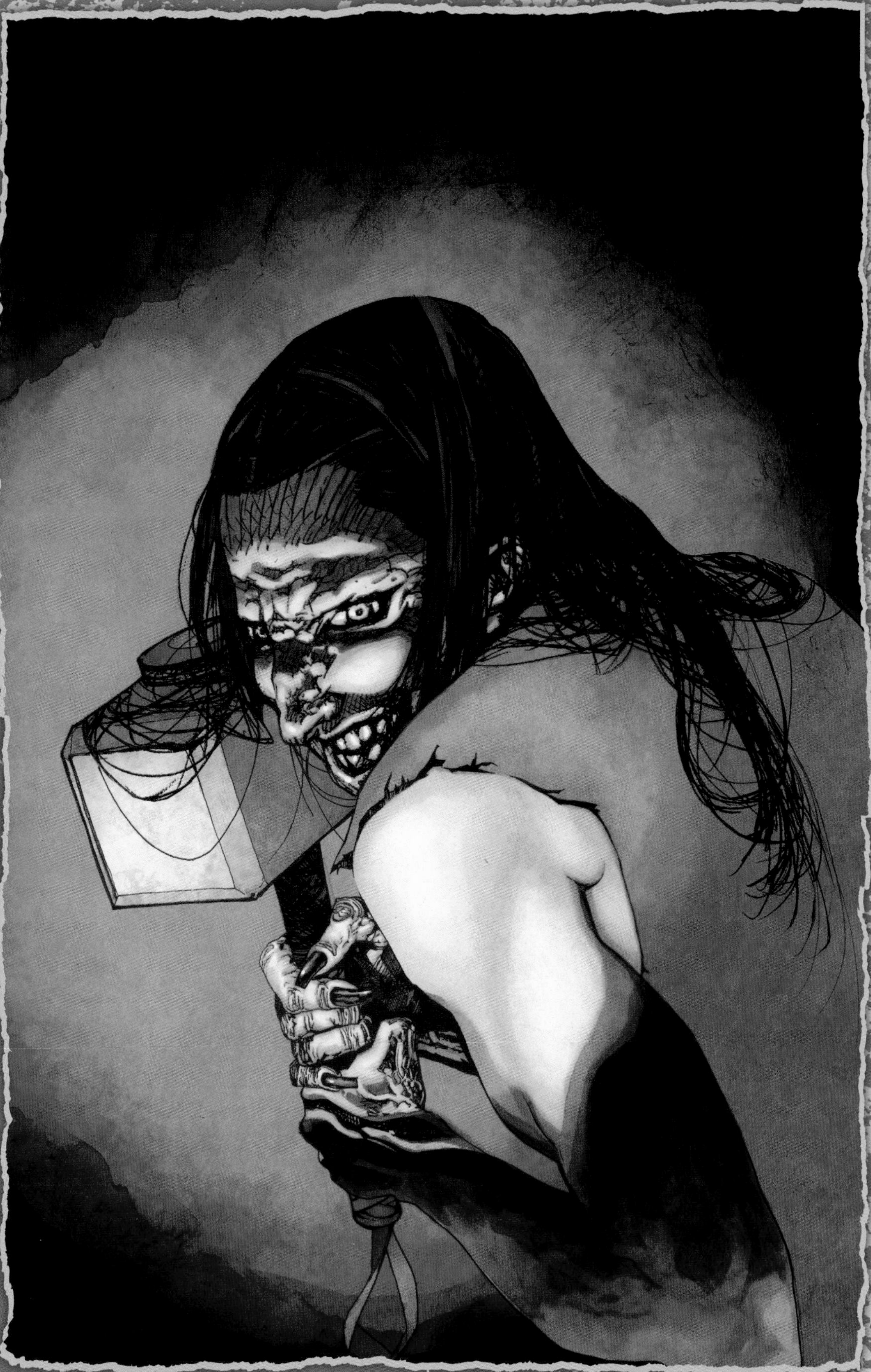

#1 VARIANT BY
TRAVEL FOREMAN & NATHAN FAIRBAIRN

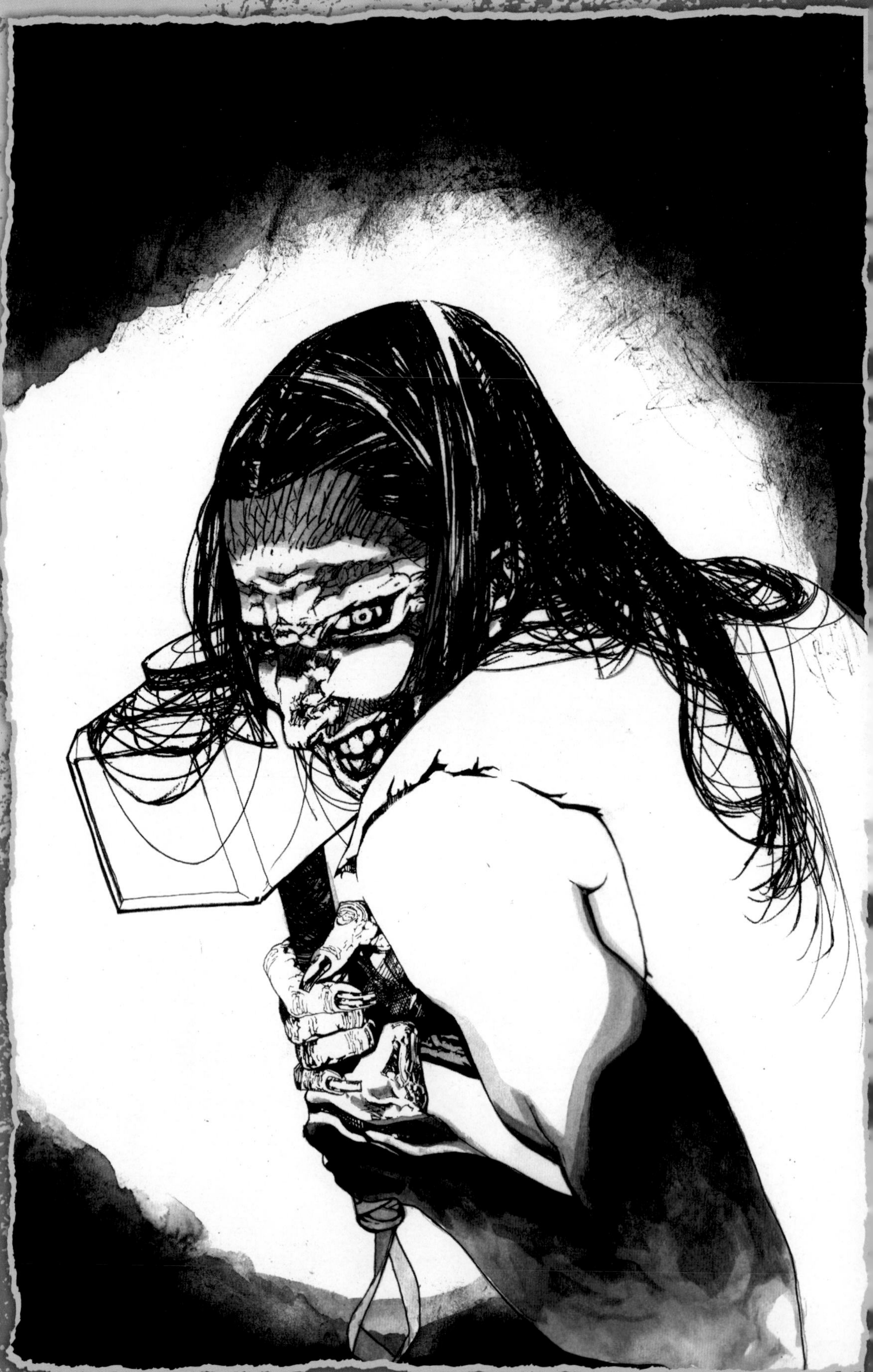

#1 VARIANT PENCILS BY
TRAVEL FOREMAN

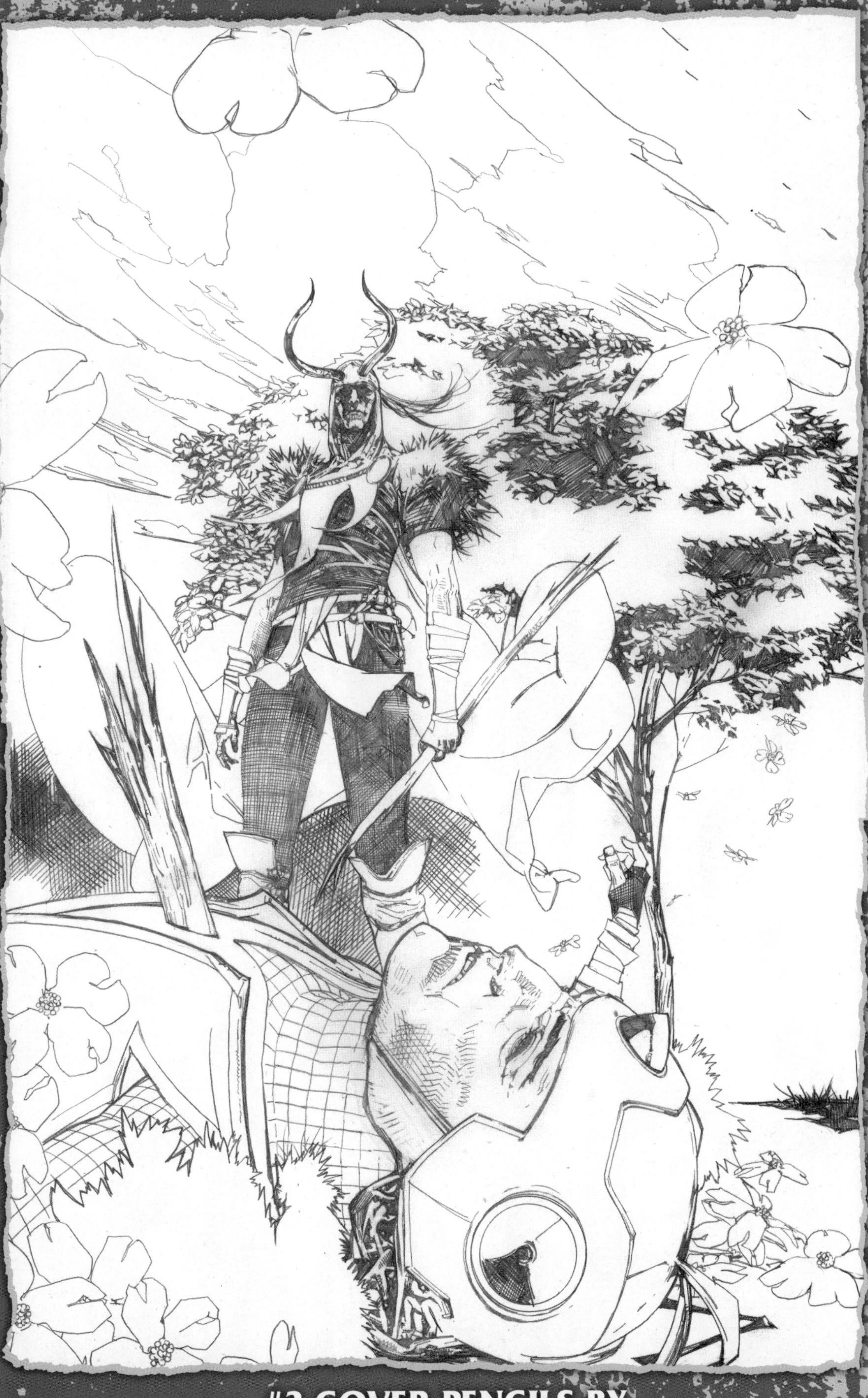

#2 COVER PENCILS BY
TRAVEL FOREMAN

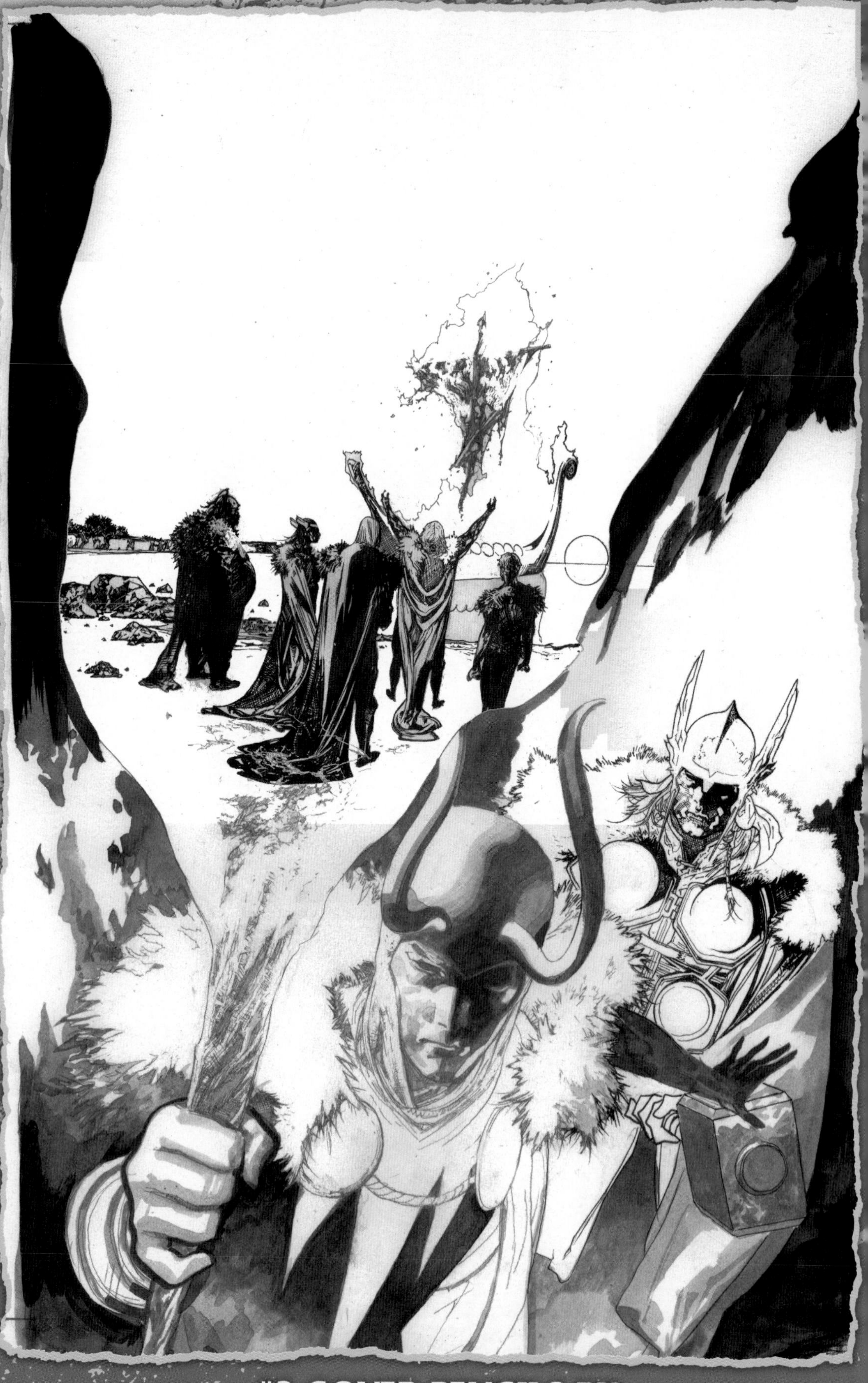

#3 COVER PENCILS BY
TRAVEL FOREMAN

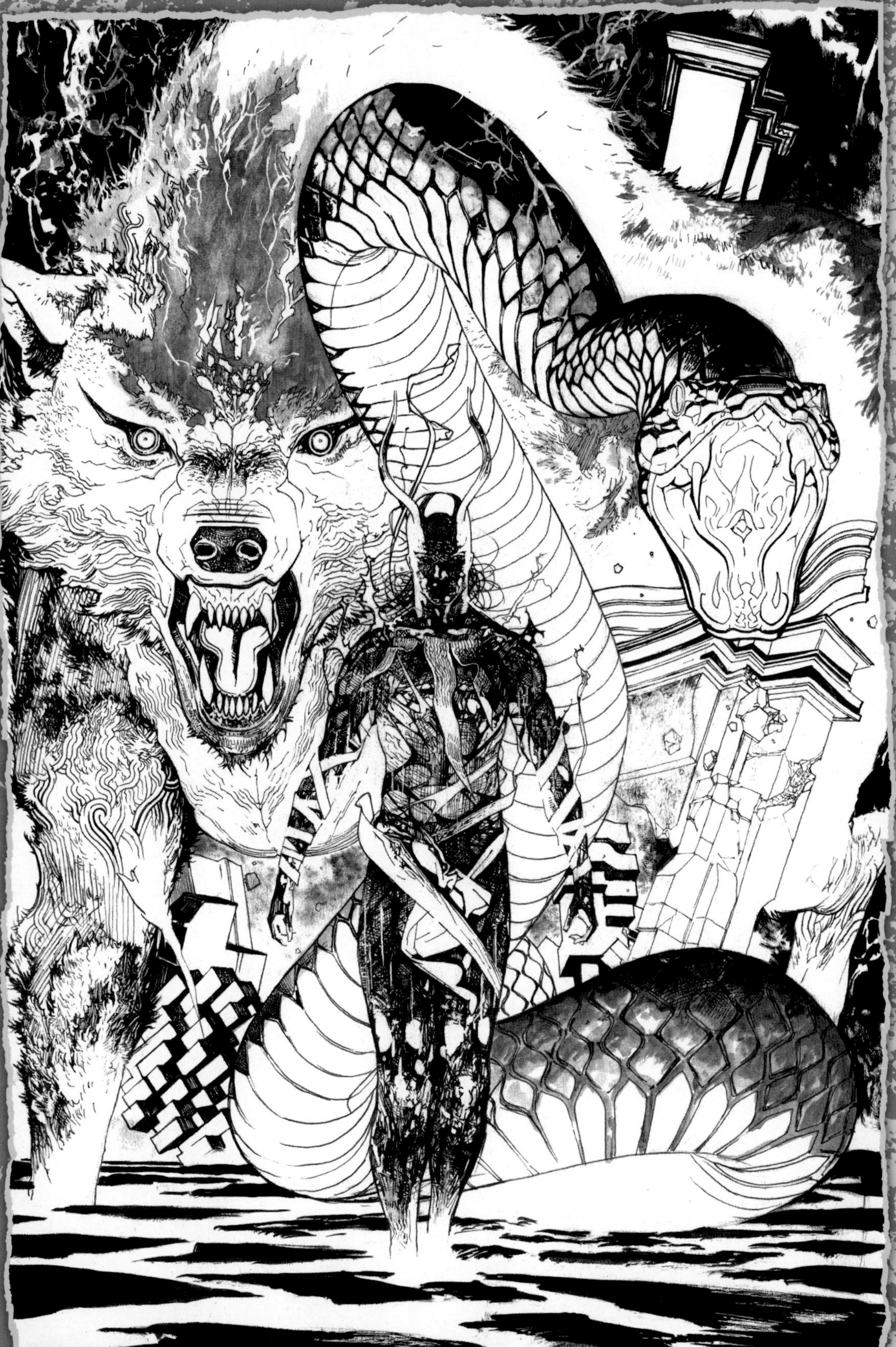

#4 COVER PENCILS BY
TRAVEL FOREMAN

SEBASTIÁN FIUMARA SKETCHBOOK

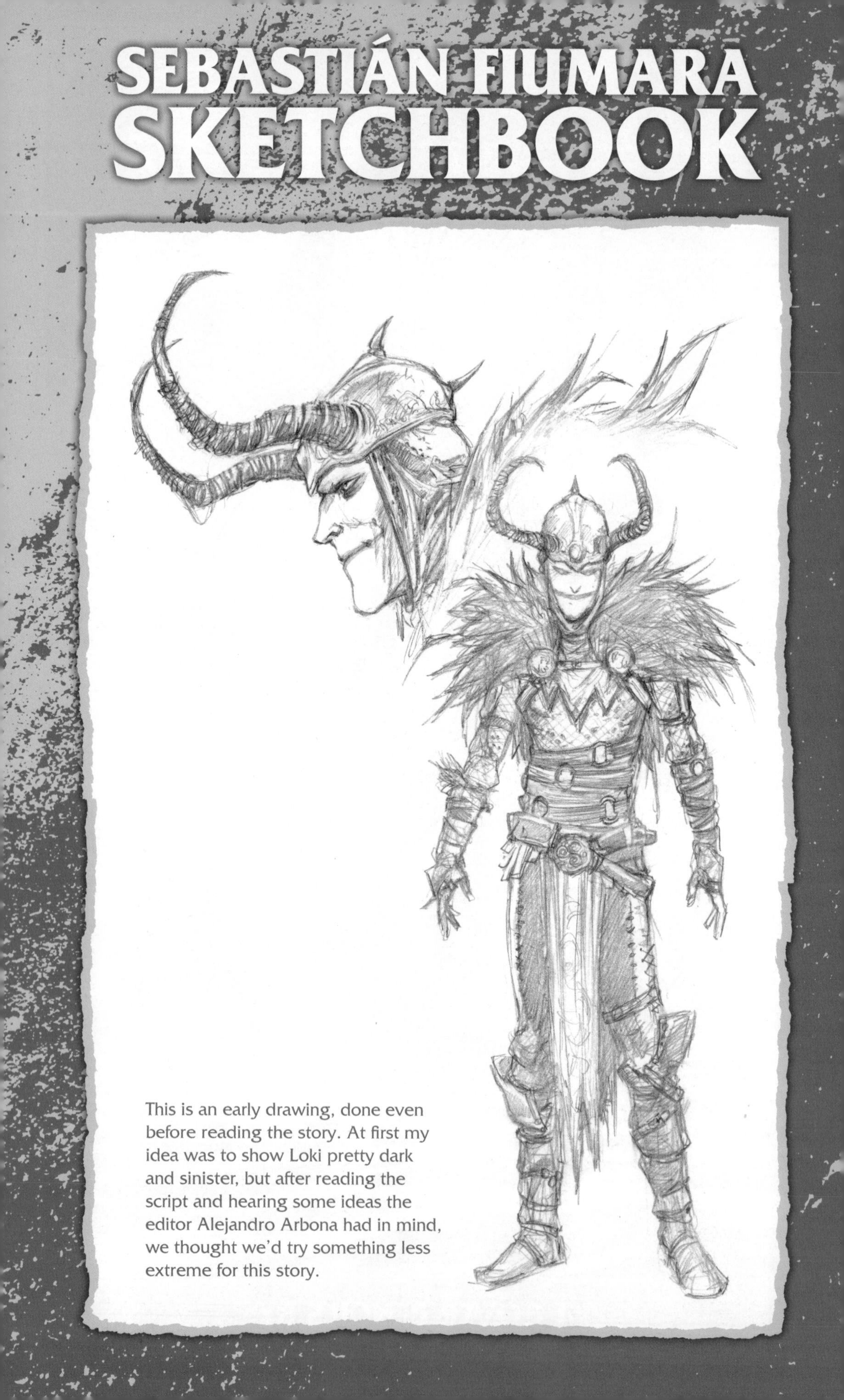

This is an early drawing, done even before reading the story. At first my idea was to show Loki pretty dark and sinister, but after reading the script and hearing some ideas the editor Alejandro Arbona had in mind, we thought we'd try something less extreme for this story.

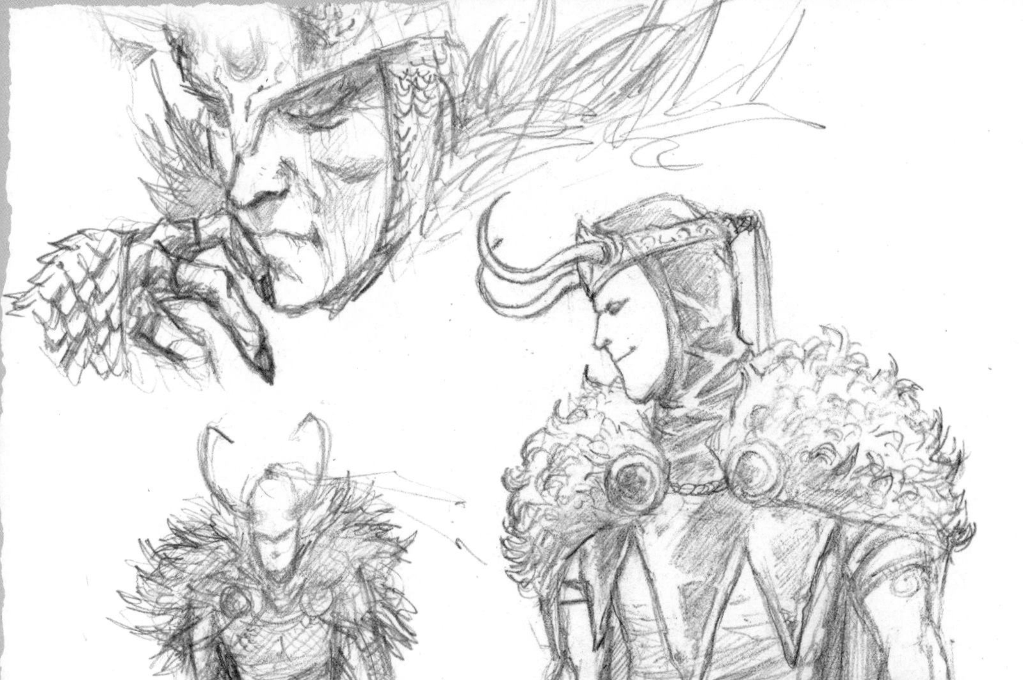

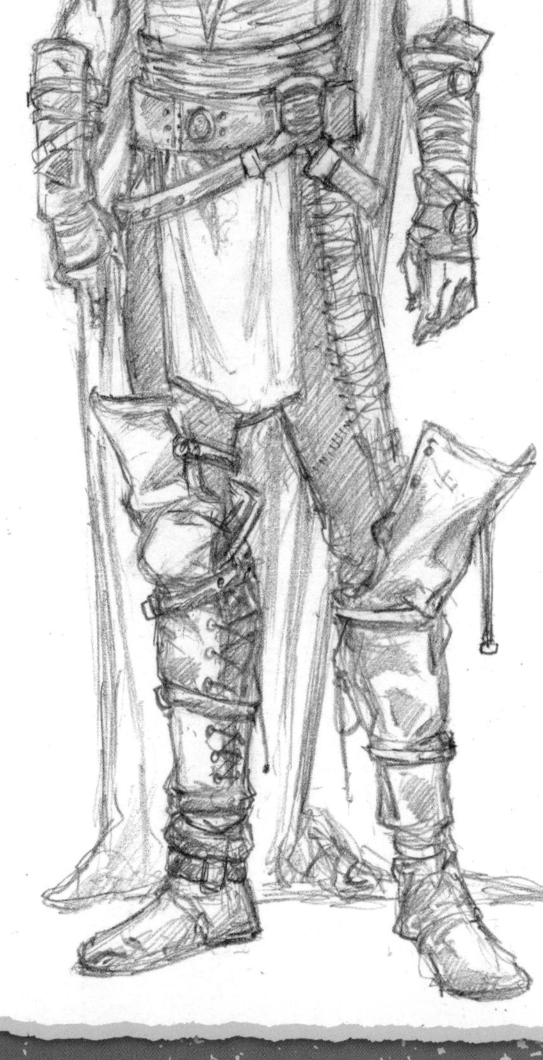

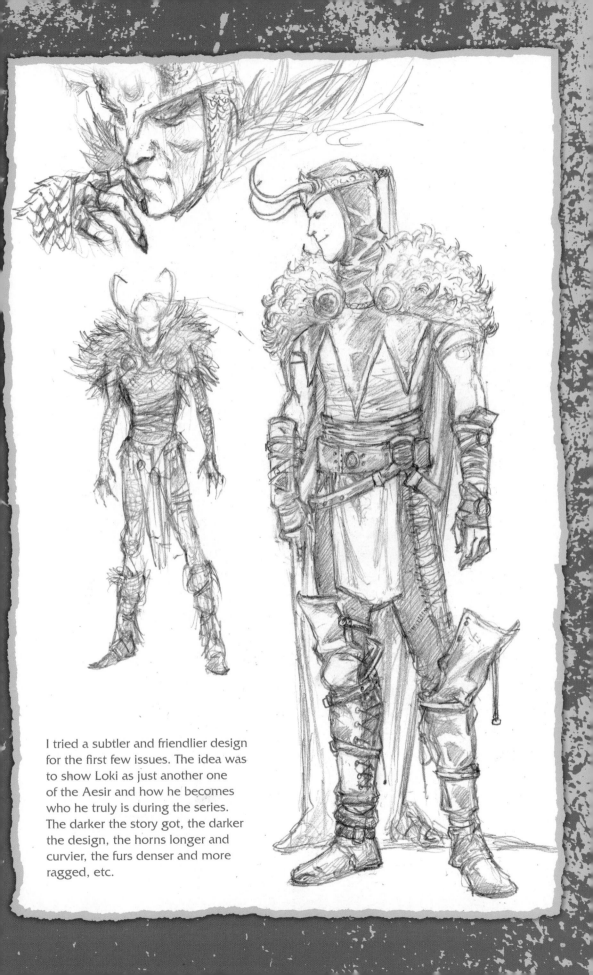

I tried a subtler and friendlier design for the first few issues. The idea was to show Loki as just another one of the Aesir and how he becomes who he truly is during the series. The darker the story got, the darker the design, the horns longer and curvier, the furs denser and more ragged, etc.

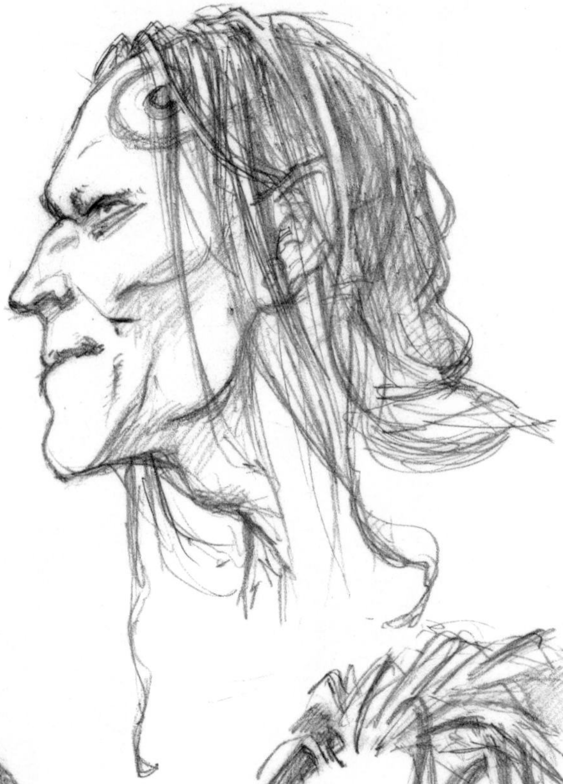

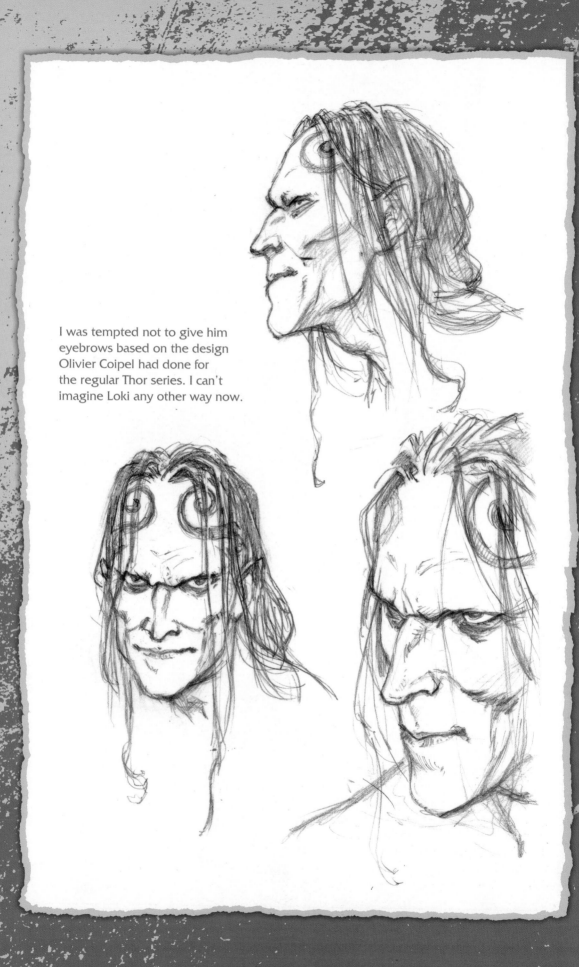

I was tempted not to give him eyebrows based on the design Olivier Coipel had done for the regular Thor series. I can't imagine Loki any other way now.

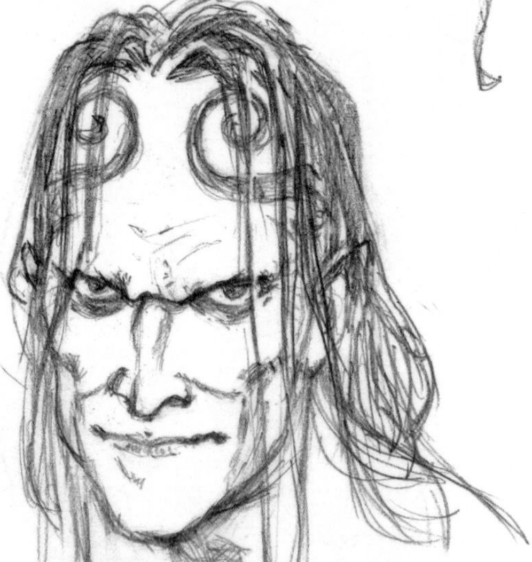

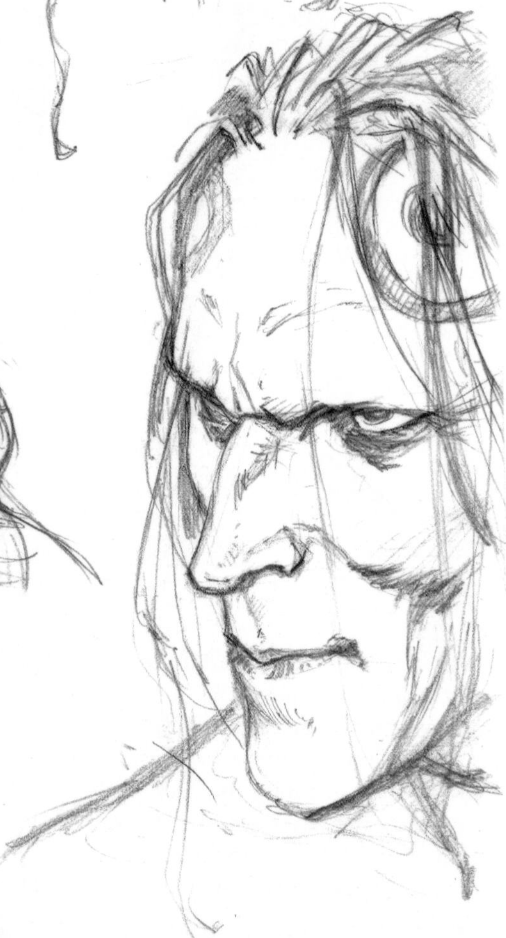

A lot of the essence of Loki depends on what's going through his mind. I thought the best way to translate that to images was to give a lot of importance to his gaze. It didn't matter if he was in costume or not, with or without horns, his gaze should always be intense and tell us what's happening.

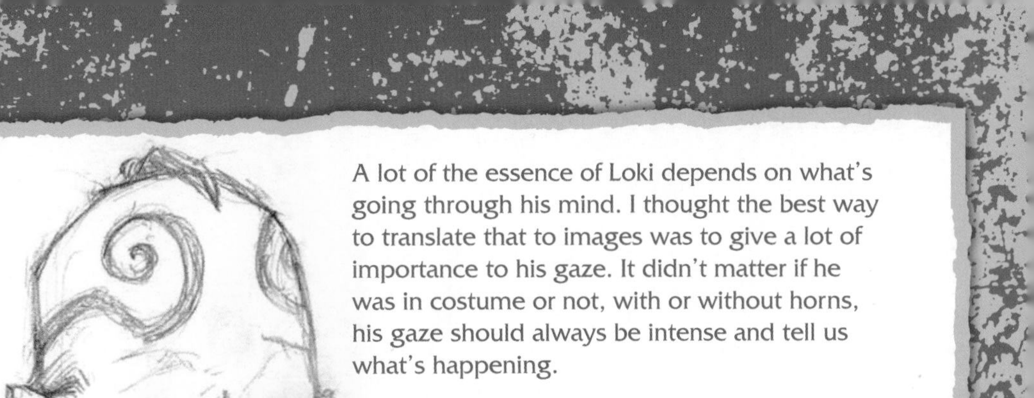

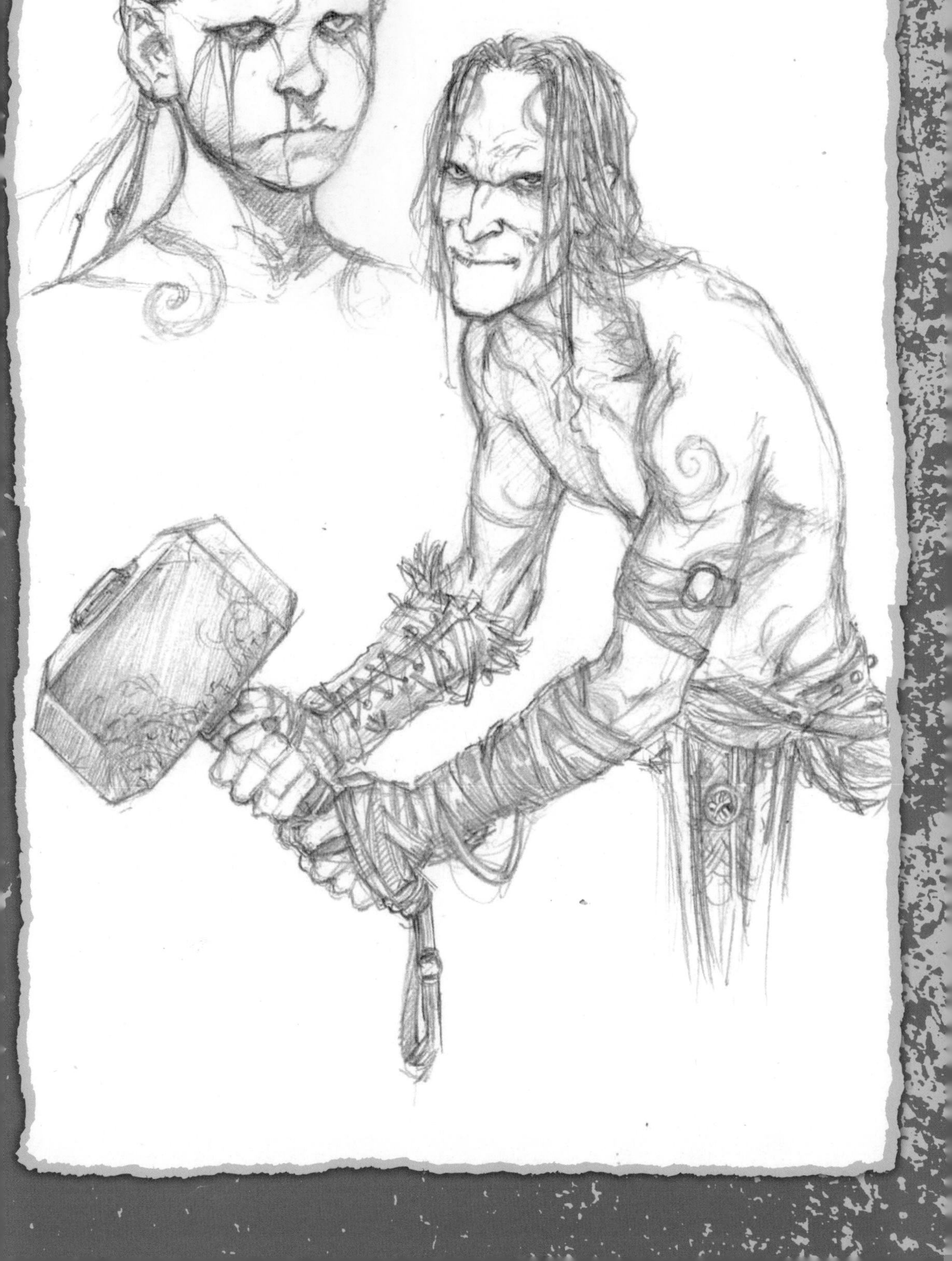

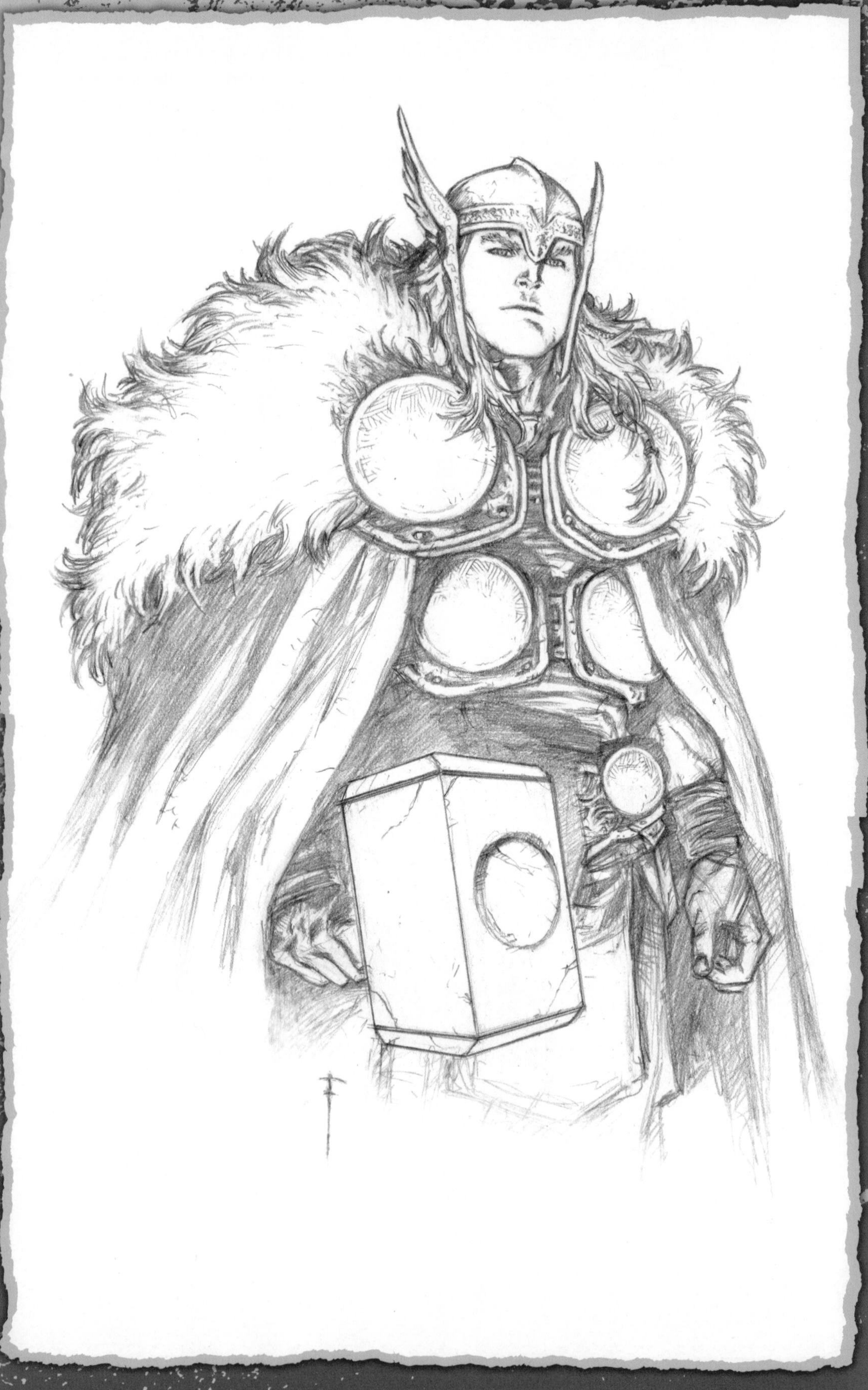

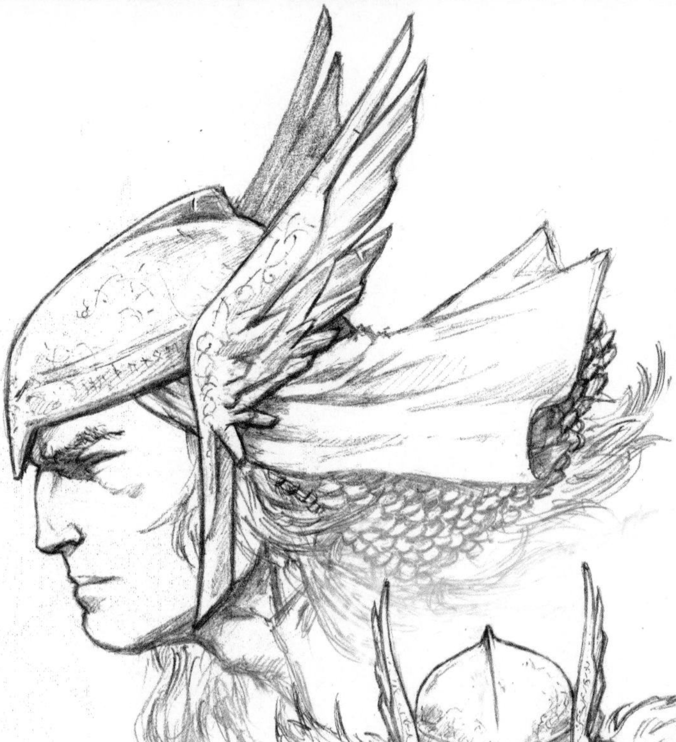

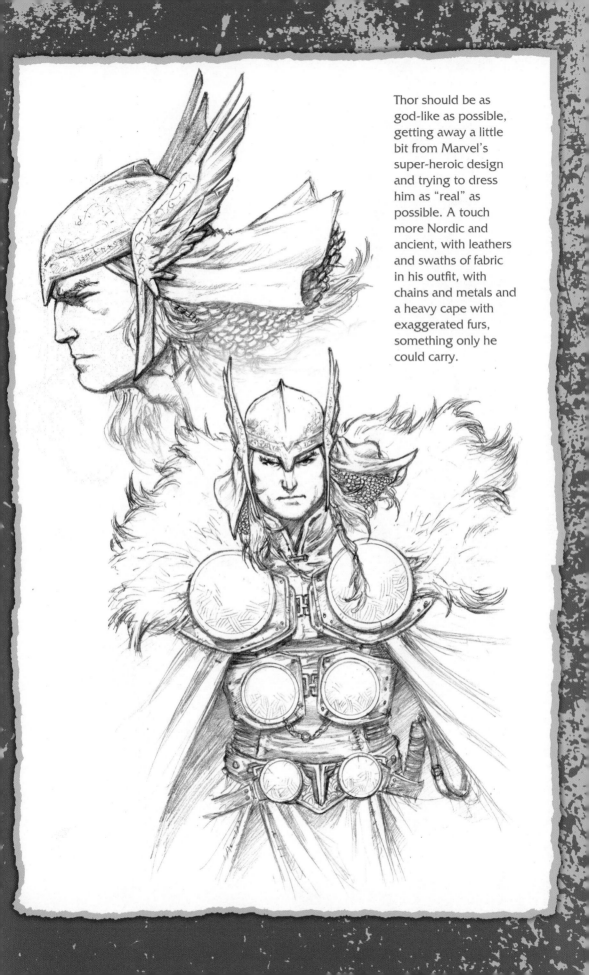

Thor should be as god-like as possible, getting away a little bit from Marvel's super-heroic design and trying to dress him as "real" as possible. A touch more Nordic and ancient, with leathers and swaths of fabric in his outfit, with chains and metals and a heavy cape with exaggerated furs, something only he could carry.

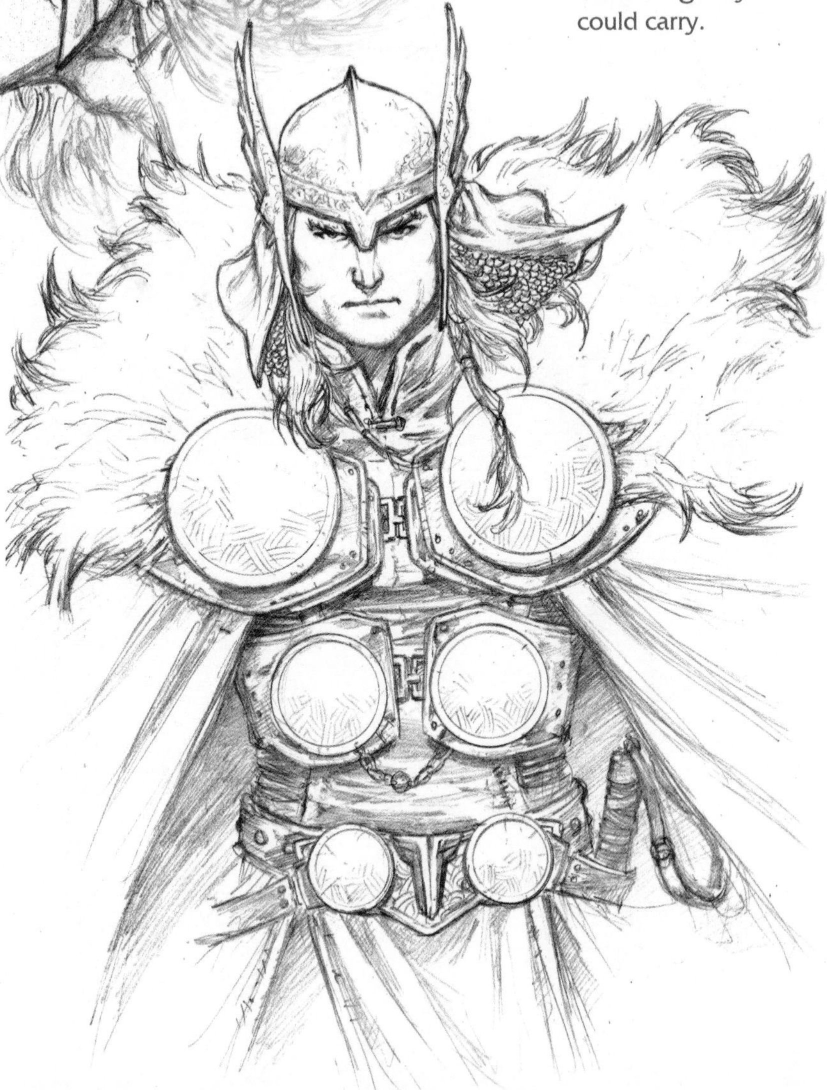

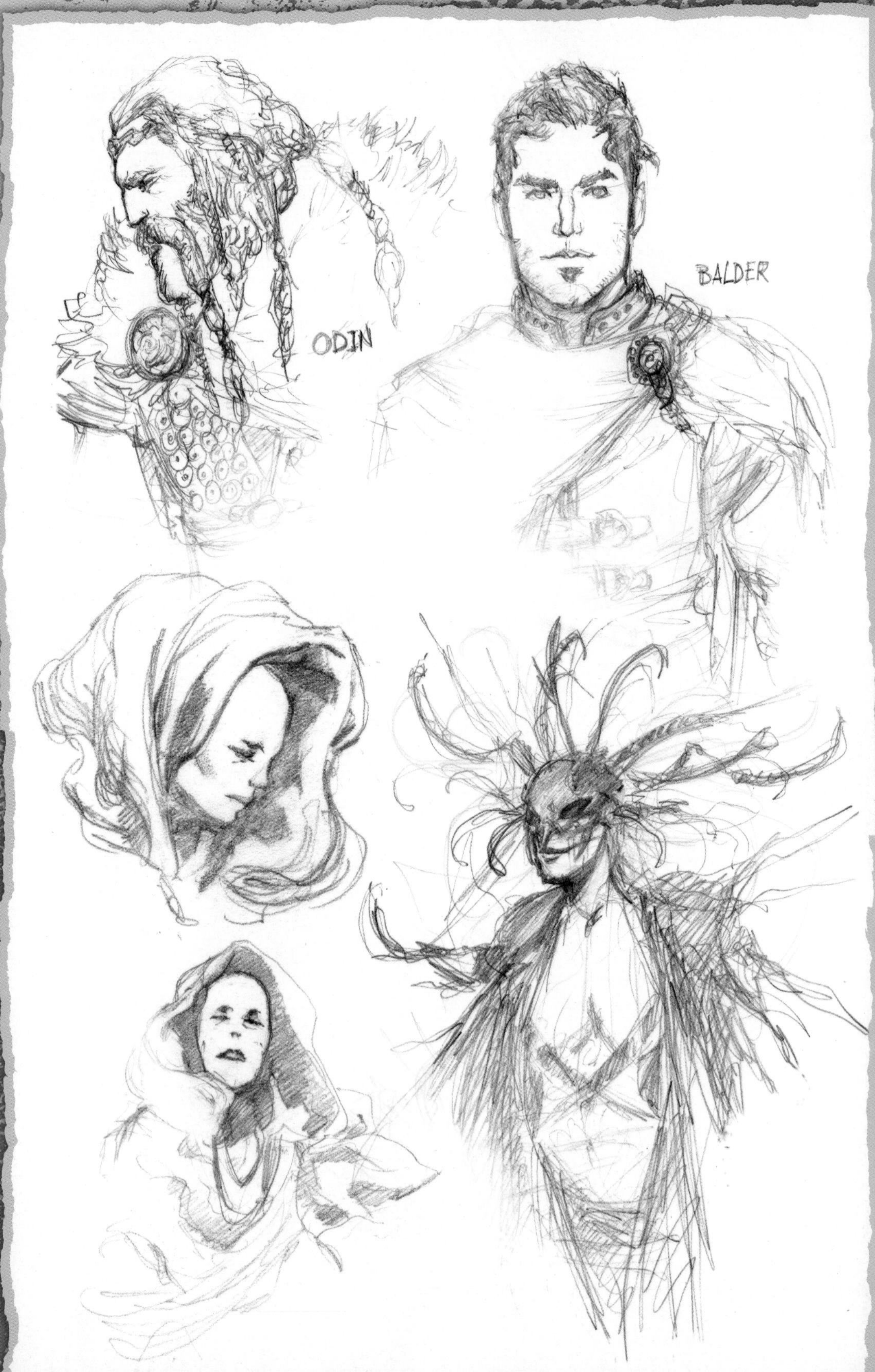
ODIN
BALDER

BROKE
BROKK

EHRI

IVALDI #1

IVALDI #2

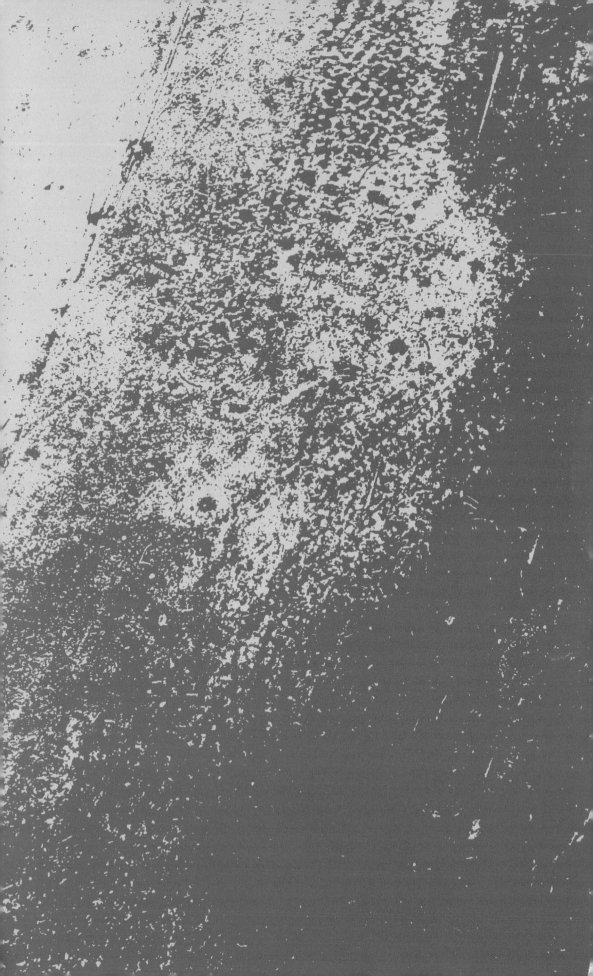